Annotated Teacher's Edition

P9-DGT-580

Be A Better Reader

Level F/Seventh Edition

Contents

Be A Better Reader—A Classroom Tradition	T2
Sample Lessons	T4
Basic Reading Skills	T9
Comprehension and Study Skills in the Content Areas	T11
Administering Level Assessment Tests	T15
Answer Key and Skills Correlation	T15
Annotated Student's Edition	1-176
Reproducible Assessment Tests	AT1
Student Answer Sheet	AT15
Class Record-Keeping Chart	AT16

Printed in the United States of America

 5 6 7 8 9 10   04 03 02 01 00

ISBN 0-8359-1931-5

C12

Globe Fearon

Be A Better Reader

By Nila Banton Smith

NEW! *The Seventh Edition of Nila Banton Smith's Classic Program*

- *Diagnostic and Placement Guide* offers diagnostic and placement tests to help you assign students to the proper *Be A Better Reader level*.

- Teaches the reading, comprehension, and study skills that students in grades 4–12 need.

- Applies these skills to the content areas:
  - Literature
  - Social Studies
  - Science
  - Mathematics

- **Lessons always begin with instruction** so that students learn successfully (and independently) before they apply a skill.

- **Focuses on one important skill in each Lesson** so that students concentrate on a skill and master it—independently.

- **Reading, comprehension, and study skills include:**

  literal comprehension

  interpretive and inferential comprehension

  critical and creative reading

  main idea

  cause and effect

  fact and opinion

  sequencing

  details

  literary concepts (such as plot and theme)

  following directions

  graphic and pictorial aids

  locating information

  reading symbols

  previewing

  outlining

  classifying

  problem solving

  reading rate

  and much more

- **Student independence** Instruction is in the student's book, so that students work and learn *independently*.

- **Each unit follows the same structure** so that students know what to expect and can work independently:

  A Lesson with a literature selection

  A Lesson with a social studies selection

  A Lesson with a science selection

  A Lesson with a mathematics selection

  Several brief "worksheet" Lessons that reinforce important phonics (in levels A–C), comprehension, and study skills

- **Vocabulary Instruction** Students learn vocabulary words *before* they read. Students also learn to use different types of *context clues* to increase vocabulary power: definitions, synonyms, antonyms, appositives, details, comparisons and contrasts, examples, and similes.

- **Easy to manage in your classroom** Use with individual students, small groups, or the entire class. *Be A Better Reader* is used successfully with students working below level, on level, and above level. (Level A—grade 4 reading level, Level B—grade 5, and so on to Level F—grade 9.)

- **Lessons may be used in any order** Correlate Lessons to your curriculum. Use them for reinforcement of specific skills or as a complete program.

- **Each Lesson ends with a Real Life Connection** that applies what students have learned to their own lives, communities, or interests.

- **Each unit ends with a brief Lesson on a practical life or school-to-work skill,** such as how to fill out a job application and order form; how to read a bus schedule, floor plan, map, and help wanted ads; and how to follow directions.

- **Assessment tests are free in the *Annotated Teacher's Edition* (Level A—F).**

First, a sample
Be A Better Reader

Lesson with

Instruction first on one comprehension or study skill, then on vocabulary

A content area reading selection

Written comprehension activities

A written activity on the Lesson skill

(See Level A, Lesson 44)

Sample Lessons

T3

Lessons begin with instruction.

Lesson 44

 1 Primary Source

Reading a Social Studies Selection

2 ▶ **Background Information**

The Nez Percé lived in the plateau country, an area that is now where the states of Washington, Oregon, and Idaho meet. The Nez Percé originally called themselves Nee Me Poo, which means "the Real People." French-Canadian fur trappers called them Nez Percé and the people adopted the name, pronouncing it *nez purse*.

The most famous chief of the Nez Percé was Chief Joseph, whose Indian name was Thunder Traveling to Loftier Mountain Heights. Joseph was 31 years old when he became chief after the death of his father.

In this lesson, you will read about Chief Joseph. You will also read the stirring speech that he delivered to President Hayes in Washington, D.C.

3 ▶ **Skill Focus**

Using a **primary source** will help you learn about past events. A primary source is a firsthand account. It is usually written by a person who took part in the event being described. Primary sources give facts about events. They also give insight into the thoughts and feelings of the

people in the events. Letters, speeches, and newspaper articles, are primary sources.

Often textbooks, magazines, encyclopedias, and so on, will contain excerpts, or pieces, of primary source materials. These excerpts are usually set apart in some way from the rest of the text.

When reading a primary source, use the following two steps.

1. **Find out all you can about the primary source.** Ask yourself the following questions.
   a. What type of document is it? Is it a letter, a report, an article, or a speech?
   b. Who wrote it? Was the author part of the event?
   c. When was it written?
2. **Study the primary source to learn about a past event.** Try to distinguish facts from opinions. A fact can be proven. An opinion is a judgment that reflects a person's feelings or beliefs.
   a. What facts can I learn from this document?
   b. What was the author's opinion about what was reported?

4 ▶ **Word Clues**

Read the sentences below. Look for context clues that explain the underlined word.

> As the early <u>settlers</u> moved west, they came into conflict with the Indians who lived there. The settlers had left their homes to find new land. They wanted land for farming and for raising cattle.

If you do not know the word *settlers* in the first sentence, read the next two sentences. They give details about the settlers. The details tell more about the word so that you understand it.

Use **detail** context clues to find the meaning of the three underlined words in the selection.

5 ▶ **Strategy Tip**

As you read Chief Joseph's words, keep in mind the two steps for using a primary source. Reading this speech will give you insight into the thoughts and feelings of Chief Joseph and his people.

Lesson 44 *Using a primary source* **123**

1

Lessons and skills are easy to find—Lessons are numbered and give the skill in the title.

2

Background Information—provides students with important content, cultural, and historical information and tells students what the selection is about.

3

Skill Focus—Instruction comes first—so that students are successful later.

4

Word Clues—Vocabulary instruction—before students read and need help.

5

Strategy Tip—gives students background and reminds them to use the Lesson skill.

A Great and Honorable Leader

The Gold Rush

The Nez Percé lived peacefully in their country for hundreds of years. They had experienced good relations with the white trappers and explorers. But in 1860, white prospectors illegally entered Nez Percé territory and found gold. During the gold rush, thousands of miners settled on Nez Percé reservation lands, disobeying an earlier treaty. For the first time, friction developed between whites and the Nez Percé.

In 1863, under pressure from the gold miners to remove the Nez Percé from valuable mineral sources, the U.S. government demanded that the Nez Percé cede, or give up, about 6 million acres of reservation land. The majority of Nez Percé refused. A government commissioner bribed several chiefs who sold the land and signed the treaty. The government official reported to the U.S. government that he had secured all lands demanded "at a cost not exceeding 8 cents per acre."

As a result of the land sale, the Nez Percé divided into "treaty" and "nontreaty" bands. Among those who were angry about the selling of Indian land was Tuekakas, also known as Old Joseph. By 1871, thousands of settlers had moved onto reservation land, as was allowed by the new treaty. Near his death, Old Joseph spoke to his son Young Joseph about their homeland:

My son, my body is returning to my mother earth, and my spirit is going very soon to see the Great Spirit Chief. When I am gone, think of your country. You are the chief of these people. They look to you to guide them. Always remember that your father never sold his country. You must stop your ears whenever you are asked to sign a treaty selling your home.

. . . My son, never forget my dying words. This country holds your father's body. Never sell the bones of your father and your mother.

Chief of Peace

Upon his father's death, Joseph became the civil, or peace, chief of his father's band. Joseph held many councils, or meetings, with civil and military officials. In 1873, Joseph convinced the government that it had not legally secured title to the reservation lands. The government ordered the whites to move out of the territory. However, the government then reversed its decision under pressure from Oregon politicians and settlers.

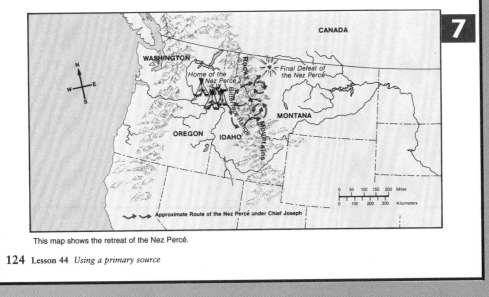

This map shows the retreat of the Nez Percé.

124 Lesson 44 *Using a primary source*

6

Primary Sources—In social studies selections, primary source materials aid comprehension, as well as provide valuable first-hand accounts of events and people.

7

Illustrations, photos, and captions increase interest and aid comprehension.

Understanding the dilemma of the U.S. government, Joseph continued to strive for a peaceful solution to the land problem. In 1877, General Oliver O. Howard concluded that the only solution was to force all the Nez Percé off their land and onto a reservation in Washington.

Many of the "nontreaty" Nez Percé wanted to fight for their land. Chief Joseph didn't want to fight. He knew that fighting would only bring death and sadness to his people. Joseph believed that he had no other choice but to lead his people to the reservation. So in the spring of 1877, Joseph agreed to the demands of the U.S. government. Several other nontreaty bands joined Joseph's for one last gathering on their land. While there, several men decided to seek revenge on white settlers for the death of one's father and for other grievances. They killed four white settlers.

Knowing that General Howard would send troops after them, the bands withdrew to Whitebird Canyon. Thus began a remarkable <u>retreat</u>, in which the Nez Percé fought, alluded, and outwitted one military force after another for four months. With about 750 people, including sick and elderly people, women, and children, the Nez Percé circled over a thousand miles trying to reach safety in Canada.

8

The soldiers who fought Chief Joseph thought that he was a great and honorable man. The soldiers knew that the Nez Percé never killed without reason. They could have burned and destroyed the property of many settlers, but they did not. Joseph and his people fought only to defend themselves and their land. The white soldiers were also impressed with their ability to allude the army for so many months and over so many miles.

"I Will Fight No More, Forever"

But the end finally came. Unaware that the army under Colonel Nelson A. Miles was in close <u>pursuit</u>, the Nez Percé camped less than 40 miles south of the Canadian border. At the end of a five-day siege, Chief Joseph decided to <u>surrender</u> to Miles on October 5, 1877. He rode into the army camp alone and handed his rifle to the soldiers. He said:

I am tired of fighting. My people ask me for food and I have none to give. It is cold and we have no blankets, no wood. My people are starving. . . . Hear me, my chiefs. I have fought, but from where the sun now stands, Joseph will fight no more, forever.

After Joseph's surrender, the U.S. government ordered them onto a reservation in Kansas, then to a disease-ridden reservation in Oklahoma. Many of the Nez Percé died of malaria and other sicknesses.

Chief Joseph pleaded on behalf of his people to gain permission to return to a reservation in the Northwest. In 1879, Chief Joseph traveled to Washington to plead his case to President Hayes.

Chief Joseph's Speech

If the white man wants to live in peace with the Indian, he can live in peace. There need be no trouble. Treat all men alike. Give them the same laws. Give them all an even chance to live and grow.

All men are made by the same Great Spirit Chief. They are all brothers. The earth is the mother of all people, and all people should have equal rights upon it. You might as well expect all rivers to run backward as that any man born a free man should be contented penned up and denied liberty to go where he pleases. If you tie a horse to a stake, do you expect he will grow fat? If you pen an Indian

Chief Joseph of the Nez Percé Indians.

Lesson 44 *Using a primary source* 125

126 Lesson 44 *Using a primary source*

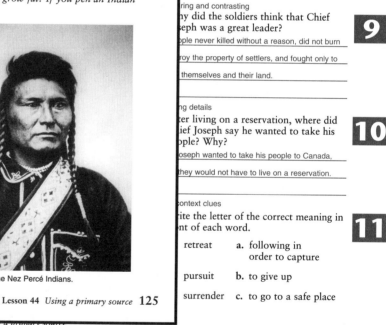

wars. We shall all be alike—brothers of [fa]*ther and mother, with one sky above us* [and] *one country around us and one* [gover]*nment for all. Then the Great Spirit* [Chief] *who rules above will smile upon this* [land] *and send rain to wash out the bloody* [spots] *made by brothers' hands upon the face* [of the] *earth. For this time, the Indian race are* [waiting] *and praying. I hope no more groans* [of wo]*unded men and women will ever go to* [the ea]*r of the Great Spirit Chief above, and* [that a]*ll people may be one people.*

[In] 1885, after eight years of campaigning [on be]half of his people, Joseph and the other [Nez] Percé were allowed to return to the [North]west. Unable to join the treaty bands on [the Id]aho reservation, Joseph and the others [were] escorted to the Colville Reservation in [Wash]ington Territory. It was there that [Josep]h died in 1904, reportedly from a [broke]n heart.

[F]ACTS

[Compa]ring and contrasting
[Wh]y did the soldiers think that Chief [Jo]seph was a great leader?

[Peo]ple never killed without a reason, did not burn

[or dest]roy the property of settlers, and fought only to

[defend] themselves and their land.

9

[Recallin]g details
[Af]ter living on a reservation, where did [Ch]ief Joseph say he wanted to take his [pe]ople? Why?

[J]oseph wanted to take his people to Canada,

[where t]hey would not have to live on a reservation.

10

[Using]context clues
[Wr]ite the letter of the correct meaning in [fro]nt of each word.

11

    retreat   **a.** following in order to capture

    pursuit   **b.** to give up

    surrender   **c.** to go to a safe place

8

Word clues—Unfamiliar words are defined using context clues, such as synonyms, appositive phrases, comparisons, and details, to aid reading and comprehension.

9

After reading, students complete written activities.

10

Recalling Facts—checks students' literal comprehension of the selection. (In the *Annotated Teacher's Edition,* each question has a skill label and answer for the teacher's benefit.)

11

Vocabulary Skills—The last item in "Recalling Facts" is a vocabulary check.

The lesson ends with a skills check.

12

Identifying point of view

1. For each pair of sentences, circle t[...]
Joseph's thoughts and opinions in [...]

   (a.) The white man can live in peace [...]
same law.

   b. Because so many promises have [...]
man and the Indian.

   a. There will be no more wars wh[...]

   (b.) There will be no more wars wh[...]

Drawing conclusions

2. Decide whether Chief Joseph is a g[...]
must look carefully at Chief Josep[...]
are listed in order below. For each [...]

   a. Chief Joseph first agrees to lead[...]
He knows that the small number of Nez Pe[...]

   b. Chief Joseph decides to lead his[...]
He wants to escape the army's punishment[...]
put on reservations.

   c. Chief Joseph will fight the army[...]
He knows that the battle will end only in de[...]

   d. Chief Joseph leads his people o[...]
He is trying to avoid battle and being captu[...]

   e. During this time, Chief Joseph [...]
He knows that the skills of his warriors will [...]

   f. Chief Joseph says that he will "[...]
reservation.
The army has trapped them. His people hav[...]
They must either surrender or die.

   g. Two years later, Chief Joseph sp[...]
even though he led his people t[...]
He believes that taking away a people's fre[...]
live "penned up." Yet, he has given his wor[...]

Now answer this question: Do you think that Chief Joseph was a great and honorable leader? In your answer, first tell what you mean by the words *great* and by *honorable*. Then tell why you think Chief Joseph was or was not a great and honorable leader.

Conclusions will vary, but all answers should include the following: (a) Student's definition of *great* and *honorable* and

(b) student's conclusion about Chief Joseph should be consistent with their definitions of *great* and *honorable* and

should cite facts in the selection and speech that led to the conclusion.

_____

_____

_____

_____

_____

_____

13

Reread Chief Joseph's speech. Pay special attention to what it tells you about Chief Joseph's feelings and motives. Then answer the questions below.

1. *Find out all you can about the primary source.*

What type of document is this? _____ a speech _____

Who wrote it? _____ Chief Joseph _____

Was the author involved in the event? _____ yes _____

When was it written? _____ 1879 _____

2. *Study the primary source to learn about a past event.*

What facts can you learn from this document? Indian lands were being overrun by white men; many Indians were dying and being treated as outlaws.

_____

_____

What was the author's opinion about what was reported? Chief Joseph believed that the Indians and white men could live in peace if all were subject to the same laws. He thought that his people would prosper if they could be moved back to the Pacific Northwest (Oregon).

_____

 ▶ **Real Life Connections** Write an interesting fact or story about the history of your community. List your primary sources.

14

128 Lesson 44 *Using a primary source*

12

Interpreting Facts—checks students' comprehension on *inferential* and *critical* levels.

13

Skill Focus—checks students' understanding of the Lesson skill. In the "Skill Focus" at the beginning of the Lesson, students learned about the Lesson skill. Now students

complete a written activity that applies the skill to the reading selection.

14

Real Life Connections— asks students to apply what they have read or learned to their own lives, communities, or interests.

Brief end-of-unit Lessons follow.

15

Lesson 40

Main Idea and Suppo[rt]

Many times in reading, you will l[earn]
details. Details give more informati[on]
supporting details because they sup[port]

Below is a paragraph about how the brakes w[ork]
the supporting details are listed.

Braking a car is an interesting process. I[n]
most cars, a liquid called brake fluid begi[ns]
the steps that stop the moving automobil[e].
When the brakes are not being used, the flu[id]
rests in the master cylinder and the brak[e]

Main Idea   Braking a car is an interesti[ng]
Supporting Details

a. In most cars, a liquid called brake flu[id]
   automobile.

b. When the brakes are not being used, t[he]
   tubes.

c. When the driver steps on the brake pe[dal]

d. The brake shoe presses against the bra[ke]

e. Each wheel has its own braking syste[m]

On the next page, write the main idea and t[he]

16

1. In the United States, almost everyone[']s
life is linked to the auto industry. Most peopl[e]
depend on a car, bus, or truck fo[r]
transportation. More than 12 million peopl[e]
earn their living in some part of the ca[r]
industry by building, shipping, servicing, [or]
selling cars, buses, or trucks. These peopl[e]
account for about one tenth of the labor forc[e.]
In fact, there are 500,000 automobile-relate[d]
businesses in the United States.

2. Several steps go into designing a ne[w]
car model. Automobile designers creat[e]
hundreds of sketches on computers. Final idea[s]
for the new model come from these sketche[s.]
Then a full-sized clay model is made. Furthe[r]
improvements are made in the design. [A]
fiberglass model is made. Finally, when eve[ry]
part has been approved, blueprints of the ca[r]
are drawn so that the car can be cut out of ste[el]
and built.

3. Most of the early automobile builder[s]
were mechanics or knew about machine[s]

Lesson 42

Comparing Car Ads

17

If you are interested in buying a new car, reading ads in newspapers and magazines should start you in the right direction. The details in ads can help you decide what kind of car will suit your needs and your budget. After you decide on the best car for your needs, you shop around for the best price.

Carefully read the following ads to compare the two cars.

PASHUBI: WE DESIGNED OUR CAR FOR ■ YOU ■ THE DRIVER

At Pashubi, we think you are very important. So we created the 630-X, a fully equipped luxury sports car. The 630-X surrounds the driver with more window than other sports cars. The 630-X has a steering wheel and instrument panel that can be moved up or down.

The roomy bucket seats can be easily moved and can tilt back as far as you like. And the large storage area in back lifts up to become two additional seats.

There are 30 standard equipment features, including power disc brakes, power windows, electrically heated outside rearview mirror, two-tone paint, and CD player.

At $20,025, the 630-X offers more than other imported cars. And you'll save on gas—an exceptional 43 EST HWY MPG, 28 EST MPG. Use MPG for comparison. Mileage may differ depending on conditions. Highway mileage may be less.

The 630-X. By Pashubi. It's *not* for everyone—but it is for *you.*

TILTON:
The American way to get more for your money.

You get more for your money with our cars. Take the Star, for example. This compact car uses 3,000 computer-assisted robot welds, more than any other car. This helps to create an easy-to-maintain car which will give you more for your money for years to come.

The Star gives you more for your money because it's sensibly priced. It starts as low as

$16,999*. The Star gives you more for your money with front-wheel drive. With the engine pulling in front and rack-and-pinion steering, you get the real feel of the road.

The six-passenger Star gives you more for your money with comfort.

And the Star gives you more for your money when you study the mileage figures:

41 EST HWY, 26 EST MPG.+

The Star's standard equipment includes power disc brakes, CD player, and 5-speed transmission (3-speed automatic is extra). Among the other extras are two-tone paint, luggage rack, leather steering wheel, power windows, and more.

Last year's Star was the best-selling compact car. See the Star today—and learn how to get more for your money the American way.

* $19,698 as shown in photograph

+ Use EST MPG for comparison. Mileage may vary depending on speed, trip length, and weather. Actual highway mileage lower.

15

Each brief Lesson focuses on one important skill and begins with instruction.

16

Students benefit from skills practice and reinforcement without full-length reading selections. (In Levels A, B, and C, phonic skills are reviewed in the Lessons.)

17

The last Lesson in each unit is on a practical skill—such as reading a bus schedule, filling out a job application, or following directions.

(See Level A, Lessons 40 and 42)

Basic Reading Skills

Whether students are reading a story for pleasure, skimming newspapers or magazines for information, or studying a chapter in a textbook, they need the following basic reading skills.

Word Recognition: the ability to recognize words.

Comprehension: the ability to derive stated and implied meanings from printed symbols.

Reading Rate: the ability to adjust reading rate to content and purpose.

Study Skills: the ability to apply what is already understood in a new context.

Word Recognition

In *Be A Better Reader*, specific skills instruction in word recognition is designed to provide students with a variety of word attack strategies needed to read an unfamiliar word.

Phonetic Analysis: recognizing and identifying the sounds of consonants, consonant blends, and digraphs; recognizing and identifying vowel sounds and their variant spellings.

Structural Analysis: recognition of root words, prefixes and suffixes, compound words, multi-syllabic words, accent marks, and syllabication.

Context Clues: determining word meaning from a particular context clue.

Respellings, Footnotes, and Other Word Helps: using vocabulary aids typical of content-area textbooks.

Comprehension

Reading comprehension is a process that begins with word recognition, but does not end until students have derived meaning from the ideas both stated and implied in the text and have been able to evaluate these ideas. In *Be A Better Reader*, each lesson focuses on a specific reading skill that helps students recognize and understand a text pattern that is typical of a content area, as well as a variety of other reading materials that students encounter in their daily lives.

Literal Comprehension

Literal questions are included to help students process information that is stated explicitly in the text. These questions require students to recall from memory or to select from the text specific answers; in other words, to reproduce what has been stated in the text.

The literal comprehension activities and questions in the Understanding Facts and Skill Focus activities sections require students to do the following.

1. Identify stated main idea
2. Identify stated main idea and details
3. Recall details
4. Identify stated cause and effect
5. Recognize sequence of events
6. Recognize fact and opinion
7. Recognize elements of a short story (plot, character, setting, theme, etc.)
8. Recognize variety of literary types or genres (fiction, play, nonfiction, biography, primary sources, etc.)

Inferential and Critical Comprehension

Numerous activities and questions are included to encourage students to probe for deeper meanings that are implied but not explicitly stated in the text. These questions require students to think about the meanings that can be derived from their reading, not just reproduce what the text has stated. Inferential and critical comprehension begins with literal meanings, but advances to higher-level thinking and reasoning skills that require students to go beyond the printed symbol.

The inferential and critical comprehension questions in the Interpreting Facts and Skill Focus activities sections require students to do the following.

1. Infer unstated main idea
2. Infer cause and effect
3. Infer details
4. Infer conclusions
5. Infer comparisons and contrasts
6. Distinguish fact from opinion
7. Infer information about elements of a short story (plot, character, setting, theme, etc.)
8. Draw conclusions and make generalizations
9. Evaluate validity of ideas
10. Predict outcomes

Reading Rate

Studies indicate that students are ready for a variety of reading rates by the latter part of fifth grade or by sixth grade. Students who have acquired reading skills through reading fiction only need to learn that there are different rates at which they should read different content. Practice in adjusting reading rate is introduced in Level C of *Be A Better Reader*. Emphasis is placed on adjusting the rate of reading to the content and the purpose of the material.

Study Skills

An analysis of questions, exercises, explanations, visuals, and directions in the various content area textbooks reveals that certain basic study skills are called for again and again in all subject areas. Most of these skills involve using comprehension skills to study and understand information in the content area. As students work with materials in literature, social studies, science, and mathematics, *Be A Better Reader* provides instruction and practice in the following study skills.

Selecting and Evaluating Information: the ability to select items from context and evaluate them in terms of conditions or specifications.

Organizing Information: the ability to put together or organize similar ideas.

Locating Information: the ability to find information in reference books and periodicals.

Reading Visuals: the ability to understand information presented in visuals, such as diagrams, maps, and graphs.

Following Directions: the ability to follow a specific sequence of steps.

Previewing: the ability to use previewing skills to understand the meaning and organization of a selection before reading it.

Reading Special Materials: the ability to read materials other than classroom textbooks.

Selecting and Evaluating Information

Just as word recognition skills are basic to reading, selection and evaluation are basic to study skills. Textbooks in the content areas contain many questions and directions that call for selection and evaluation skills. The skill of selecting and evaluating information requires students to select a piece of information and judge its worth in meeting the specifications of an activity or question. The answers to most literal comprehension questions need only to be selected from the text. However, inferential questions require students to go beyond the selection process to evaluation, the highest level of critical comprehension. In *Be A Better Reader*, lessons on fact and opinion, primary sources, and propaganda teach students selection and evaluation skills.

Organizing Information

The skill of organizing information is important because of the frequency with which students must apply it in studying textbooks, listening in class, and writing papers and tests. This skill provides opportunity for applying comprehension of content to a different format. Organizing information calls for putting together systematically items or ideas that belong to a whole. *Be A Better Reader* includes lessons on the procedures most often used in organizing information: (1) classifying items that belong to one group or that occur in a certain order; (2) outlining to show the relationship among ideas; (3) summarizing important ideas.

Locating Information

The skill of locating information includes activities that range from using a table of contents and an index to using a dictionary, an encyclopedia, and the library database system. Skill in locating information begins with recognizing alphabetical order and advances to finding information in complex reference books. In *Be A Better Reader*, lessons on locational skills are self-contained and include representative examples of typical dictionary and encyclopedia entries, indexes, and tables of contents.

Reading Visuals

Most content-area textbooks require students to read a variety of visuals, such as maps, timelines, diagrams, and graphs. Throughout *Be A Better Reader*, in all content areas, students are taught how to extract specific information from visuals and how to compress textual information into a brief visual presentation.

Following Directions

Reading to follow directions is a fundamental skill needed in studying all content areas. In *Be A Better Reader*, students are given directions for carrying out the activities that follow the reading selections. Thus, in addition to specific lessons in following directions, students acquire abundant experience in reading and following directions throughout each level of the program.

Previewing

Previewing a selection is another organizational skill. Previewing results in an organized "picture" or understanding of the structure of the selection. In *Be A Better Reader*, students learn to preview a selection by noting headings of sections, main ideas, and visuals.

Reading Special Materials

Students must be able to read special materials that they encounter outside the classroom. The last lesson in each unit of *Be A Better Reader* provides specific directions on how to read the yellow pages, a recipe, a floor plan, a travel brochure, and so on. Practice with these materials helps students make the transition from relatively controlled classroom reading situations to everyday reading situations.

Reading research has shown that different types of content require specialized reading skills. In preparing *Be A Better Reader*, textbooks in four different content areas were analyzed.

Literature

Social Studies

Science

Mathematics

Books were analyzed for text patterns, visual programs, and study aids typical of each content area. The specific skills situations that occurred most often in each content area were selected for inclusion in *Be A Better Reader*. The situations in which the skills were used were more abstract and higher levels of thinking were required in the books intended for the higher grades, but the skills situations are basically the same at all grade levels at which each subject is taught.

Literature

The literature selections in *Be A Better Reader* were carefully selected to appeal to student interest and are written at appropriate reading levels. The basic goal of the lessons with literature selections is threefold: (1) to acquaint students with various literary genres; (2) to increase students' awareness of the literary elements; and (3) to provide practice in applying comprehension skills to reading literature. A variety of genres is included in each level of *Be A Better Reader*. In the instructional section of each lesson, an important literary concept is stressed in terms appropriate to the particular level.

Each level of *Be A Better Reader* provides a lesson that develops one of the following special skills required in understanding and appreciating literature.

Recognizing plot

Recognizing character

Recognizing conflict

Recognizing setting

Recognizing theme

Plot

Most short stories have a plot, or sequence of events. They have a beginning, a middle, and an end, and events are arranged to build to a climax. As students read stories, it is important for them to keep the events in order, to notice how one event leads to the next, and to be able to identify the climax, or turning point of the story.

Character

The characters in a story are as important as the plot. Students need to be able to identify the main character, or protagonist, in a story. They should think about what motivates characters to act as they do. They should also notice how characters develop and change by contrasting how the characters behave at the beginning of a story with how they behave at the end.

Conflict

Students should be able to recognize a story's central conflict, or problem. Most stories are built around one of three common conflicts.

1. The main character is in conflict with himself or herself.
2. The main character is in a conflict with other characters.
3. The main character is in conflict with nature, society, or some outside force over which he or she may not have any control.

Setting

Setting is the time and place of the events in a story. Awareness of setting is essential to understanding the characters and their conflicts. Students must be shown how to interpret setting and its impact on the story's characters and events.

Theme

The theme, or idea, of a story is usually the most difficult concept for students to formulate by themselves. Students need to use higher-level comprehension skills to infer the author's underlying message.

Social Studies

Social studies texts have their own characteristic text patterns that require special reading skills. For example, social studies texts include frequent references to visuals, such as maps, graphs, and pictures. These references may require students to find information in a specific visual and then combine that information with information in the text.

Students need to become familiar with the text patterns typical of social studies textbooks. *Be A Better Reader* teaches some of the skills that are necessary to aid in comprehension of the patterns.

Reading visuals, such as pictures, maps, and graphs

Recognizing cause-and-effect relationships

Understanding sequence of events

Making comparisons and contrasts
Understanding detailed statements of fact
Thinking and reading critically

Visuals

Pictures in social studies textbooks are selected to depict historical concepts and events. The ability to read pictures and captions that accompany them results in students gaining information and implied meanings that go beyond the text. Reading pictures requires close attention to detail.

Reading maps and graphs is a highly specialized kind of reading skill. Map reading requires recognition and interpretation of symbols for rivers, mountains, lakes, towns and cities, boundary lines, and such features as scales of miles, color keys, and meridians. When reading graphs, students need to know how to extrapolate data and use it to make generalizations, thereby supplementing information in the text.

Cause and Effect

While the cause-and-effect text pattern occurs to some extent in most content areas, it occurs with the highest frequency in social studies, especially history. Every major event in history comes about as the result of some cause or set of causes, and when the event happens its effect or effects are felt. Sometimes the effect of one event becomes the cause of another event. Thus, the student often encounters a chain of causes and effects. Students who are adept at recognizing cause-and-effect patterns will find this to be a valuable asset in studying social studies textbooks.

Sequence of Events

Another text pattern encountered in social studies presents events in specific time sequences accompanied by dates. Students should read this pattern for two purposes: (1) to grasp the chronological order of large periods or whole blocks of events and (2) to grasp times of important happenings within each period or block—stopping long enough to associate events with dates and to think about how each event led to others.

Social studies textbooks include several kinds of visual aids designed to help students understand time relationships. These aids include charts of events and dates, chronological summaries, timelines, outline maps with dates and events, and so on. Each of these visual aids requires special reading skills.

Comparison and Contrast

A text pattern calling for the comparison of likenesses and/or contrast of differences is common in social studies textbooks. This pattern occurs most frequently in discussions of such topics as the theories of government or policies of different leaders; physical features, products, or industries of different countries; and so on. Students who recognize a comparison and contrast chapter or section of a text can approach it with the foremost purpose of noting likenesses and differences.

Detailed Statements of Fact

Much social studies text contains many details and facts. Facts, however, are usually included within one of the characteristic text patterns already discussed. The facts in social studies textbooks are not as dense as they usually are in science textbooks, nor are they as technical. Because they are often associated with sequential events or with causes and effects, they are more easily grasped.

Critical Thinking

Many social studies texts require students to interpret material critically. Students are expected to make inferences from facts, to distinguish fact from opinion, to analyze propaganda, to interpret primary sources, to draw conclusions and make generalizations, and to answer open-ended questions. Students need specific instruction and practice in these skills if they are to probe for deeper meanings and respond to higher-level questions.

Combination of Patterns

A single chapter in social studies may contain several text patterns. For example, a chapter may contain biographical material similar to the narrative pattern, a chronology of events during a certain time period, maps and charts depicting those events, and cause-and-effect relationships. If students who start to study such a chapter have not acquired the skills necessary to recognize and process each of these text patterns and instead use the same approach in reading all of them, the resulting understandings of the concepts presented will be extremely limited.

Science

Science text, like all other types of text, calls for the use of such comprehension skills as identifying main ideas and making inferences. However, an analysis of science textbooks reveals text patterns unique to science text that call for other approaches and special reading skills.

As in social studies textbooks, science texts include frequent references to such visuals as diagrams and pictures. Students need continued practice in combining text reading with visual reading in order to process all the information that is available on a science text page.

Be A Better Reader provides lessons on the following special reading skills that are needed for science textbooks.

Understanding classification

Reading an explanation of a technical process

Recognizing cause and effect relationships

Following directions for an experiment

Understanding detailed statements of fact

Recognizing descriptive problem-solving situations

Understanding abbreviations, symbols, and equations

Reading text with diagrams

Classification

The classification pattern is characteristic of science text. In this pattern, living things, objects, liquids, gases, forces, and so on are first classified in a general grouping that has one or more elements in common. This group is further classified into smaller groups, each of which varies in certain respects from every other group in the general grouping. Students who recognize the classification text pattern will concentrate on understanding the basis of the groupings and the chief characteristics of each one.

Explanation of a Technical Process

Another text pattern particularly characteristic of science is the explanation of a technical process. Explanation is usually accompanied by diagrams, necessitating very careful reading of text with continuous references to diagrams. The diagrams themselves require students to use special reading skills in addition to those needed to grasp the text explanations.

Cause and Effect

A text pattern sometimes encountered in science textbooks, but not unique to science, is the cause-and-effect pattern. In this pattern the text gives information that explains why certain things happen. In reading this type of pattern, students first read to find the causes and effects. A careful rereading is usually necessary to determine how and why the causes had the effects that they did.

Following Directions for an Experiment

This text pattern consists of explicit directions or instructions that must be carried out exactly. The common study skill of following directions is essential in reading this science pattern, but experiments also call for the mental activities of making discriminating observations, understanding complex explanations, and drawing considered conclusions.

Detailed Statements of Fact

Another pattern frequently encountered in science textbooks is detailed statements of fact. This pattern in science differs from factual text in the other content areas in two respects: (1) the facts are more dense and (2) they frequently lead to or embody a definition or a statement of a principle.

In reading this text pattern, students can make use of the reading skill of finding the main ideas and supporting details. Students first locate the most important thought or main idea in each paragraph, then proceed to find details that reinforce the main idea— noting particularly any definitions or statements of principles.

Descriptive Problem Solving

This text pattern describes problem-solving situations by taking the reader through a series of scientific experiments conducted by one or by many people. Students should approach this pattern with the idea of finding out what each successive problem was and how it was solved.

Abbreviations, Symbols, and Equations

Another science text pattern that requires a special kind of reading makes liberal use of abbreviations, formulas, and equations. For example, grasping the meaning of the symbol ° (degree) and the formula $CaCO_3$ (calcium carbonate) when they are integrated with words in the text calls for special recognition skills in addition to the usual recognition of word symbols. This pattern is still further complicated when symbols and abbreviations are involved in equations or number sentences.

Diagrams

Science textbooks usually contain many diagrams. Students need to learn how to go from the text to the diagrams and back to the text if they are to understand the meaning of scientific concepts. Reading diagrams requires an understanding of the purpose of diagrams, ability to interpret color and other visual devices used to highlight parts of a diagram, and comprehension of labels.

Combination of Patterns

As in social studies textbooks, a single chapter of a science text at the higher levels may contain several text patterns. If students who start to study such a chapter have not acquired the skills necessary to recognize and process each of these patterns and instead use the same approach in reading all of them, then the resulting understandings of the concepts presented will be extremely limited.

Mathematics

The reading skills needed for reading mathematics are sharply different from the skills needed in other content areas. Many students who read narrative with relative ease have great difficulty in reading mathematics, especially word problems and abstract mathematical symbols. The mathematics selections in *Be A Better Reader* are not included for the purpose of teaching mathematics. Their function is threefold: (1) to develop in students an awareness of the difference between reading mathematics texts and reading other texts; (2) to give students practice in reading the different types of text and symbols used in mathematics textbooks; and (3) to apply basic reading skills to mathematics text.

One of the special characteristics of mathematics text is compactness. Every word and every symbol is important. Unlike reading in other content areas, skipping an unfamiliar word or guessing its meaning from context will impair students' progress in mathematics. Students should be aware of this difference.

Another adjustment students have to make in reading mathematics is a change in basic left-to-right eye movement habits. Mathematics text often requires vertical or left-directed eye movements for rereading portions of the text for better understanding or for selecting certain numbers or symbols. While some students read mathematics more rapidly than others, text patterns in mathematics are not appropriate for speed reading.

Reading in mathematics makes heavy demands on the comprehension skills that call for interpretation, critical reading, and creative reading. Many mathematical situations call for a careful weighing of relationships. Of great importance is the ability to discover principles as a result of studying pictures and diagrams.

The inferential reading skills and the study skills of reading pictures and diagrams emphasized throughout *Be A Better Reader* should transfer to the following skills and attitudes specifically needed in working with mathematics.

> Reading word problems
>
> Reading mathematical terms, symbols, and equations
>
> Reading graphs and other mathematical visuals
>
> Reading explanation for processes or principles, such as fractions, decimals, and percents

Word Problems

Because problem solving is a priority in mathematics and closely related to basic reading skills, the Seventh Edition of *Be A Better Reader* includes in each level two lessons on problem solving. A five-step strategy is introduced in the first problem-solving lesson and used throughout the series. The steps in the strategy closely parallel the steps used in most mathematics textbooks. However, *Be A Better Reader* emphasizes the reading and reasoning skills necessary to solve word problems.

While the problem-solving strategy remains the same throughout the series, each succeeding lesson focuses on slightly more sophisticated problems. For example, the first problem-solving lesson focuses on problems that involve one mathematical operation. At a later level, problems are introduced in which two operations are necessary.

Terms, Symbols, and Equations

In mathematics, students must read sentences composed of word symbols and number symbols, such as equations. Recognizing and understanding symbols of various types is reading and should be taught as such in mathematics.

In reading equations, students have to recognize the meaning of the entire mathematical sentence, as well as the symbols $+$, $-$, $\times$, $\div$, and $=$. They also have to recognize and understand the symbols x and n, just as they have to learn to recognize and grasp the meaning of a new word in reading.

Students have to learn to recognize and understand the properties of geometric figures, such as the octagon, pentagon, prism, cube, cylinder, and pyramid. Parentheses, $>$, $<$, and other symbols are used frequently.

Graphs and Charts

Other distinctive text patterns in mathematics are graphs, such as bar graphs and circle graphs. While these visual aids are used in social studies, science, and other subjects, they almost always represent mathematical concepts.

To get the most information from a graph, students should: (1) read the title to determine exactly what is being compared; (2) read the numbers or labels to determine what the figures or labels stand for; (3) study the graph to compare the different items illustrated; and (4) interpret the significance of the graph as a whole. Due to the prevalence of graphs and similar mathematical visuals in most content area textbooks, most students profit from instruction in reading these types of text patterns.

Explanation

The explanation text pattern in mathematics texts is similar to the explanation text pattern in science textbooks, except that in mathematics text explanations describe a mathematical principle or process rather than a scientific process. Mathematical explanations are comparatively short and often contain symbols other than words. They are usually accompanied by or are preceded by a series of exercises or questions designed to guide students in discovering the principle or process. This text pattern calls for very careful reading and rereading until the process is understood.

Assessment tests for Level F are designed to measure students' level of achievement in each of the important comprehension and study skills that receive emphasis in *all* levels of *Be A Better Reader*. The tests may be used in conjunction with the tests provided in the *Diagnostic and Placement Guide* as pre-tests and/or post-tests, depending on students' needs and your particular classroom management style. Combined with an overview of student performance on each lesson, the tests should enable you to refine your assessment of students' performance and determine students' readiness to advance to the next level.

The four tests in Level F can be administered separately or at one time, depending on time available. Because directions are provided for each test, students should be able to take the tests independently.

The skill for each test item is identified in the answer key below. Following the skill is the number of the lesson or the lessons in Level F where that skill is treated as a Skill Focus. To simplify the scoring process, you can use the answer key to make a scoring mask, which when placed over the answer sheet reveals only those items that are correct. The total score is equal to the number of correct items. Criterion scores are not specified in this book, but you can refer to the Scoring Rubic in the *Diagnostic and Placement Guide* for more information on grading.

Answer Key and Skills Correlation

Test 1

1. b   Understanding character (1)
2. c   Understanding character (1)
3. b   Understanding character (1)
4. c   Understanding character (1)
5. c   Identifying conflict and resolution (16)
6. b   Identifying conflict and resolution (16)
7. b   Identifying conflict and resolution (16)
8. c   Identifying plot (10)
9. c   Identifying plot (10)
10. b   Identifying plot (10)
11. c   Identifying theme (23)
12. b   Identifying theme (23)
13. a   Identifying the stated or unstated main idea (8)
14. c   Identifying the stated or unstated main idea (8)
15. c   Making inferences (43)
16. a   Making inferences (43)
17. b   Making inferences (43)
18. c   Identifying omniscient point of view (31)
19. c   Identifying omniscient point of view (31)
20. b   Solving word problems (4, 13)
21. a   Recognizing multiple meanings of words (20)
22. a   Recognizing multiple meanings of words (20)
23. b   Using synonym context clues (17, 41)

Test 2

24. c   Identifying the main idea (7, 8, 18, 21)
25. a   Identifying the main idea (7, 8, 18, 21)
26. b   Identifying the main idea (7, 8, 18, 21)
27. b   Identifying the stated or unstated main idea (8)
28. a   Identifying the stated or unstated main idea (8)
29. c   Identifying the main idea and supporting details (18, 21)
30. c   Identifying the main idea and supporting details (18, 21)
31. a   Identifying cause and effect (3, 11, 44)
32. c   Identifying cause and effect (3, 11, 44)
33. b   Identifying cause and effect (3, 11, 44)
34. c   Comparing and contrasting (2, 24)
35. a   Comparing and contrasting (2, 24)
36. a   Comparing and contrasting (2, 24)
37. c   Distinguishing fact from opinion (36)
38. b   Distinguishing fact from opinion (36)
39. b   Distinguishing fact from opinion (36)
40. c   Making inferences (43)
41. b   Making inferences (43)
42. a   Making inferences (43)
43. c   Using a primary source (2)
44. c   Using a primary source (2)
45. b   Using a primary source (2)
46. c   Making generalizations (40)
47. a   Making generalizations (40)
48. b   Making generalizations (40)

48. b   Making generalizations (40)
49. a   Recognizing multiple meanings of words (20)
50. c   Recognizing multiple meanings of words (20)
51. a   Using detail context clues (2, 40)
52. b   Using detail context clues (2, 40)
53. a   Using synonym context clues (17, 41)
54. b   Reading a map (17)
55. a   Reading a map (17)
56. c   Reading a map (17)
57. c   Reading a map (17)

Test 3

58. b   Identifying the main idea (7, 8, 18, 21)
59. b   Identifying the main idea (7, 8, 18, 21)
60. b   Identifying the main idea and supporting details (18, 21)
61. c   Identifying the main idea and supporting details (18, 21)
62. b   Identifying cause and effect (3, 11, 44)
63. a   Identifying cause and effect (3, 11, 44)
64. a   Making inferences (43)
65. c   Making inferences (43)
66. a   Making inferences (43)
67. c   Classifying (25)
68. c   Classifying (25)
69. c   Classifying (25)
70. b   Classifying (25)
71. b   Recognizing multiple meanings of words (20)
72. c   Recognizing multiple meanings of words (20)
73. b   Recognizing multiple meanings of words (20)
74. b   Using synonym context clues (17, 41)
75. c   Using appositive context clues (3, 11, 18, 24)
76. b   Using antonym context clues (16)
77. c   Reading text with diagrams (12)
78. a   Reading text with diagrams (12)
79. b   Reading text with diagrams (12)
80. c   Reading text with diagrams (12)
81. c   Solving word problems (4, 13)
82. a   Solving word problems (4, 13)
83. b   Solving word problems (4, 13)
84. b   Solving word problems (4, 13)

Test 4

85. c   Using the dictionary (37)
86. c   Using the dictionary (37)
87. b   Using the dictionary (37)
88. b   Using the dictionary (37)
89. a   Using an index (48)
90. c   Using an index (48)
91. a   Using an index (48)
92. c   Using an index (48)
93. c   Recognizing prefixes (6)
94. b   Recognizing prefixes (6)
95. a   Recognizing suffixes (14)
96. c   Recognizing suffixes (14)
97. c   Recognizing syllables (5, 28, 35)
98. b   Recognizing syllables (5, 28, 35)
99. c   Recognizing roots (28)
100. b   Recognizing roots (28)

Be A
Better
Reader

Level F

Seventh Edition

Nila Banton Smith

Globe
Fearon

Pronunciation Key

Symbol	Key Word	Respelling
a	act	(akt)
ah	star	(stahr)
ai	dare	(dair)
aw	also	(awl soh)
ay	flavor	(flay vər)
e	end	(end)
ee	eat	(eet)
er	learn	(lern)
	sir	(ser)
	fur	(fer)
i	hit	(hit)
eye	idea	(eye dee ə)
y	like	(lyk)
ir	deer	(dir)
	fear	(fir)
oh	open	(oh pen)
oi	foil	(foil)
	boy	(boi)
or	horn	(horn)
ou	out	(out)
	flower	(flou ər)
oo	hoot	(hoot)
	rule	(rool)
yoo	few	(fyoo)
	use	(yooz)

Symbol	Key Word	Respelling
u	book	(buk)
	put	(put)
uh	cup	(kuhp)
ə	a as in along	(ə lawng)
	e as in moment	(moh mənt)
	i as in modify	(mahd ə fy)
	o as in protect	(prə tekt)
	u as in circus	(ser kəs)
ch	chill	(chil)
g	go	(goh)
j	joke	(johk)
	bridge	(brij)
k	kite	(kyt)
	cart	(kahrt)
ng	bring	(bring)
s	sum	(suhm)
	cent	(sent)
sh	sharp	(shahrp)
th	thin	(thin)
z	zebra	(zee brə)
	pose	(pohz)
zh	treasure	(treszh ər)

Be A Better Reader, Level F, Seventh Edition
Nila Banton Smith

Printed in the United States of America
5 6 7 8 9 10   04 03 02 01 00

C12
ISBN 0-8359-1930-7

Acknowledgments
We wish to express our appreciation for permission to use and adapt copyrighted materials.

The dictionary definitions in this book are reprinted with permission of Macmillan Reference USA, a Division of Simon & Schuster, from WEBSTER'S NEW WORLD DICTIONARY, Student Edition. Copyright © 1976, 1981, 1983 by Simon & Schuster Inc.

As Gyldendal Norsk Forlag for "From *Kon-Tiki*." Adapted from KON-TIKI by Thor Heyerdahl. Copyright © 1950 by Thor Heyerdahl.

Rosica Colin Limited for "We are going to see the rabbit . . ." by Alan Brownjohn from COLLECTED POEMS 1952–1983. Copyright © 1983 by Alan Brownjohn.

Henry Gibson for "The Ingredients of Expedience." Published by *National Wildlife*, December–January 1971.

ANOTHER VIEW reprinted by permission of United Feature Syndicate, Inc.

Photo Credits
p. 13: UPI; **p. 42:** George H.H. Huey; **p. 43:** George H.H. Huey; **p. 101:** (*left*) Richard Nowitz/Photo Researchers, Inc., (*right*) Jeff Greenberg/Photo Researchers, Inc.; **p. 102:** (*left*) Richard Nowitz/Photo Researchers, Inc., (*right*) Will & Demi MacIntyre/Photo Researchers. Inc.; **p. 103:** (*left*) Will & Demi MacIntyre/Photo Researchers. Inc., (*right*) Tom Carroll/Phototake; **p. 150:** (*top*) Topham/The Image Works, (*bottom*) National Geographic Society; **p. 151:** Merlin Tuttle courtesy Bat Conservation League; **p. 152:** Randall Hymen; **p. 164:** NASA; **p. 165:** UPI.

Globe Fearon

Contents

Unit One Different Worlds   6

1 Character   6
LITERATURE SELECTION
"Silent World"

2 Primary and Secondary Sources   11
SOCIAL STUDIES SELECTION
"A Voyage on a Raft" and
"From *Kon-Tiki*"

3 Cause and Effect   17
SCIENCE SELECTION
"Earthquakes and Tsunamis"

4 Word Problems   23
MATHEMATICS SELECTION
"Solving Word Problems"

5 Syllables   28

6 Prefixes   30

7 Main Idea   31

8 Stated or Unstated Main Idea   32

9 Health Insurance Application   34

Unit Two Time Future, Time Past   36

10 Plot   36
LITERATURE SELECTION
"Ask MIKE"

11 Cause and Effect   41
SOCIAL STUDIES SELECTION
"The Ancient Ones"

12 Diagrams   47
SCIENCE SELECTION
"The Electromagnetic Spectrum"

13 Word Problems   52
MATHEMATICS SELECTION
"Completing and Solving
Word Problems"

14 Suffixes   57

15 Federal Income Tax Form   58

Unit Three Freedom and Responsibility   60

16 Conflict and Resolution   60
LITERATURE SELECTION
"New Car, New Image"

17 Reading a Map   66
SOCIAL STUDIES SELECTION
"The Electoral College"

18 Main Idea and Supporting Details 72
SCIENCE SELECTION
"Genetics"

19 Similar and Congruent Triangles   78
MATHEMATICS SELECTION
"Similar and Congruent Figures"

20 Multiple Meanings   83

21 Main Idea and Supporting Details 84

22 Voter Registration Form   86

Unit Four Careers   88

23 Theme   88
LITERATURE SELECTION
"Other Times, Other Customs"

24 Comparing and Contrasting   94
SOCIAL STUDIES SELECTION
"Jobs of the Future"

25 Classifying   100
SCIENCE SELECTION
"Careers in the Sciences"

26 Understanding Probability   106
MATHEMATICS SELECTION
"Understanding Probability"

27 Word Parts   110

28 Syllables   111

29 Outlining   112

30 Reading a Résumé   114

Unit Five Laws: Written and Unwritten   116

31 Point of View   116
LITERATURE SELECTIONS
"The Chance of a Lifetime"

32 Reading a Flow Chart   122
SOCIAL STUDIES SELECTION
"How a Bill Becomes a Law"

33 Following Directions   128
SCIENCE SELECTION
"Motion"

34 Statistics   134
MATHEMATICS SELECTION
"Interpreting Statistics"

35 Accented Syllable and
Schwa Sound   138

36 Fact and Opinion   139

37 The Dictionary   140

38 Reading a Floor Plan   142

Unit Six Environmental Issues   144

39 Satire   144
LITERATURE SELECTION
"We are going to see the rabbit"
and "The Ingredients of
Expedience"

40 Making Generalizations   149
SOCIAL STUDIES SELECTION
"Making a Difference"

41 Chemical Formulas   155
SCIENCE SELECTION
"Symbols, Formulas, and
Equations"

42 Equations   160
MATHEMATICS SELECTION
"Reading Equations"

43 Inferences   164

44 Cause and Effect   165

45 Synonyms and Antonyms   167

46 Analogies   168

47 Improving Reading Rate   169

48 Using an Index   172

49 Reading a Budget   174

4

How to Use *Be A Better Reader*

For more than thirty years, **Be A Better Reader** has helped students improve their reading skills. **Be A Better Reader** teaches the comprehension and study skills that you need to read and enjoy all types of materials—from library books to the different textbooks that you will encounter in school.

To get the most from **Be A Better Reader**, you should know how the lessons are organized. As you read the following explanations, it will be helpful to look at some of the lessons.

In each of the first four lessons of a unit, you will apply an important skill to a reading selection in literature, social studies, science, or mathematics. Each of these lessons includes the following seven sections.

Skill Focus

This section teaches you a specific skill. You should read the Skill Focus carefully, paying special attention to words that are printed in boldface type. The Skill Focus tells you about a skill that you will use when you read the selection.

Word Clues

This section teaches you how to recognize and use different types of context clues. These clues will help you with the meanings of the underlined words in the selection.

Reading a Literature, Social Studies, Science, or Mathematics Selection

This section introduces the selection that you will read and gives you suggestions about what to look for as you read. The suggestions will help you understand the selection.

Selection

The selections in the literature lessons are similar to those in a literature anthology, library book, newspaper, or magazine. The social studies selec-
tions are like chapters in a social studies textbook or encyclopedia. They often include maps and tables. The science selections, like a science textbook, include special words in boldface type and sometimes diagrams. The mathematics selections will help you acquire skill in reading mathematics textbooks.

Recalling Facts

Answers to the questions in this section—the first of three activity sections—can be found in the selection. You will sometimes have to reread parts of the selection to do this activity.

Interpreting Facts

The second activity includes questions whose answers are not directly stated in the selection. For these questions, you must combine the information in the selection with what you already know in order to *infer* the answers.

Skill Focus Activity

In the last activity, you will use the skill that you learned in the Skill Focus section at the beginning of the lesson to answer questions about the selection. If you have difficulty completing this activity, reread the Skill Focus section.

The remaining lessons in each unit give you practice with such skills as using a dictionary, an encyclopedia, and other reference materials; using phonics and syllabication aids in recognizing new words; locating and organizing information; and adjusting reading rate. Other reading skills that are necessary in everyday experience are also covered, such as reading a bus schedule and a menu.

Each time that you learn a new skill in **Be A Better Reader**, look for opportunities to use the skill in your other reading at school and at home. Your reading ability will improve the more you practice reading!

Reading a Literature Selection

▶ **Background Information**

Imagine yourself talking and laughing in a room filled with people. They seem to be having a wonderful time, but you can't hear them. When you speak to them, you can't even hear yourself. Caroline lives in such a world; she is deaf, and her world is forever silent.

▶ **Skill Focus**

All fictional characters can be classified as static or dynamic. *Static* means "standing still" or "staying the same." *Dynamic* means "full of energy" or "active, changing, productive." A **static character** is the same kind of person at the end of a story as he or she was at the beginning of the story. A **dynamic character** undergoes a permanent change in some aspect of his or her personality or outlook. In most novels and short stories, the main character changes as the result of a crucial situation in his or her life.

An author may reveal how

a character either changes or remains the same through a combination of ways:

1. the character's actions and speech
2. the character's thoughts and feelings
3. the opinions and comments of other characters in the story

When you read a story, the following questions will help you distinguish between static and dynamic characters.

1. How do the character's actions, speech, thoughts, and feelings reveal what he or she is like?
2. What do other characters say or feel about the character?
3. Does the character change or remain the same in the story? Is the character static or dynamic?
4. What conclusions can you draw about the kind of person the character is?

▶ **Word Clues**

When you read a word that you do not know, look for context clues to help you.

Read the following sentences.

Elliot evaded his partner's glances; he was disgusted. What a terrific weekend this was going to be, he thought, with more than a trace of <u>sarcasm</u>.

Sometimes there are no context clues to help you clearly understand the meaning of a new word. You will need a dictionary to help you. You may find it convenient to finish what you are reading first before looking up the word.

Use a **dictionary** to find the meanings of the three underlined words in the selection.

▶ **Strategy Tip**

As you read "Silent World," be aware of the importance of communication in building a relationship and in revealing a character's personality. See whether the main characters remain static or become dynamic.

Silent World

Elliot evaded his partner's glances; he was disgusted. What a terrific weekend this was going to be, he thought, with more than a trace of sarcasm. He'd thought that it would be exhilarating to clear last winter's debris from the hiking trails with all the local high school conservation clubs. How was he to know that he would be working with a student from the Madison School for the Deaf?

✔ Elliot made numerous attempts to talk to Caroline, but it was hopeless. He couldn't understand a word she said, although he pretended that he did. He simply smiled and nodded pleasantly.

> Gallaudet College, founded in Washington, D.C., in 1864, is the only liberal arts college for deaf people in the world.

✘ As Elliot swung his <u>mattock</u> angrily, Caroline observed him out of the corner of her eye. Just because they can hear, she thought, they think they know everything. She knew that she could show Elliot how to use that mattock properly, but why bother? He'd just smile, nod ignorantly, and continue using it incorrectly. They think that we don't know anything because we're deaf.

Caroline swung her mattock easily. As the hard sod crumbled beneath her blows, Caroline relished thinking about how Elliot's arms would ache by the end of the day.

At lunch, Caroline and her friends sat on a grassy <u>knoll</u>. They "talked" animatedly, lip reading and using finger spelling and sign language. Her hands flew as she discussed the events of the morning. Caroline <u>pantomimed</u> Elliot's clumsy efforts for the benefit of her friends, and everybody laughed. The hearing students sitting nearby glanced up, startled, and pretended not to notice. But the deaf teenagers noticed.

"Who wants to talk to them anyway?" Caroline's friends signed to Mr. Soong, their counselor. Mr. Soong wasn't deaf, but he used manual communication as fluently as they did. "It's easier not talking to them, isn't it?" he said.

"I talked," Caroline scowled. "He didn't understand me."

"He didn't understand your words; you haven't learned to enunciate clearly yet. It takes time and some people won't ever understand you—but there are other ways to communicate."

"How? He doesn't understand signs or finger spelling."

"It's a problem, I know," signed Mr. Soong. "But I'm sure you can think of something."

After lunch, Elliot collected trash in the brush off the trail. He looked up, saw Caroline walking toward him, and looked away again. Caroline tramped through the brush to where Elliot was working. When she got there, she couldn't believe her eyes—Elliot was standing knee-deep in poison oak.

Caroline burst out laughing—she couldn't help it . . . until she remembered the time that she had had a reaction to poison oak. It was a horrible and painful ordeal.

As Elliot bent down to extract a stubborn bit of trash from the brush, Caroline, exasperated, yelled, "That's poison oak!"

But Elliot couldn't understand her. "Yeah, sure," he said, shrugging. Caroline glared at him. Then she gestured at the brush and yelled. Elliot ignored her.

Suddenly, Caroline began to pantomime. She pantomimed somebody whose body is itching all over. As Elliot stared at her, fascinated with her performance, Caroline pointed at the brush again. This time Elliot turned and looked where she was pointing.

✔ "Hey!" he said. "That's poison oak!" He leaped away. "I didn't even see it—is that what you were trying to tell me? I'm so allergic to that stuff, you wouldn't believe it. Listen, thanks, Caroline." He turned and stopped, realizing that Caroline was staring blankly at him, uncomprehending.

Later Elliot approached Mr. Soong and told him what had happened. As Elliot turned to leave, he said, "So would you tell her thanks for me?"

Mr. Soong just looked at him. "Why don't you tell her yourself?"

"Caroline doesn't hear," said Mr. Soong. "That doesn't mean you can't communicate. She can read lips. If you enunciate clearly, speak slowly, and look at her when you talk, she can understand you."

Elliot hesitated for a moment, and then he said, "Would you show me something?"

Later, Elliot went back to where Caroline was working. He felt foolish, but he realized that undoubtedly Caroline occasionally felt foolish too. Caroline looked up, and Elliot smiled at her. Then, putting his fingertips to his lips, palms flat, he made the gesture that Mr. Soong had said meant "thank you."

For an instant, Caroline looked quite astonished; she peered suspiciously at Elliot, looking in his face for a sign of a joke or betrayal. Uncomfortable but determined, Elliot kept beaming at her. Slowly, Caroline's face relaxed; she broke into a smile.

✘ When Elliot picked up the mattock again, Caroline took it from his hands; wordlessly, she demonstrated the correct way to hold it.

RECALLING FACTS

Write the answers to the following questions on the lines provided. You may go back to the selection to find an answer.

Identifying setting
1. Where do the events in this story take place?

They take place in an outdoor camping area with

hiking trails.

Identifying cause and effect
2. Why does Caroline tell Elliot about the poison oak?

Caroline remembers that she has suffered terribly from

poison oak and feels sorry for Elliot.

Recalling details
3. Why is Elliot angry at the beginning of the story?

He is angry because he did not expect to have to work

with a deaf student, and he dislikes the idea.

Comparing and contrasting
4. What do Caroline and Elliot have in common?

Both Caroline and Elliot are proud and love the outdoors.

Recalling details
5. List two ways in which deaf people can communicate.

They can communicate by finger spelling and by sign

language.

Using context clues
6. Match the following words with their correct meanings.

mattock   a. expressed by actions or gestures instead of words

pantomimed   b. a mound or small hill

knoll   c. a cutting and digging tool similar to an axe

Not all the questions about a selection are answered directly in the selection. For the following questions, you will have to figure out answers not directly stated in the selection. Write the answers to the questions on the lines provided.

Distinguishing fact from opinion

1. Identify the following statements by writing *fact* or *opinion* on the line provided.

_____opinion_____ Trying to communicate with the deaf is a hopeless effort.

_____fact_____ The deaf have many ways of communicating with others.

_____opinion_____ Sign language can be learned quickly.

Making inferences

2. The people in this story communicate in many ways.

   a. Which ways are deliberate? They communicate deliberately by speech, finger spelling, sign language, pantomime, lip reading, and demonstration.

   b. Which ways are unconscious? Answers may vary. Possible answers include attitudes and emotional reactions.

Inferring comparisons and contrasts

3. Why do Elliot and Caroline distrust each other at first?

Neither understands the world in which the other lives.

Inferring cause and effect

4. Why does Elliot's embarrassment enrage Caroline?

Elliot's embarrassment tells Caroline that he feels she is not his equal. Caroline is angry at being mistreated this way.

Making inferences

5. Why does Caroline look suspicious when Elliot uses sign language?

Caroline may think that Elliot is making fun of her. It's difficult for her to believe that a hearing person is sincere

when using sign language.

Making inferences

6. How do you think deafness has influenced Caroline's personality?

Caroline's anger and distrust could stem from the fact that she has had to overcome her handicap to be part of a

hearing world or could be a result of being patronized and teased.

Inferring comparisons and contrasts

7. Some people become deaf after they have learned a language; others are born deaf. Imagine that you were born deaf and that you didn't know what language was. How would life be different for you?

Answers will vary. Probably you would feel like an outsider much of the time. You would always have to watch your

surroundings, because noises could not alert you to danger. You would have to learn how to enjoy many activities,

such as dancing or movies, in a different way.

1. An author can reveal the personality of a character through a combination of ways:
   a. the character's actions and words
   b. the character's thoughts and feelings
   c. the opinions and comments of other characters

Read the following passages about the main characters in the story. On the line or lines in front of each passage, write the letter or letters of the technique that the author uses. On the line provided after each passage, tell what the passage reveals about the character.

__a__ After lunch, Elliot collected trash in the brush off the trail. He looked up, saw Caroline walking toward him, and looked away again.

Totally uninterested in Caroline, Elliot tries to ignore her by turning away as she approaches.

__b__ She . . . could show Elliot how to use that mattock . . . but . . . he'd just smile, nod ignorantly, and continue using it incorrectly.

Caroline distrusted Elliot so much that she wouldn't give him the help she knew he needed.

__b, a__ Caroline burst out laughing—she couldn't help it . . . until she remembered the time she had had a reaction to poison oak. It was a horrible and painful ordeal. As Elliot bent down to extract a stubborn bit of trash from the brush, Caroline, exasperated, yelled, "That's poison oak!"

Once she remembered how she had suffered from a reaction to poison oak, Caroline felt she must tell Elliot

about it, even though they weren't exactly friends.

2. Reread the two passages with check marks next to them. What do these passages reveal about the kind of person Elliot is?

Elliot's attitude toward, or opinion of, Caroline has changed, especially since she helped him.

3. Read the two passages with Xs next to them. What do these passages reveal about the kind of person Caroline is?

Caroline's attitude toward, or opinion of, Elliot changed, especially since he made a sincere effort to communicate

with her through sign language.

4. Are Elliot and Caroline static or dynamic characters? Write a paragraph of four or five sentences for each character. Explain how each character does or doesn't change during the story.

Elliot Dynamic. At first, Elliot felt that the deaf should stick to themselves, and he was startled by their

strange noises. Later, after Caroline warns him about the poison oak, he learns that the deaf and the hearing have

the same feelings. He even makes an effort to understand the deaf by speaking to Mr. Soong.

Caroline Dynamic. At first, Caroline shuts out the hearing world. Later, she becomes more trusting and less

angry, especially after Elliot attempts to learn sign language.

▶ **Real Life Connections** Research the basics of American Sign Language, including the ASL Alphabet. Practice signing a message with a partner.

Primary and Secondary Sources

__Reading a Social Studies Selection __

▶ **Background Information**

On April 28, 1947, six men set out across the Pacific Ocean on a log raft called the *Kon-Tiki*. The leader of the expedition was Thor Heyerdahl, a Norwegian anthropologist. For more than three months, Heyerdahl, his crew, and their pet parrot drifted on the *Kon-Tiki* westward across the Pacific Ocean.

The following selections tell about Heyerdahl's voyage. The first, "A Voyage on a Raft," was written by someone who did not participate in the voyage. The second is Heyerdahl's own account of a portion of the voyage, taken from his book *Kon-Tiki*, published in 1950.

▶ **Skill Focus**

Information about an event can be found in both **primary sources** and **secondary sources**. Primary sources (meaning first or original sources) are accounts that give firsthand information. They are written by eyewitnesses to history, usually at the time an event occurred. Diaries, letters, autobiographies, newspapers, and photographs are all primary sources. Secondary sources are descriptions or interpretations of an event by someone who did not witness the event. Often they are written long after the event occurred. History books, biographies, encyclopedias, and other reference works are secondary sources.

Because original information sometimes offers the best historical evidence, historians use mostly primary sources when studying or investigating a past period or event.

When comparing information from two different sources, follow these guidelines:

1. **Identify the source.**
   a. Who wrote the information?
   b. When was it written?
   c. How was the author involved in the event?
   d. Is it a primary or a secondary source?

2. **Analyze the information.**
   a. What event is described?
   b. What time period is covered?
   c. How reliable is the information?

3. **Evaluate the information.**
   a. Why is one source apt to be more accurate than the other?
   b. Why is one source apt to be more biased than the other?
   c. What conclusions can you draw based on both sources of information?

▶ **Word Clues**

Read the sentence below. Look for context clues that explain the underlined word.

> Finally, in one <u>surge</u>, the sea rose and lifted them inside the reef.

The word *surge* is explained by the words that follow it. These words give details to help you understand the meaning of *surge*.

Use **detail** context clues to find the meanings of the three underlined words in the selection.

▶ **Strategy Tip**

As you read these primary and secondary sources, compare the information in them. Which selection is the primary source? The secondary source? Use the questions in the Skill Focus to help you compare the two sources.

A Voyage on a Raft

While visiting Fatu Hiva, a Polynesian island in the Pacific Ocean, Thor Heyerdahl heard a fascinating legend—a tale about an ancient god and chief named Tiki, who had brought people to the islands many centuries ago. Before that time, they had inhabited "a big country beyond the sea."

The old legend seized Heyerdahl's scientific curiosity. He wondered where these people might have come from and how they had crossed the ocean. Heyerdahl went to Peru, where he heard a legend about Kon-Tiki, the sun king, who once led a group of people across the Pacific Ocean. This legend was similar to the Polynesian story about the god Tiki. Could the two legends be descriptions of the same event?

After years of research and speculation regarding these questions, Heyerdahl formulated a startling theory. He proposed that the first settlers on the Polynesian Islands had traveled over 4,000 miles (6,400 kilometers) from Peru.

✗ The facts supported Heyerdahl's theory. First, the wind blows constantly toward the west from South America. Second, the Polynesian settlers had once carved huge stone statues similar to statues found in South America. Third, the ancient Incas of Peru had gone to sea in rafts, sailing over 50 miles (80

> *For almost four months, they would not encounter another human being.*

kilometers) from the coast to catch fish. At that distance, they were in the Humboldt Current, which runs north along the coast of Peru and then swings west just below the equator to join the South Equatorial Current, which goes straight to the Polynesian Islands. Tiki could have reached those islands on a raft.

Heyerdahl was determined to test his theory, even if he had to cross the Pacific on a raft himself.

✗ With five other men, he built a raft exactly like those described in ancient records. They chose nine of the thickest balsa logs that they could find. They cut deep grooves into the wood to prevent the ropes holding the whole raft together from slipping; not a single spike was used. In the middle of the raft, they erected a small, open bamboo cabin. The men then set up a sail and a steering oar. When the raft was completed, they stocked it with a four-month supply of food.

On April 28, 1947, the six men and their parrot began their voyage from Callao, Peru. A tug towed them about 50 miles (80 kilometers) from shore into the Humboldt Current. For almost four months, they would not encounter another human being.

At first, the raft tossed about in the treacherous sea. When the water became calm, the men caught fish for food. At night,

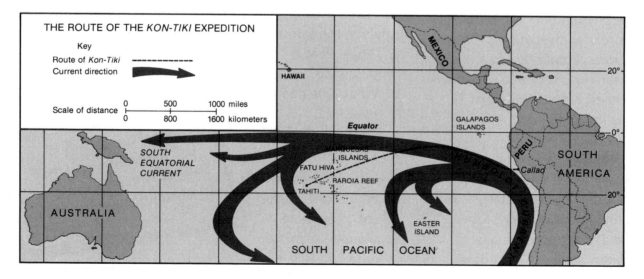

THE ROUTE OF THE *KON-TIKI* EXPEDITION

Key
Route of *Kon-Tiki* - - - - - - - -
Current direction →

Scale of distance
0   500   1000 miles
0   800   1600 kilometers

HAWAII
MEXICO
Equator
GALAPAGOS ISLANDS
PERU
Callao
SOUTH AMERICA
SOUTH EQUATORIAL CURRENT
MARQUESAS ISLANDS
FATU HIVA
RAROIA REEF
TAHITI
AUSTRALIA
EASTER ISLAND
SOUTH PACIFIC OCEAN
20°
0°
20°

they charted their progress by the stars and found that the current was carrying them—just as Heyerdahl had predicted—westward toward the Polynesian Islands.

On July 3, 1947, the crew saw land birds for the first time. Several weeks later, they saw a small cloud on the horizon. It did not move with the wind but rose steadily like a column of smoke; it was caused by the warm air rising from an island.

On July 30, the crew saw land, but they couldn't reach it because the wind and currents carried them away from it. They soon passed another remote island and headed toward it. The raft hit the coral wall of the reef innumerable times. Finally, in one surge, the sea rose and lifted them inside the reef. Although the raft was severely damaged, the men were not injured.

Maps showed that they had landed on Raroia Reef in the Polynesian Islands. Their voyage did not prove that such a voyage had been made centuries ago. It did prove, though, that it could have been made. Thor Heyerdahl, however, was satisfied that his theory was <u>valid</u>.

From *Kon-Tiki*

As the troughs of the sea gradually grew deeper, it became clear that we had moved into the swiftest part of the Humboldt Current. This sea was obviously caused by a current and not simply raised by the wind. The water was green and cold and everywhere about us; the jagged mountains of Peru had vanished into the dense cloud banks astern. When darkness crept over the waters, our first duel with the elements began. We were still not sure of the sea; we were still uncertain whether it would show itself a friend or an enemy. . . .

About midnight, a ship's light passed in a northerly direction. At three, another passed on the same course. We waved our little paraffin lamp and hailed them with flashes from an electric torch. But they did not see us, and the lights passed slowly northward into the darkness and disappeared. Little did we on board the raft realize that this was our last ship and the last trace of men we should see till we had reached the other side of the ocean.

We clung like flies, two and two, to the steering oar in the darkness and felt the fresh sea water pouring off our hair while the oar hit us and our hands grew stiff with the exertion of hanging on. We had a good schooling those first days and nights; it turned landlubbers into seamen. For the first twenty-four hours, every man, in unbroken succession, had two hours at the helm and three hours' rest. We arranged that every hour a fresh man should relieve one of the two steersmen who had been at the helm for two hours.

✔ The next night was still worse; the seas grew higher instead of going down. Two hours of struggling with the steering oar was too long. A man was not much use in the

Kon-Tiki, shown leaving Callao Harbor, Peru, was named after the Peruvian sun god, who long ago vanished westward across the sea.

second half of his watch, and the seas got the better of us and hurled us round and sideways, while the water poured on board. Then we changed over to one hour at the helm and an hour and a half's rest. So the first sixty hours passed, in one continuous struggle against a <u>chaos</u> of waves that rushed upon us, one after another, without <u>cessation</u>. . . .

After a week or so the sea grew calmer, and we noticed that it became blue instead of green. We began to go west-northwest instead of due northwest and took this as the first faint sign that we were out of the coastal current and had some hope of being carried out to sea.

The very first day we were left alone on the sea we had noticed fish around the raft, but we were too much occupied with steering to think of fishing. The second day, we went right into a thick shoal of sardines, and soon

afterward an eight-foot blue shark came along and rolled over with its white belly uppermost as it rubbed against the raft's stern. . . . It played round us for a while, but disappeared when we got the hand harpoon ready for action.

Next day, we were visited by tunnies, bonitos, and dolphins, and when a big flying fish thudded on board we used it as bait and at once pulled in two large dolphins weighing from twenty to thirty-five pounds each. This was food for several days. On steering watch we could see many fish we did not even know. One day, we came into a school of porpoises which seemed quite endless. The black backs tumbled about, packed close together, right in to the side of the raft, and sprang up here and there all over the sea as far as we could see from the masthead.

RECALLING FACTS

Write the answers to the following questions on the lines provided. You may go back to the selection to find an answer.

Recalling details
1. Why did Heyerdahl name the raft *Kon-Tiki* after the Peruvian sun king?

The raft, like the Peruvian sun king, was taking a

group of people westward across the sea.

_____

Recalling details
2. Heyerdahl and his men kept the raft going in the right direction by which of the following ways? Check two items.

✔ _____ a. charting their movement according to the stars

_____ b. always looking for the equator

✔ _____ c. sailing with the Humboldt Current

Reading a map
3. Sequence the events below in the order in which they happened.

__4__ *Kon-Tiki* travels on the Humboldt Current.

__2__ After research in Peru, Heyerdahl formulates his theory.

__3__ *Kon-Tiki* leaves Peru.

__1__ Heyerdahl first visits Polynesia.

__5__ *Kon-Tiki* arrives at a Polynesian island.

Reading a map
4. What ocean current moves in a northwest direction along the coast of South America?

The Humboldt Current moves in this direction.

_____

Reading a map
5. Between which two latitude lines did the *Kon-Tiki* sail?

0° and 20°

Identifying the main idea
6. Reread the two paragraphs that have Xs next to them. Then in each paragraph underline the sentence that states the main idea of the paragraph.

Using context clues
7. Draw a line to match each word with its meaning.

cessation   based on evidence

chaos   ceasing

valid   confusion

Not all the questions about a selection are answered directly in the selection. For the following questions, you will have to figure out answers not directly stated in the selection. Write the answers to the questions on the lines provided.

Distinguishing fact from opinion.

1. Identify each of the following statements as fact or opinion by writing *F* or *O* on the line provided.

___F___ The crew of the *Kon-Tiki* risked their lives to make the voyage.

___O___ Heyerdahl was wrong to risk the lives of his crew members.

Drawing conclusions

2. The crew sighted land birds and a small cloud that didn't move with the wind but rose steadily like a column of smoke. What did the crew conclude?

The crew realized that they were near land.

Inferring the unstated main idea

3. Reread the paragraph with a check mark next to it. Write a sentence describing its main idea.

The beginning of the voyage was a life and death struggle between the crew and the ocean.

Making inferences

4. From what you have read about Thor Heyerdahl, how would you describe his character?

Heyerdahl had a strong scientific curiosity, combined with a courageous and adventurous spirit.

Making generalizations

5. Write a generalization based on the three facts below.

   Facts a. The crew of the *Kon-Tiki* was alone on the vast Pacific Ocean.

   b. The ocean waves crashed across the small raft with great force.

   c. Sharks swim up close to the raft.

   Generalization The *Kon-Tiki*'s crew risked their lives on the voyage.

Making inferences

6. Look at the sail of the *Kon-Tiki* in the photograph on page 13.

   a. Whose face do you think is on the sail?

the Peruvian sun king, Kon-Tiki

   b. Why do you think it is appropriate?

Kon-Tiki's face on the sail is very appropriate; the raft was going westward across the ocean as the ancient

sun king had done centuries before.

SKILL FOCUS

To answer the questions below, compare the information presented in "A Voyage on a Raft" on pages 12–13 and "From *Kon-Tiki*" on pages 13–14.

1. **Identify the source.**

   a. Who wrote the information?

   "A Voyage on a Raft" author not given

   "From *Kon-Tiki*" Thor Heyerdahl

b. When was the information written?

"A Voyage on a Raft" <u>after the expedition</u>

"From *Kon-Tiki*" <u>probably during and after the expedition</u>

c. How was the author involved in the event?

"A Voyage on a Raft" <u>The author researched information.</u>

"From *Kon-Tiki*" <u>The author took part in the event.</u>

d. Is it a primary or a secondary source?

"A Voyage on a Raft" <u>secondary source</u>   "From *Kon-Tiki*" <u>primary source</u>

2. **Analyze the information given.**

   a. What event is described?

   "A Voyage on a Raft" <u>The background of Heyerdahl's voyage and the voyage itself is described.</u>

   "From *Kon-Tiki*" <u>The events of a few days of the voyage are described.</u>

   b. What time period does the source cover?

   "A Voyage on a Raft" <u>several years</u>   "From *Kon-Tiki*" <u>several days</u>

   c. How reliable is the source's information?

   "A Voyage on a Raft" <u>The author researched the facts of the event.</u>

   "From *Kon-Tiki*" <u>It is more reliable than "A Voyage on a Raft" because the author experienced the</u>

   <u>event.</u>

3. **Evaluate the information given.**

   a. Why is one source apt to be more accurate than the other?

   <u>The primary source ("From *Kon-Tiki*") is more accurate because the author had firsthand information as an eyewitness.</u>

   <u>The author of the secondary source ("A Voyage on a Raft") merely gathered available information.</u>

   b. Why is one source apt to be more biased than the other?

   <u>The primary source is more biased because the author was totally involved in the event. The secondary source is</u>

   <u>comprised of facts and details gathered after the event occurred.</u>

   c. Is the photograph on page 13 a primary or a secondary source of information? Explain.

   <u>The photograph, taken during the actual expedition, is a primary source.</u>

   d. What conclusions can you draw based on both sources of information?

   <u>Possible answers: Heyerdahl's mission proved that the trip most likely was made and that ancient people in</u>

   <u>primitive vessels could cross large bodies of water.</u>

▶ **Real Life Connections** Locate a firsthand and a secondhand account of an event reported in your local newspaper. Compare the two accounts. How are they similar? How are they different?

Cause and Effect

__ Reading a Science Selection __

▶ **Background Information**

Earthquakes and tsunamis are powerful natural forces. "Earthquakes and Tsunamis" examines these explosive and destructive powers of nature. It also examines what scientists are doing to find ways to predict these natural forces.

▶ **Skill Focus**

A **cause** is a reason, condition, or situation that makes an event happen. An **effect** is the result of a cause. For example, earthquakes may uproot trees. Earthquakes are the cause, and uprooted trees are the effect.

Sometimes one effect may be the result of many causes, or one cause may have many effects. When an effect becomes the cause of another effect, a chain of causes and effects is formed. Read the following sentences.

> An earthquake caused gas lines in the ground to break. The gas that was released caused a fire.

The first cause, an earthquake, results in broken gas lines. This effect is then the cause of the second effect, a fire.

The diagram below shows the chain of causes and effects.

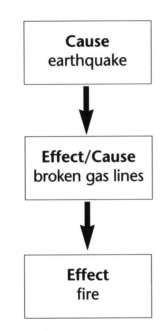

Causes and effects are often directly stated in textbooks. Sometimes, however, you have to **infer**, or figure out, an effect.

▶ **Word Clues**

Read the sentence below. Look for context clues to help you understand the underlined word.

> This chain reaction continues until all the energy is <u>expended</u>, or used up.

If you do not know the meaning of the word *expended*, the phrase *or used up* can help you. The phrase *or used up* is an appositive phrase. An appositive phrase explains a word coming before it and is set off by commas or dashes.

Use **appositive phrases** to find the meanings of the three underlined words in the selection.

▶ **Strategy Tip**

As you read "Earthquakes and Tsunamis," use your knowledge of cause and effect to understand the causes of earthquakes and tsunamis. Think about how chains of cause and effect relate to these natural phenomena.

Earthquakes and Tsunamis

On January 17, 1995, a powerful earthquake hit the city of Kobe, Japan. Although the quake lasted only 20 seconds, it killed more than 5,000 people and injured 26,000 more. Over 50,000 buildings were destroyed or severely damaged, leaving 310,000 people—one fifth of the city's population—without homes. In January 1994, an earthquake struck Northridge, California, a suburb of Los Angeles. This quake killed more than 50 people, injured 7,000, and left 20,000 homeless.

In September 1992, a mild undersea earthquake in the eastern Pacific Ocean triggered seismic sea waves, or **tsunamis** (tsoo NAH meez), that rushed with jet-plane speed toward Nicaragua. As 30-foot waves crashed into the coast, 170 people drowned, houses were washed into the sea, leaving more than 13,000 people homeless, and boats were carried inland like bathtub toys.

What Are Earthquakes?

If you throw a pebble into a pond, you see waves moving outward in all directions. When rocks in the earth break, something similar happens; waves travel through the earth in all directions, causing the ground to shake. During a severe earthquake, the ground can rise and fall in a way that is similar to the movement of waves in the ocean. The motion of the ground causes trees and buildings to sway and fall.

Most earthquakes are caused by **faulting**, which occurs when sections of the earth's crust are pushed or pulled in different directions.

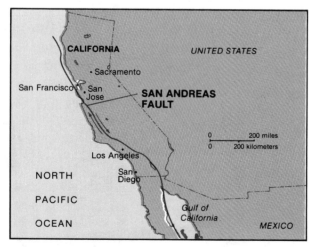

Figure 1. The San Andreas Fault runs through California.

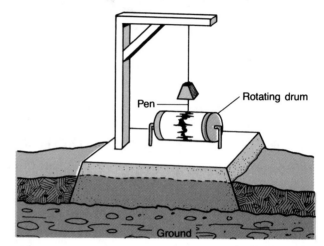

Figure 2. A seismograph measures an earthquake's strength.

During faulting, rocks break and slide past one another, releasing energy. The movement in an earthquake is caused both by the movement and the vibration of rocks. As the rocks move or vibrate, they cause nearby rocks to move or vibrate. This chain reaction continues until all the energy is expended, or used up.

A break in the earth's surface where faulting occurs is called a **fault**. The San Andreas Fault runs north and south from the Gulf of California to San Francisco. As shown in Figure 1, the land west of this fault is slowly moving north, and the land east of it is slowly moving south. However, the rocks along the fault do not all move simultaneously, or at the same time, nor do they all necessarily move at the same pace. During a severe earthquake in San Francisco in 1906, rocks on both sides of the San Andreas Fault moved.

Faults can be close to the earth's surface or up to 74 kilometers deep. The point beneath the surface where rocks break and move is called the **focus** of an earthquake. The point on the earth's surface directly above the focus is called the **epicenter** (EP ə sen tər). The most violent movement during an earthquake is at its epicenter.

Detecting and Measuring Earthquakes

Rock movement and vibration can be measured by an instrument called a **seismograph** (SYZ mə graf), shown in Figure 2. This instrument has a recording sheet on a

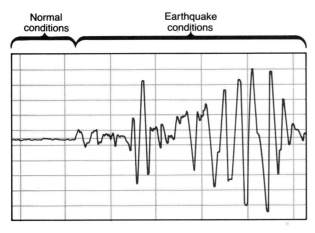

Figure 3. A seismograph records a straight line when the earth is not moving and a wavy line during an earthquake.

rotating drum. Above the drum, a pen is attached to a heavy object. When all is quiet, the pen draws a straight line on the recording sheet. When the earth moves, the base vibrates, but the weighted pen does not. As a result, the pen leaves a wavy line on the drum. The degree of side-to-side movement of the wavy line depends on the strength of the earthquake. Figure 3 shows recordings under both normal and earthquake conditions.

The Richter scale, which was designed in 1935 by Charles F. Richter, an American scientist, is used to measure how much energy an earthquake releases. This scale numbers earthquakes from 1 to 10, based on how violent they are, and each number indicates an earthquake that is ten times stronger than the <u>preceding</u> number, or the number that comes before. For example, an earthquake that registers 2 on the scale is ten times stronger than an earthquake that registers 1. Any quake registering more than 6.0 on the Richter scale is termed destructive. The Kobe, Japan, earthquake registered 7.2. The Northridge, California, quake registered 6.8.

What Is a Tsunami?

When an earthquake occurs on the ocean floor, an area of the ocean floor may rise. If, for example, an area the size of Indiana or Ohio rises about 2 meters, it sends vibrations through the water, and the waves caused by the vibrations form a **tsunami**. Tsunamis move very fast—1,000 to 1,300 kilometers per hour! Their waves have a long wavelength; a wavelength is the distance from the crest of one wave to the crest of another.

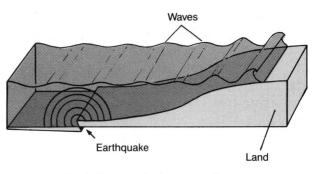

Figure 4. An earthquake in the ocean floor can cause a tsunami.

As long as the waves are over the deep ocean, however, they are not very high. Figure 4 shows a tsunami forming.

As tsunamis rush toward land, the shallow water slows them down. This slowdown, in turn, causes the water to pile up, forming a towering wave that may be over 30 meters high. The power behind the wave sends it crashing against the shore and makes the water flood the land.

Predicting Earthquakes and Tsunamis

Scientists can quickly determine the epicenter of a quake that has occurred, but they still don't understand earthquakes well enough to predict them. However, every earthquake that occurs provides scientists with data that bring them closer to understanding these natural disasters. From these data, scientists hope to find a pattern of natural events that are related to earthquakes and that take place before the actual quake. If scientists can identify such a pattern, perhaps they can predict earthquakes. Certain areas are more <u>susceptible</u> to, or easily affected by, earthquake activity, and scientists are studying these areas carefully.

In their studies, scientists use various instruments, one of which is called a **tiltmeter.** This device records any changes in the land's slope that could indicate the movement of rocks. Sensitive gravity meters measure tiny changes in gravity that indicate an increase or decrease in the elevation of an area. Electronic devices are used to detect increased stress on underground rock that may cause the rock to break or shift. Lasers are used to detect slight shifts in the earth's crust.

In addition to these scientific methods, scientists are also examining folklore about earthquakes. Animals have been reported as behaving strangely hours before a quake, and strange lights and loud sounds have supposedly occurred before an earthquake. Scientists are trying to find out how reliable these signs are.

Since tsunamis occur after earthquakes, they are less difficult to predict. Earthquakes occurring on the ocean floor usually produce tsunamis, but strong quakes on land can also produce tsunamis if they disturb the ocean floor.

The most important aim in the study of tsunamis is a warning system to let people in coastal areas know when these waves are coming. Such a warning system operates in Hawaii; it sends information to the entire Pacific area. This station receives seismograph readings from many other stations. Equipped with a computer, the station determines the position of the earthquake's epicenter and <u>calculates</u>, or figures out, the time that the tsunami is expected to arrive at land bordering the Pacific.

The study of earthquakes is a relatively young area of science. Yet scientists around the world are working hard to learn how to predict these disasters and reduce the loss of life.

RECALLING FACTS

Write the answers to the following questions on the lines provided. You may go back to the selection to find an answer.

Identifying cause and effect
1. What causes the earth's movements in an earthquake?

The movement and vibration of underground rocks causes an earthquake.

Recalling details
2. What is a fault?

A fault is crack in the earth's crust.

Identifying cause and effect
3. What causes most earthquakes?

Most are caused by faulting, when sections of the earth's crust are pushed or pulled in different directions.

Recalling details
4. What is the focus of an earthquake?

The focus is the point deep in the earth where rocks break and move.

Recalling details
5. What is the epicenter of an earthquake?

The epicenter is the point on the earth's surface directly above an earthquake's focus.

Recalling details
6. What information does a seismograph provide?

It tells whether there is movement or vibration of the rocks in the area of the seismograph.

Recalling details
7. What does the Richter scale measure?

The Richter scale measures the energy released in an earthquake, or the strength of an earthquake.

Identifying cause and effect
8. What causes a tsunami?

A tsunami is caused by an earthquake on the ocean floor that raises the surface of a large area of the ocean floor;

a strong quake on land can disturb the ocean floor and produce a tsunami.

Identifying cause and effect
9. What makes the low ocean waves of tsunamis become towering waves near a coast?

The waves are slowed down in the shallow water near a coast. Water from other incoming waves piles up, creating

a towering wave.

Recalling details

10. What two means are scientists using to study earthquakes? Give an example of each.

They are using scientific instruments (tiltmeter, gravity meter, electronic devices, lasers) and folklore (animals' strange

behavior, strange lights, loud noises before a quake).

Using context clues

11. Complete each sentence by filling in the correct word from below.

preceding   susceptible   calculates

   a. A computer _____calculates_____ faster than a person.

   b. He slept late because he had worked hard the _____preceding_____ day.

   c. If you don't eat properly, you are more _____susceptible_____ to colds.

INTERPRETING FACTS

Not all the questions about a selection are answered directly in the selection. For the following questions, you will have to figure out answers not directly stated in the selection. Circle the letter next to the correct answer.

Making inferences

1. An earthquake that registers 5.5 on the Richter scale is ten times weaker than a quake that registers _____.

   a. 4.5   **b.** 6.5   **c.** 55   **d.** 6.0

Making inferences

2. An earthquake registering 8.0 would _____.

   a. do little damage

   b. cause extensive damage

   c. be the strongest earthquake known

   d. cause leaves to flutter

Inferring cause and effect

3. Aftershocks are felt in an area for weeks, months, and sometimes even years after an earthquake occurs. Although they can do damage, they usually register lower on the Richter scale than the earthquake itself. Aftershocks are an indication that _____.

   a. the rocks around the earthquake's focus are still using up released energy

   b. the rocks around the epicenter of the earthquake are stable again

   c. the rocks in areas where earthquakes occur are always stable

   d. another earthquake will not occur

Inferring cause and effect

4. In which of the following areas is an earthquake most likely to result in a tsunami?

   a. Colorado

   b. central Canada

   c. the Pacific Ocean

   d. Arizona

Inferring cause and effect

5. Why can't scientists predict earthquakes?

   a. Since earthquakes have not occurred for very long, scientists have not had much time to study them.

   b. Earthquakes occur in more than just one part of the world, so scientists don't know where a quake will hit.

   c. Scientists have not been able to find a pattern that is common to all earthquakes and that would help them make predictions.

   d. Scientists do not have the instruments necessary to measure the vibrations of the earth's crust.

Complete the chains of causes and effects below by choosing the appropriate sentence from the box below. Write each sentence on the appropriate line. The middle effect and cause for each chain has been done for you.

> **Areas that are susceptible to earthquakes are identified.**
> **Shallow water along the coasts slows the waves, making them towering giants.**
> **An earthquake raises a large area of land on the ocean floor.**
> **Rocks in the earth's crust move.**
> **A wavy line is recorded on the seismograph.**
> **An earthquake occurs in the Pacific Ocean.**
> **The earth's surface trembles.**
> **Scientists collect data that help them understand earthquakes.**
> **Rocks in the earth's crust move.**
> **A tsunami warning is sent to the land along the Pacific.**

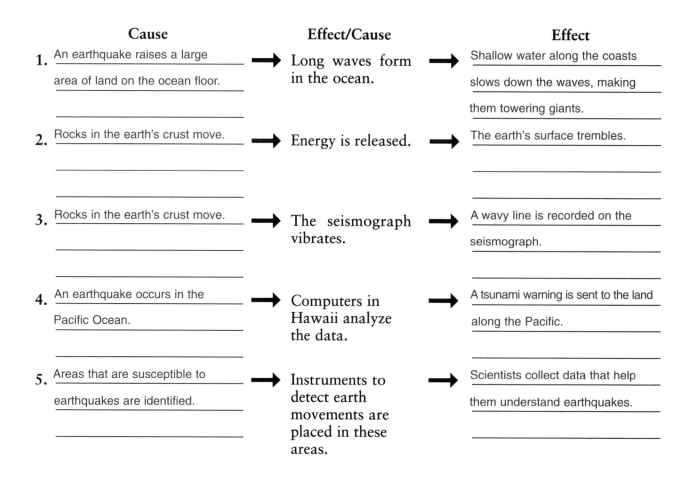

Cause	Effect/Cause	Effect
1. An earthquake raises a large area of land on the ocean floor.	→ Long waves form in the ocean.	→ Shallow water along the coasts slows down the waves, making them towering giants.
2. Rocks in the earth's crust move.	→ Energy is released.	→ The earth's surface trembles.
3. Rocks in the earth's crust move.	→ The seismograph vibrates.	→ A wavy line is recorded on the seismograph.
4. An earthquake occurs in the Pacific Ocean.	→ Computers in Hawaii analyze the data.	→ A tsunami warning is sent to the land along the Pacific.
5. Areas that are susceptible to earthquakes are identified.	→ Instruments to detect earth movements are placed in these areas.	→ Scientists collect data that help them understand earthquakes.

▶ **Real Life Connections** Investigate the most recent earthquake in your geographic area. What did it register on the Richter scale?

Word Problems

Reading a Mathematics Selection

▶ Background Information

In most mathematical word problems, some kind of unit label is attached to each number. Sometimes the unit is a number of things, such as apples or books. At other times the unit is a unit of measurement, such as meters, grams, or seconds. Sometimes the answer depends on the units being of the same kind. Adding a length expressed in meters to one expressed in kilometers results in the wrong answer. At other times, the units may be different. For example, dividing a number of kilometers by a number of hours is reasonable, as long as the solution is expressed in kilometers per hour.

▶ Skill Focus

Use the following five steps in solving word problems.

1. First, read the problem. Be sure that you are familiar with all of the words used in the problem. Think about the question that is asked or the information that you are to supply. Also try to picture in your mind the information given in the problem. Then read the problem again carefully to be sure that you understand what information you are to supply. It may help to draw a diagram.

2. Decide how to find the solution to the problem. You may find it helpful to write a sentence that describes each fact given in the problem. Often there are two or more steps to a problem. When a problem involves three steps, you will need to write three mathematical sentences, or equations, to find the solution. Key words can help you decide which operations will be used in the equations.

3. Estimate the answer. Use rounded numbers to make an estimate for each mathematical sentence, or equation.

4. Carry out the plan. Solve each of the mathematical sentences, or equations.

5. Reread the problem. Then write the complete solution, being careful to label the numbers in the solution with the units they describe. Check your solution. Is it logical? How close is it to your estimate?

▶ Word Clues

Be alert for key words as you read mathematics problems. The word *per* is often used to signal division in mathematics problems. To find kilometers per hour, you divide the total number of kilometers by the total number of hours. Similarly, to find one amount per another amount, you divide the first amount by the second. The word *difference* often signals that subtraction is the operation needed to find the answer. The words *entire,* *total,* or *sum* often signal addition.

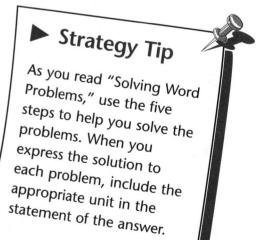

▶ Strategy Tip

As you read "Solving Word Problems," use the five steps to help you solve the problems. When you express the solution to each problem, include the appropriate unit in the statement of the answer.

Solving Word Problems

The Europeans who explored the New World found sophisticated Native American civilizations and the remains of earlier cultures. These explorers wrote accounts of their discoveries. The accounts include mathematical descriptions. Word problems about these discoveries are often based on these accounts.

Use the following five steps in solving word problems.

1. Read the problem.
2. Decide how to find the answer.
3. Estimate the answer.
4. Carry out the plan.
5. Reread the problem.

READ THE PROBLEM

When Alexander von Humboldt, a German naturalist, visited South America in the early nineteenth century, he was amazed by the roads built by the Incas. One stretch of the main road crossed a pass that was 4,041 meters above sea level. The road rose over a course of 295 kilometers from an elevation of only 1,084 meters. How many meters did the road rise per kilometer traveled?

Reread the problem. Be sure that you know the unit label that is used for each number in the problem. Are there any words that you do not know? If so, look those words up in a dictionary to find their meanings. Does the problem ask a question, or does it call for you to supply some information? What question does the problem ask? Often the last sentence of a problem asks the question. *How many meters did the road rise per kilometer traveled?*

DECIDE HOW TO FIND THE ANSWER

In this problem, you need to use more than one operation to obtain the solution. First, list the facts that you know as separate sentences. Then decide on the operations to use.

1. The high pass crossed by the road was 4,041 meters above sea level.
2. The point where the road started to rise was 295 kilometers from the pass.

3. The point where the road started to rise was 1,084 meters above sea level.

Be sure that you know how the rise of a road per kilometer is calculated. The amount of the rise is divided by the number of kilometers over which it rises. You need to do two mathematical operations to find the answer. First, you must find the difference between the elevations of the high pass and the place where the road started to rise. Then you must divide this difference by the total distance between the two places.

Each operation can be shown as an equation. Let d be the difference between the two elevations and m be the rise per kilometer.

$$4{,}041 - 1{,}084 = d$$
$$d \div 295 = m$$

ESTIMATE THE ANSWER

You can estimate this answer easily with rounded numbers.

$$4{,}000 - 1{,}000 = 3{,}000$$
$$3{,}000 \div 300 = 10$$

Your estimate, 10, is the estimated number of meters per kilometer. Do you think that a rise of 10 meters per kilometer is reasonable? Another way to state this estimate is 10 meters per 1,000 meters, which is equivalent to a rise of 1 meter for every 100 meters. This rise is not unreasonably steep.

CARRY OUT THE PLAN

First operation: $4{,}041 - 1{,}084 = 2{,}957$
Second operation: $2{,}957 \div 295 = 10.02$

The answer of 10.02 is given to the nearest hundredth.

REREAD THE PROBLEM

After rereading the problem, write the complete solution: *The road rises at a rate of 10.02 meters per kilometer.*

Notice that the solution is very close to the estimate. You should expect it to be close, since 4,041 is close to 4,000, 1,084 is close to 1,000, and 295 is close to 300.

Use the five steps to solve the following problem. With problems of this type, it may be helpful to draw a diagram like the one shown below.

Read: The temple mound at Cuicuilco, in the Valley of Mexico, may be the oldest large building still standing in the Americas. It was covered by a hill of ash from a volcano thousands of years ago. Like many ancient temples in Central America, it is a stepped pyramid. From top to bottom, the steps are the following heights: 14 meters, 7.3 meters, 1.2 meters, and 1.5 meters. The hill that was excavated to find the temple was only 18.5 meters higher than the surrounding area. The top of the temple was found 2.1 meters beneath the top of the hill. A more recent lava flow had raised the area surrounding the base of the hill. Find out the thickness of the later lava flow.

Make sure that you know what all the words in the problem mean. If you do not know the meanings of the words *lava* or *stepped pyramid*, look them up in a dictionary.

Decide: You are asked to supply the depth of a lava flow using the dimensions of the stepped pyramid as a guide. From the information about the pyramid, you can calculate how tall the pyramid is. From the information about the hill, you can find out how far the pyramid extends beneath the lava flow that surrounds the hill. This depth is the same as the depth of the lava flow around the hill.

The problem requires three equations. You must first find the height of the pyramid h, the distance from the lava layer to the top of the pyramid e, and the thickness t of the lava layer, which is the difference between h and e. The equations are as follows:

$$14 + 7.3 + 1.2 + 1.5 = h$$
$$18.5 - 2.1 = e$$
$$h - e = t$$

Estimate: You can make a good estimate by rounding all the decimals to whole numbers.

$$14 + 7 + 1 + 2 = 24$$
$$18 - 2 = 16$$
$$24 - 16 = 8$$

Carry Out:

$$14 + 7.3 + 1.2 + 1.5 = 24$$
$$18.5 - 2.1 = 16.4$$
$$24 - 16.4 = 7.6$$

Reread: The later lava flow is 7.6 meters thick.

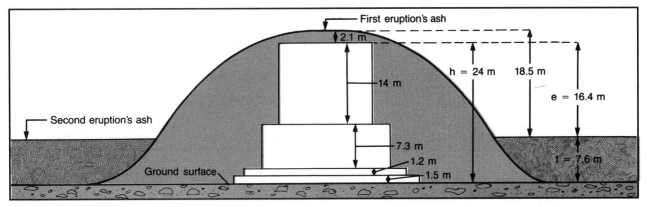

First eruption's ash
2.1 m
h = 24 m   18.5 m
14 m
e = 16.4 m
Second eruption's ash
7.3 m
1.2 m
Ground surface
1.5 m
t = 7.6 m

RECALLING FACTS

Write the answers to the following questions on the lines provided. You may go back to the selection to find an answer.

Recalling details
1. What mathematical operation is indicated by the word *per*?

division

Recognizing sequence of events
2. What is the last step you should perform in solving a word problem?

Reread the problem.

Recalling details
3. If you do not understand some words in a problem, what should you do?

Look them up in a dictionary.

4. What is a good way to estimate the solution to a word problem?

Use rounded numbers.

5. When you arrive at an estimate, what should you ask yourself?

Is it reasonable?

6. In the decide step, how do you express your plan of action?

You write equations.

7. What do you call the step in which you solve the equations that describe a problem?

It is called carrying out the plan

INTERPRETING FACTS

Not all the questions about a selection are answered directly in the selection. For the following questions, you will have to figure out answers not directly stated in the selection. Write the answers to the questions on the lines provided.

Making inferences

1. If you estimate the answer to the sum of 5,430, 9,397, and 3,486 by rounding to the nearest thousand, would you expect your estimate to be close to the actual sum or fairly far from it? Explain.

The estimate would be fairly far from it, because none of the actual numbers is very close to the rounded numbers.

Making inferences

2. If a problem calls for you to find the number of temple ruins per hundred square kilometers in Yucatan, what mathematical operation is required? Division is required.

Making inferences

3. In solving a problem, you find that a lava flow is 9 kilometers thick. What would you suspect about your answer?

It is probably wrong because 9 kilometers is an unreasonable thickness for a lava flow. A correct answer might be

9 meters.

Making inferences

4. Each of two tasks takes 75 seconds and 1.4 minutes to complete. The problem asks you to find the total time taken by both tasks. Before writing the equations for the solution of the problem, how should you change the problem?

Rewrite the times in the same units, either seconds or minutes.

Making inferences

5. What is meant by the elevation of a geographic feature?

The elevation of a geographic feature is its height above sea level.

1. **Read:** In the mid-1920s, the explorer Thomas W. F. Gann discovered that the Mayas, like the Incas, built extensive roads. The road from Cobá to a point near Chichen Itzá stretches for 97 kilometers. It is 9.75 meters wide and built with stone and rubble to an average height of 1.5 meters above the ground. In cubic meters, what is the volume of stone used in making such a road? (There are 1,000 meters in a kilometer. The formula for volume is length × width × height.)

Decide: $97 \times 1{,}000 = m; m \times 9.75 \times 1.5 = y$

Estimate: $100 \times 1{,}000 = 100{,}000; 100{,}000 \times 10 \times 2 = 2{,}000{,}000$

Carry Out: $97 \times 1{,}000 = 97{,}000; 97{,}000 \times 9.75 \times 1.5 = 1{,}418{,}625$

Reread: The volume of stone was 1,418,625 cubic meters.

2. **Read:** Every 3 kilometers along the Incan roads was a chasqui, a small hut where messengers could rest or sleep. It is estimated that the Incan road system included 16,000 kilometers of roads. About how many chasquis were there?

Decide: $16{,}000 \div 3 = x$

Estimate: $15{,}000 \div 3 = 5{,}000$

Carry Out: $16{,}000 \div 3 = 5{,}333$

Reread: There were about 5,333 chasquis.

3. **Read:** The archaeologist Sylvanus G. Morley discovered an ancient Mayan inscription whose date in the Mayan system is equivalent to April 9, 328 A.D. He discovered the inscription on May 10, 1916, which was the 131st day of the year 1916. How many days had passed since the inscription had been made until it was discovered? (Ignore leap years, and simply count every year as 365 days. Include the days in the year that came before the discovery.)

Decide: $1916 - 328 = y; y \times 365 = d; d + 131 = n$

Estimate: $1{,}900 - 300 = 1{,}600; 1{,}600 \times 400 = 640{,}000; 640{,}000 + 100 = 640{,}100$

Carry Out: $1{,}916 - 328 = 1{,}588; 1{,}588 \times 365 = 579{,}620; 579{,}620 + 131 = 579{,}751$

Reread: The number of days that had elapsed when Morley discovered the inscription was 579,751.

▶ **Real Life Connections** If you want to find the number of cars per hundred square kilometers in your school parking lot, what mathematical operation would you use?

Syllables

To help you pronounce long words, divide the words into syllables. Then pronounce each syllable until you can say the whole word. There are several different ways of deciding how a word should be divided.

Guide 1: Compound Words

One of the easiest guides to use in dividing words is the one for a compound word. Because a compound is made up of two words, it must have at least two syllables. Always divide a compound word into syllables by separating it between the two smaller words first. If one or even both of the smaller words in a compound word have more than one syllable, it may be necessary to use another guide. However, you can pronounce most compound words if you divide them into two words.

snowstorm   snow storm

Read each of the following compound words. Divide the word into two syllables, writing the two smaller words separately on the line to the right of each compound word.

1. doghouse ___dog house___
2. highway ___high way___
3. downtown ___down town___
4. bedspread ___bed spread___
5. sidewalk ___side walk___
6. toothpaste ___tooth paste___

Guide 2: Words with Double Consonants

Another guide that you may use is for words with double consonants. Divide the word into two syllables between the two consonants and read each syllable.

lettuce   let tuce

Use this guide to divide the following two-syllable words into syllables. Write each syllable separately on the line to the right of the word.

1. common ___com mon___
2. muffin ___muf fin___
3. kitten ___kit ten___
4. tunnel ___tun nel___
5. splatter ___splat ter___
6. pillow ___pil low___

Guide 3: Words with a Prefix or Suffix

A prefix or suffix always has at least one sounded vowel. Therefore, a prefix or suffix always contains at least one syllable. You can divide a word that has a prefix or suffix between the prefix or suffix and the root word.

preheat   pre heat
cloudy   cloud y

Divide each of the words below into two syllables between the prefix or suffix and the root word. Write the syllables separately on the line to the right of the word.

1. rethink ___re think___
2. pitcher ___pitch er___
3. monthly ___month ly___
4. unfair ___un fair___
5. misspell ___mis spell___
6. worthless ___worth less___

Guide 4: Words With Two Consonants Between Two Sounded Vowels

A word that has two consonants between two sounded vowels is usually divided into syllables between the two consonants.

helmet   hel met

Divide each of the words below into two syllables by writing the syllables separately on the line to the right of the word.

1. cactus ____cac tus____   3. chapter ____chap ter____   5. magnet ____mag net____

2. picture ____pic ture____   4. pencil ____pen cil____   6. plaster ____plas ter____

Guide 5: Words with One Consonant Between Two Sounded Vowels

Guide 5a: A word that has one consonant between two sounded vowels, with the first vowel long, is usually divided into syllables before the consonant.

robot   ro bot

Guide 5b: A word that has one consonant between two sounded vowels, with the first vowel short, is usually divided into syllables after the consonant.

venom   ven om

Say each of the words below to yourself. If the first vowel is long, use Guide 5a to divide it into two syllables. If the first vowel is short, use Guide 5b. Write the syllables separately on the line to the right of the word.

1. canine ____ca nine____   3. flavor ____fla vor____   5. closet ____clos et____

2. seven ____sev en____   4. critic ____crit ic____   6. climate ____cli mate____

Guide 6: Words with Blends

The word *trophy* has two consonants between two sounded vowels. Because *ph* is a consonant digraph, you do not divide the word between the two consonants. The letters *ph* should be treated as one consonant. When dividing the word *trophy* into syllables, use Guide 5a.

tro   phy

If three consonants are in the middle of a word, two of the consonants may be a blend or digraph. You treat the blend or digraph as one consonant. For example, *complex* has a *pl* blend. You divide the word between the consonant and the blend.

com   plex

Circle the blend or digraph in each of the words below. Then divide the word into two syllables, writing the syllables separately on the line to the right of the word.

1. pan(th)er ____pan ther____   3. li(ch)ens ____li chens____   5. men(th)ol ____men thol____

2. com(pl)aint ____com plaint____   4. far(th)er ____far ther____   6. de(gr)ee ____de gree____

When a word ends in *-le,* the *-le* and the consonant before it make up a syllable, as in *han dle.*

Divide each of the words below into two syllables, writing the syllables separately on the line to the right of the word.

1. trample ____tram ple____   3. marble ____mar ble____   5. trouble ____trou ble____

2. noble ____no ble____   4. stable ____sta ble____   6. uncle ____un cle____

Prefixes

A **prefix** is a word part that is added to the beginning of a word to change its meaning. Ten prefixes and their meanings are given below.

Prefix	Meaning		Prefix	Meaning
bi	having two, or happening every two		non	not
de	undo		pre	before
dis	away or opposite of		re	again or do over
mid	middle		tri	having three
mis	wrong or badly		uni	having one

Read each word below and the meaning that follows it. Then write the correct prefix before each word.

1. _bi_monthly — happening once every two months

2. _mis_trust — to trust wrongly

3. _tri_angles — shapes that have three angles

4. _pre_cautions — cautions taken beforehand

5. _de_code — undo a code

6. _re_possess — to possess again

7. _uni_cycle — one-wheeler that is used for riding

8. _dis_connect — the opposite of connect

9. _non_fiction — not fiction

10. _mid_day — the middle of the day

Use one of the words above to complete each sentence below.

1. The spy was able to _decode_ the secret message from the head of state.

2. On weekdays, we eat our _midday_ meal in the school cafeteria.

3. Maria Alonzo publishes a _bimonthly_ magazine that comes out six times a year.

4. The automobile company will _repossess_ your car if you do not make payments on time.

5. Sarah had to _disconnect_ the stereo because the wire looked worn.

6. Geometry includes measurement of squares, _triangles_, and circles.

7. Carla took _precautions_ against burglary by installing an alarm in her house.

8. The acrobat in the circus rode a red _unicycle_.

9. _Nonfiction_ is a form of writing that deals with real people and events.

10. _Mistrust_ is a natural attitude to have toward someone who lies.

Main Idea

The main idea often appears in the first or last sentence of a paragraph. However, the main idea can also be found in any of the sentences in a paragraph.

To find the sentence with the main idea, you first need to read the paragraph carefully. Try to figure out what most of the sentences are about. Then look for the sentence that tells the main idea.

Each of the following paragraphs is about a different subject. Read each paragraph, and underline the sentence that tells its main idea.

Paragraph 1

In February 1987, grave robbers dug a pit into a mud-brick platform near the village of Sipán in Peru. They found an ancient tomb and looted it of gold and silver ornaments. Scientists learned of the tomb when the robbers sold their loot. Peruvian archaeologist Walter Alva began excavating the looted tomb and others he found later. The tombs of Sipán proved to be one of the richest archaeological finds in the New World.

Paragraph 2

Africa's population includes many distinct peoples and cultures. The northern part of the continent is primarily Arab. South of the Sahara desert, the population is predominantly black African. Not counting European languages introduced by colonists, about 1,000 different languages and distinct dialects are spoken. Most people in North Africa speak Arabic. Major languages in black Africa include Swahili, Amharic, Yoruba, Hausa, and Xhosa.

Paragraph 3

Edwin L. Drake drilled an oil well near Titusville, Pennsylvania, in 1859. This oil well was the first successful oil well to be drilled in our country. Using a steam-operated drill and a wooden rig, Drake struck oil at a depth of $69\frac{1}{2}$ feet (20.9 meters). His well produced approximately 10 to 35 barrels of oil a day. Soon wells were drilled in other parts of the country. The sticky black petroleum was taken to refineries, where kerosene oil was extracted from the petroleum. When the automobile came into use, the refineries began making gasoline.

Paragraph 4

Do you know the origin of the word *cereal*? The ancient Romans prayed to Ceres, the goddess of agriculture. They believed that Ceres guarded their food plants and was responsible for the growing season. Once a year, they held a festival in her honor, called the *Cerealia*. From the names of the goddess and of her festival came the word *cereal*. The word is now used to describe various kinds of grain, from plants such as oats, corn, wheat, and rice.

Paragraph 5

Tecumseh, a Shawnee chief, attempted to unite midwestern Native American tribes to oppose European-American settlement of tribal lands. Famous for his military skill, Tecumseh joined the British army against the United States in the War of 1812. He was defeated and killed in the battle of the Thames River in Ontario in 1813.

Paragraph 6

A firefly winks its light in the summer night. A bird migrates thousands of miles to its winter home in the south. A dolphin swims fast enough to outrace some boats. An ape uses a stick to draw ants out of an anthill that cannot be captured otherwise. Each of these animals can do something that people can do. A firefly creates light; people do the same thing with fire or with electric light bulbs. A bird can travel great distances; so can people with their airplanes or ships. A dolphin speeds through water, just as people speed through water in a motorboat. An ape makes a tool for food-gathering, just as humans make tools to perform functions that they cannot do otherwise.

Stated or Unstated Main Idea

When you read a chapter in a textbook, the main idea of each paragraph is often stated in a sentence. However, sometimes the main idea of a paragraph is not stated in one of the sentences. You need to use the information in the paragraph to **infer**, or figure out, the main idea. To do so, you need to ask yourself what the paragraph is about.

Read the following paragraph about deaf people interacting in a hearing world. Because the main idea is not stated, you will need to infer it.

> Deaf people do not wear signs that identify them as handicapped. They function in a sound-oriented world. Sometimes, though, when others learn that someone is deaf or profoundly hard of hearing, they scream at the deaf person. They seem to think that shouting will solve the communication problem. Others ignore the attempts of the deaf to be included. They turn away lips that might be read.

Underline the phrase that tells what this paragraph is about.

a. methods of coping for deaf people

b. a basic problem that deaf people encounter

c. lessons that handicapped people teach each other

If you chose b, you are correct. The paragraph tells about a basic problem that deaf people have. The following sentence is a main idea sentence for this paragraph.

> One of the main problems that deaf people have is the insensitivity of the hearing community.

Read the following selection about deaf individuals.

Help for the Deaf

1. <u>People who are deaf have unique problems.</u> Unlike blind people with seeing eye dogs or white walking sticks, deaf people do not show any outward signs of their handicap. Drivers may use their horns without any positive effect. Trains may be announced over public address systems, but the deaf never hear the announcements. Sirens go unnoticed. Hearing people who try to communicate with the deaf may be cruel without meaning to be because they think that deaf people are not paying attention. A ringing phone, a blaring alarm clock, an oven timer going off—all these things may be meaningless to the deaf.

2. Many deaf individuals use lip reading as an aid in receiving information from others. Deaf people learn to watch a person talking and understand what that person is saying from mouth movements. Many hearing people also use lips as an aid to understanding in a very casual and unconscious way. Deaf people actively and carefully watch others' lips to "get the message." Sometimes, however, other people talk in such a fashion that reading their lips may be very difficult. Following a conversation between two or more other people is also difficult for a deaf person if the conversation bounces back and forth very quickly. Part of what is said gets lost because it is never seen. A person whose lips are being read may carelessly turn his or her head away. The entire process is then abruptly halted for the deaf person.

3. Signing is a two-way conversation and communication process that deaf people use. It

is a language that is expressed by use of the hands. The positioning of the fingers and the movement of the hands give the meaning; fingers and hands can spell out entire words and phrases. A single sign can also give a complete word or phrase. Signing is a good method, but it has its limitations. Signers can communicate only with other people who know how to sign. Unlike lip reading, signing does not help deaf people understand individuals who cannot sign. On the other hand, signers can often communicate where hearing people cannot—such as on a noisy bus!

4. Two important electronic devices—TTY and TDD—are available to enable deaf people to communicate over long distances. TTY stands for teletypewriter. TDD stands for telephone device for the deaf. Both devices are basically variations of the same machine. A TTY is a device that has a keyboard and some type of readable display. Just as a telephone links up with other telephones, a TTY links up with other TTYs. Deaf people type what they want to say, and the message comes up on someone else's readable display. The other person types a response and sends it back to the first person. Police departments and many other types of public services are now literally at deaf people's fingertips.

5. Deaf people used to sit in front of a television and try to figure out what was going on by watching the movements of the people and by trying to read their lips. This method was haphazard at best. Most of what happens on television is conveyed by the dialogue. Lip reading television conversations is very difficult, because the speakers often turn their backs or talk off-camera. Then closed-caption television was developed. Through the use of a decoding device, deaf people can display the dialogue in printed subtitles on their television screens so they can read what is being said. In 1992, Congress passed a law that all television sets with screens 13 inches or larger sold after July 1, 1993, must include a built-in decoding device.

6. Seeing Eye dogs are no longer the sole canine aids for the handicapped. Trained hearing ear dogs are also now in use. These dogs are trained to respond obediently to silent hand signals. They alert their deaf owners to such sounds as doorbells, smoke alarms, crying babies, whistling teakettles, oven timers, alarm clocks, auto horns, and any unusual sounds at night. Hearing ear dogs give their deaf owners freedom to live independently. The dogs are good companions, too.

A. In paragraphs, 1, 3, and 4, the main idea is stated. Underline the main idea sentence in each of these paragraphs.

B. In paragraphs 2, 5, and 6, the main idea is unstated. For each of these paragraphs, do the following.
  1. Underline one of the phrases in the list below that tells what the paragraph is about.
  2. Write a main idea sentence on the lines provided.

Paragraph 2
a. numbers of people who use lip reading
b. advantages and disadvantages of lip reading
c. how to lip read

Answers may vary. Lip reading is helpful but of limited value.

Paragraph 5
a. how deaf people can enjoy television
b. getting more deaf people on TV
c. getting more television shows about deaf people on the air

Answers may vary. Deaf people are now able to enjoy television through closed-caption systems.

Paragraph 6
a. the companionship provided by hearing ear dogs
b. the training of hearing ear dogs
c. how hearing ear dogs help their owners

Answers may vary. Hearing ear dogs enable their owners to respond to sounds that they cannot hear.

Health Insurance Application

Most people carry health insurance to absorb some of the costs for doctors, hospitals, and medicine. When choosing a health insurance policy, be sure that you understand how much coverage, or protection, it provides and how much it costs. Most important, you must answer all the questions before you sign the application.

Study the part of a completed health insurance application on page 35.

A. Determine if the health insurance application asks for each of the following items of information. Write *yes* or *no* on the line next to the number of each item. For each *yes* response, find the section on the form that contains the required information. Then write the section number on the line following the item.

_____ no _____ **1.** the applicant's employer's address _____

_____ yes _____ **2.** what the applicant does at his job ____ 1 ____

_____ no _____ **3.** the eye color of the applicant's child _____

_____ yes _____ **4.** if any insurance policy has been denied to the applicant or to any of his

dependents ____ 3 ____

_____ yes _____ **5.** the name of the company with which the applicant or any of his

dependents now has health insurance ____ top ____

_____ no _____ **6.** whether the applicant or any of his dependents has ever been treated for

a broken arm or leg _____

_____ no _____ **7.** the amount of money that must accompany the application _____

_____ yes _____ **8.** the name of the doctor who treated the applicant or any of his

dependents for a disease during the past five years ____ 9 ____

_____ yes _____ **9.** whether the applicant or any of his dependents has high blood pressure ____ 6[b] ____

_____ no _____ **10.** the amount of money that an insurance company paid the applicant or a

dependent for an injury or illness _____

B. Complete each sentence using the information from the health insurance application.

1. The person applying for health insurance is _____ Arthur E. Lewis _____.

2. The applicant works at the _____ Holiday Hotel _____.

3. The applicant has ____ 2 ____ dependents.

4. You can tell that the applicant wishes his dependents to be covered by the health insurance

policy because _____ he completed section 2 of the application _____.

5. The oldest person on the applicant's policy is _____ Arthur _____.

6. According to the application, the only medical condition(s) that the applicant and his

dependents have been treated for is(are) _____ asthma _____.

7. Person(s) treated for the above condition(s) is(are) _____ Martin _____.

| APPLICATION TO: | ☐ UNITED CASUALTY COMPANY | ☑ VALLEY HEALTH INSURANCE COMPANY |

1. APPLICANT (PRINT) Arthur E. Lewis	HEIGHT 5'-10"	WEIGHT 155	SEX M	AGE 46
ADDRESS 120 Waverly Drive	CITY Linwood	STATE & ZIP CODE NJ 08221	BIRTH DATE 6/11/50	
EMPLOYER Holiday Hotel	OCCUPATION tennis coach	DUTIES give tennis lessons		
SEND PREMIUM NOTICE TO: Arthur E. Lewis	ADDRESS: 120 Waverly Drive, Linwood, NJ 08221			

2. IF YOU ARE APPLYING FOR FAMILY DEPENDENTS TO BE COVERED, COMPLETE THIS SECTION.

FIRST NAME	RELATIONSHIP	BIRTH DATE	AGE	HEIGHT	WEIGHT	FIRST NAME	RELATIONSHIP	BIRTH DATE	AGE	HEIGHT	WEIGHT
Jennifer	wife	12/26/53	43	5'5"	119						
Martin	son	110/14/79	17	5'11"	138						

3. To the best of your knowledge and belief have you or any dependent named ever made application for, or had issued, any type of insurance which has been declined, postponed, withdrawn, modified or rated up? ☐ Yes ☑ No

4. To the best of your knowledge and belief do you or any dependent named now carry any disability income, hospital, surgical insurance or service plan or have an application pending for such insurance or plan? ☐ Yes ☑ No

5. To the best of your knowledge and belief have you or any dependent named ever made a claim for, or received indemnity on account of an injury or illness? (If Yes to Questions 3, 4 or 5 complete the following) ☐ Yes ☑ No

Question No.	Name of Company	TYPE (Income, Hosp., etc.)	Date	Reason & Amount Paid	Person Pertaining to

6. To the best of your knowledge and belief have you or any dependents named, ever been medically treated for or medically advised for any of the following:

a.) Alcoholism, epilepsy, or any nervous, mental or emotional disorder ☐ Yes ☑ No

b.) Abnormal blood pressure, heart attack, stroke or any other blood or circulatory disorder. ☐ Yes ☑ No

c.) Asthma, emphysema, or any other lung or respiratory disorder. ☑ Yes ☐ No

d.) Ulcer of the stomach or duodenum, rectal disorder, liver disorder, gallbladder disorder or any other digestive disorder. ☐ Yes ☑ No

e.) Kidney disorder or any other urinary disorder, prostate disorder or female disorder. ☐ Yes ☑ No

f.) Thyroid disorder, diabetes, gout, or any eye or ear disorder. ☐ Yes ☑ No

g.) Arthritis, rheumatism, any disorder of the back, spine, bones, muscles or joints. ☐ Yes ☑ No

h.) Cancer, tumor, growth or any skin disorder. ☐ Yes ☑ No

7. To the best of your knowledge and belief have you or any dependents named, been a user of marijuana, amphetamines, barbiturates, hallucinogens or narcotics, except upon a physician's prescription? ☐ Yes ☑ No

8. To the best of your knowledge and belief have you or any dependent named had medical or surgical advice or treatment, or been hospital confined during the past 5 years other than admitted in answer to question 6. ☐ Yes ☑ No

9. To the best of your knowledge and belief have you or any dependent named ever had any physical impairment, deformity or disease during the past 5 years other than admitted in question 6. (If Yes to question 6 a-h, 7, 8 or 9 complete the following.) ☐ Yes ☑ No

Question No.	First Name	Med. Condition	Dates	Results	Doctors or Hospitals
6C	Martin	asthma	since 1989	on medication	Dr. Sherman

10. If you are applying for disability income protection complete the following.

What portion of your average monthly earnings does the disability indemnity under all policies you have or are applying for represent? ☐ Less than 50% ☐ 50% to 66 2/3% ☐ More than 66 2/3%

I understand and agree that no coverage shall be in force unless the policy is issued, and if issued, that coverage will be in force as of the effective date shown on the issued policy. Dated 1/6/96 At Valley Health-Linwood office

Signature of applicant X Arthur E. Lewis

I hereby certify that information supplied me by the applicant has been truly and accurately recorded hereon.

Agent or Broker Maria Soto code 6247009

CHECK OR CURRENCY MUST ACCOMPANY APPLICATIONS

Lesson 10 _____

Plot

Reading a Literature Selection _____

▶ Background Information

The last year of high school can be a stressful one because students have to make many important decisions. This story tells what happens to a student who wishes someone else would make the decisions for him.

▶ Skill Focus

Plot is the plan of action or series of events in a story. The plot in most stories follows a basic pattern consisting of five parts.

3. Climax

2. Rising Action

4. Falling Action

1. Beginning

5. Conclusion

Sometimes an author gives clues about events that will happen later in the plot. This technique is called **foreshadowing**. Hints about

future events can be found in the dialogue, descriptions, or reactions of characters. Read the example below.

> "I've always been afraid of spiders," laughed Carl, "but I don't imagine we'll find any around here."
>
> "Probably not!" answered Peter.

The dialogue between Carl and Peter foreshadows an event that is likely to happen later in the story. The author is hinting at their future encounter with spiders.

Use the questions below to help you follow the events in a story's plot.

1. What are the main events in the story's plot?
2. Does the author hint at an event before it occurs in the story? If so, which event?
3. Is the story's conclusion expected or unexpected? Explain.

▶ Word Clues

Read the following sentence. Look for context clues that explain the underlined word.

> Nothing about my life these days seemed to synchronize, to run in time with itself, anymore.

If you do not know the meaning of the word *synchronize* in the first part of the sentence, read on. The rest of the sentence explains what the word *synchronize* means. A word meaning that is stated directly can often be found near a new word.

Use **definition** context clues to find the meanings of the three underlined words in the story.

▶ Strategy Tip

As you read, look for hints that foreshadow the action to come. Pay special attention to the twist in the story's ending. Watching for clues to upcoming turns in the plot can make your reading more interesting and enjoyable.

Ask MIKE

I was ready to give up. I'd been curled up on the canvas sling chair in my room for so long that my knees felt permanently locked into position. I was becoming aware that, for the past half hour, I'd been staring at a nearly microscopic speck on the ceiling. Nothing about my life these days seemed to synchronize, to run in time with itself, anymore. I was in my last year in high school, the deadline for college applications was approaching, and I hadn't decided about going on to college.

"Frank! Still <u>procrastinating</u>, putting off, finishing your applications? You can't do that forever!" My mother had caught me wasting time again.

"I just wish I had a computer that was programmed to make all the important decisions for me!"

Mom wasn't impressed—I could tell. "Would you be satisfied with a decision that was made for you? I wouldn't want a machine to control my life. Looks like you need more time to think about your future. By yourself." With that, she left me alone.

I surveyed the piles of college brochures around my room. Halfheartedly, I sat down with an application and stared at the first question: "Why do you wish to attend Appleton University?"

Before long, I was staring at that speck on the ceiling again. Suddenly, the speck grew larger and began to change color. Soon it turned into a pinwheel of spiraling colors, pulling me into its center with the force of a whirlpool. The next thing I knew, I was in a brightly lit and immaculate <u>anteroom</u>, a reception area, filled with waiting teenagers. By the door, a man was stationed at a video display terminal. I approached him.

"Name?" he inquired pleasantly when he saw me.

"Frank Olsen," I responded.

He tried to scroll it up on the computer display, as if my name should be in the records.

"Don't see it here. Are you sure you have the date right—November 12, 2046?"

I gasped—"2046? I've just lost the rest of the century! Where am I?"

"Well, young man," he said snappishly, "right now you're in the Life Determination Resources Center." He went on. "Now let me see. Olsen . . . Olsen . . . I don't have you here. But I think the Micro Interviewer for Career Evaluation—nicknamed MIKE by some of your disrespectful friends over there—could see you in a few moments. Have a seat over there."

The next instant, my name was called. The door whooshed open on unseen gliders, and I entered. I found myself in a thickly carpeted, warm room. I was alone in the hushed atmosphere, except for a computer terminal that faced me.

"Mr. Olsen, sit down please."

The voice startled me. It was calm and reassuring, and emanated from the computer.

"It will take just a few nanoseconds—ah, yes—here we are. Sorry for the delay, but sixty years is a bit out of the ordinary."

I nodded dumbly.

"My clients call me MIKE," the computer continued in its genial, friendly tone. "We're here to determine your future. Let's see . . . math four years . . . science fair winner . . . mmm . . . very good, if a bit dated. You tinker with motorcycles and once fixed your parents' dishwasher. All right. Now let's see what's available for you. Yes. You'll study microelectronics at Future Tech for two years, then take a position as a robotic repair technician. In seven years, you'll be earning enough to support a family, and you'll be allowed to take out a marriage license. At that time, SAM—that's an acronym for Standardized Acquisition of Mate—will find you a suitable mate."

I began to stammer. "I don't . . ."

The computer spoke. "Is there a problem? Perhaps your file is incorrect—a human error during input, of course."

I interrupted. "I don't want to be a technician, and I'm not interested in robotics. At least, not now. I might want to be something else—maybe a construction engineer! And I had been thinking of a four-year college . . ."

"That's impossible," MIKE interrupted. "Technicians do not require four years of school. As for engineering, we cannot have an excess of workers in any field. We don't need any more engineers. You must understand that, in your day, people made all their own life decisions and all their own mistakes. Some people were unemployed because they were trained in fields with no future. In other areas, jobs went begging for workers. People married for all the wrong reasons, and the divorce rate skyrocketed. We have solved these problems by removing human error from the decision-making process."

"But I don't know if I even want to be a technician," I repeated, "and I certainly don't want a computer choosing a wife for me!"

"Oh, we do very well in that regard. It takes all the tension and stress out of dating."

I was getting more and more upset.

"There is no further recourse," MIKE said. The light blinked, and the room grew dimmer. "Your appointment time is up. Your life decisions have been made."

"Wait!" I screeched. "I don't want a computer to control my life!"

All of a sudden, I found myself back in my room. I realized that I had had a bad dream. In my panic, I had knocked over a pile of college brochures. On top of the pile was a catalog for Future Tech. Perhaps I'd take a two-year course; perhaps not. It was a possibility to think about. As I started to contemplate the decisions that I had to make, the phone rang.

"Hello," I said.

"Is this Frank Olsen?" the caller inquired.

"Yes, it is."

"Well, congratulations, Frank. You're the lucky winner of our new personal decision-making microcomputer. It will be delivered tomorrow. We know you will enjoy letting the computer make your decisions for you. Congratulations, Frank!"

"No, no, I don't want it," I tried to say, but, before I finished, the caller hung up. When the microcomputer was delivered the next day, no one could understand why I would not accept it.

RECALLING FACTS

Identifying setting
1. a. Where does the story begin?
It begins in the present, in Frank Olsen's room.

b. Where does the action move?
It moves to a computer guidance center in the

year 2046.

Identifying point of view
2. a. Who is the narrator of the story?
Frank is the narrator.

b. Is the narrator a participant in the events or an outside observer?
He is a participant.

c. From which point of view is the story told—first or third person?
It is told in the first person.

Identifying cause and effect
3. Why does Frank wish he had a computer to make important decisions for him?
Because Frank can't make up his mind about college,

he wishes a computer could do it for him.

Using context clues.
4. Complete each sentence with the correct word below.

genial   anteroom   procrastinating

a. It's time to stop ——procrastinating—— and finish your assignment.

b. Visitors are met in the ——anteroom—— then escorted into the office.

c. Jessica is a warmhearted and ——genial—— friend.

INTERPRETING FACTS

Understanding character
1. a. Circle two of the words below that best describe Frank's character in the beginning of the story.
(undecided)   (procrastinating)   forceful

b. Circle two words below that best describe Frank's character after his dream.
(decisive)   carefree   (determined)

c. Is Frank a static or a dynamic character? Explain.
Dynamic. Frank is changed by the end of the story.

At the end, he is willing to accept the responsibility of

making his own decisions.

Making inferences
2. Why does Frank decide he'd rather not have MIKE make his career decisions?
MIKE gives Frank no alternatives, does not consult him,

and makes sweeping, long-range, permanent decisions

that Frank dislikes.

Inferring comparisons and contrasts
3. How do Frank and the others respond to MIKE?
Frank gets upset when MIKE makes personal decisions

for him. The other teenagers take MIKE's decision

making for granted, acting very casually about it; in fact,

they have given the microcomputer its nickname.

Making inferences
4. Why might some people like having MIKE make their decisions?
Most students will answer that some people can't

handle the pressures involved in making decisions.

They prefer the less stressful alternative of having a

computer make decisions for them.

Understanding character
5. Does Frank understand why he must make his own decisions about college? Explain.
Yes. Frank's experience with MIKE has shown him that

decision making is a personal matter that can affect

one's entire future.

1. On the diagram below, identify the five parts of the plot structure. Then fill in the letter of the appropriate event.

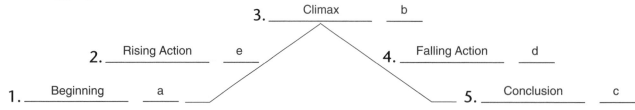

3. _____ Climax ___ b

2. _____ Rising Action ___ e   4. _____ Falling Action ___ d

1. _____ Beginning ___ a   5. _____ Conclusion ___ c

   a. Frank wishes that a programmed computer would make all his important decisions.

   b. Upset when the computer makes decisions that affect his future, Frank decides he doesn't want a computer to control his life.

   c. Frank doesn't accept the microcomputer when it's delivered.

   d. Frank wakes up from his dream, only to learn that he has won his own personal decision-making computer.

   e. In the Life Determination Resources Center, MIKE makes decisions for Frank: Frank will go to Future Tech for two years, and a suitable mate will be selected for him seven years later.

2. a. Which event does the author hint at before it occurs in the story?
He hints that Frank would have a personal decision-making computer.

   b. Go back to the story and circle the statement that foreshadows this event.

3. Is the story's conclusion expected or unexpected? Explain.
Answers will vary. It is unexpected because at first, Frank wanted a computer programmed to make his personal

decisions, but, when he could really have one, he didn't want it; expected especially after Frank's dream experience.

4. Here are some sentences from a very short story. In this story, one event foreshadows another that occurs later in the story. Circle the letter of the foreshadowing event. Then, on the lines provided below, rewrite the story so that the ending is unexpected.

   a. The Carsons always had quiet Sunday dinners in the dining room.

   (b.) Junior forgot to feed the dog and to put it outside.

   c. "Dinner time!" sang Mrs. Carson.

   d. While the Carsons ate their dinner, the dog enjoyed their dessert—the ice cream cake.

   e. Junior is grounded and will have no desserts for a week.
Answers will vary.

_____

_____

_____

_____

_____

▶ **Real Life Connections** Write a persuasive paragraph for or against using a computerized program to help you make decisions.

Cause and Effect

Reading a Social Studies Selection

▶ **Background Information**

The Anasazi inhabited parts of the American Southwest from about the year C.E. 1 to 1300. These ancient people were the ancestors of modern Pueblo Indians.

Preview the selection by reading the headings of its main sections. As you read about the Anasazi, look for a chain of causes and effects in which an effect becomes a cause of another effect.

In reading textbooks, you may find words that you do not know how to pronounce. These words are usually respelled. In this selection, for example, the word *metate* is respelled "mə TAHT ee." The pronunciation key on page 2 will help you pronounce this and other words.

▶ **Skill Focus**

A **cause** is an underlying reason, condition, or situation that makes an event happen. An **effect** is the result, or outcome, of a cause. Sometimes a cause brings about an effect that in turn

becomes the cause of another effect. This chain of causes and effects occurs frequently.

Look for a chain of cause and effect relationships in the following paragraph.

Because these early settlers made finely crafted baskets, archaeologists named them the Basket Makers. The tightly woven baskets were used for carrying and storing food and water and even for cooking. Stones heated in a fire were dropped into a basket containing water and food. The hot stones made the water boil, which then cooked the food. However, this method was slow and often cooked the food unevenly.

The diagram below shows this chain of causes and effects. Causes and effects are often directly stated. Sometimes, however, you may have to infer a cause or an effect.

▶ **Word Clues**

Read the sentence that follows. Look for context clues that explain the underlined word.

Wetherill had discovered cliff <u>dwellings</u>, or homes, built by people who had vanished from the area more than 500 years earlier.

If you don't know the meaning of the word *dwellings,* the words following the word *or* can help you. Dwellings are homes. The word *dwellings* is explained in the appositive phrase set off by commas. Appositive phrases may also be set off by dashes.

Use **appositive phrases** to find the meanings of the four underlined words in the selection.

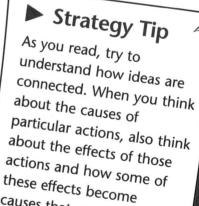

▶ **Strategy Tip**

As you read, try to understand how ideas are connected. When you think about the causes of particular actions, also think about the effects of those actions and how some of these effects become causes that result in other effects.

Cause		Effect/Cause		Effect/Cause		Effect
Heated stones were dropped into a basket.	→	The hot stones made the water boil.	→	The boiling water cooked the food.	→	The food cooked slowly and unevenly.

The Ancient Ones

One cold winter day in 1888, Colorado rancher Richard Wetherill was trying to find some cattle that had strayed. As he stood on the rim of Mesa Verde and looked at the canyon wall on the opposite side, he spotted what seemed to be the ruins of an ancient town. Wetherill had discovered cliff dwellings, or homes, built by people who had vanished from the area more than 500 years earlier.

Who were these ancient people? What were their lives like? Why did they build their towns high on cliff walls? And why did they abandon their homes?

The First Settlers

The earliest Americans living in the Southwest were <u>nomads</u>, people who had no permanent homes. They moved from place to place as they hunted animals and <u>foraged</u>, or searched, for food. Then, almost 2,000 years ago, these nomadic people learned how to grow corn and squash, and their way of life

changed. Although they still hunted, they could now settle in one place with a reliable supply of food.

One group of people settled in what is today the Four Corners region of southern Colorado. The region is named Four Corners because Colorado and three other states—Arizona, New Mexico, and Utah—meet there. No one knows what these early people called themselves. Today we call them the **Anasazi** (a nə SAH zee), from a Navajo word meaning "the ancient ones."

Changing Ways of Life

When the Anasazi first settled in the Four Corners region, small family groups lived in rock <u>alcoves</u>, or shallow recesses. Because these early settlers made finely crafted baskets, archaeologists named them the Basket Makers. The tightly woven baskets were used for carrying and storing food and water and even for cooking. Stones heated in a fire were dropped into a basket containing water and food. The hot stones made the water boil, which then cooked the food. However, this method was slow and often cooked the food unevenly.

About 550 C.E., some Anasazi moved to Mesa Verde. There they began to build permanent houses. Archaeologists call these structures **pithouses** because the floors were formed by digging shallow pits in the ground. The sloping walls and the roof were made of wooden poles covered with mud. Archaeologists have found the remains of several pithouses close together.

Another important change during this time was that the people learned to make pottery. Clay pots and bowls improved the way food was cooked. Unlike baskets, which burn, clay containers could be placed

The Cliff Palace at Mesa Verde National Park in Colorado is the largest Anasazi pueblo ruin in North America. It has 217 rooms and 23 kivas.

directly over a fire. Thus, food could be cooked more quickly and thoroughly than before.

The Anasazi's way of life changed again in about 750. Instead of pithouses, they began building square rooms with vertical walls. These rooms were often connected together to form a small community of homes. This type of building is called a **pueblo** (PWEB loh), from the Spanish word for "village."

Pueblos at Mesa Verde were constructed on top of the mesa. The walls and roofs were built from wooden posts covered with **adobe** (ə DOH bee), which is sun-dried mud. Some buildings had a row of stones around the base. Later, the Anasazi built the entire walls of stone, which made the buildings sturdier and more permanent.

> Foods were flavored with salt and wild plants such as onion and mustard.

About 1100, small villages began to join together to form large towns. Pueblos were built with many connected rooms used for sleeping, storage, and social gatherings. The people stored water in ditches and reservoirs for drier times.

In front of each pueblo was a single room dug into the ground, much like the earlier pithouses. This room, called a **kiva** (KEE və), was used for community meetings and religious ceremonies. People would gather in the kiva to conduct healing ceremonies and to pray for rain, a good harvest, and success in hunting.

Between 1150 and 1200, the Anasazi began building their pueblos in large alcoves in the canyon walls. Many pueblos consisted of hundreds of rooms built in rows on top of one another. The roof of one room formed a porch for the room above it. The families who lived in the upper rooms had to climb ladders to reach them.

In the canyon alcoves, the cliff ledges offered protection against the weather. Pueblos were often built on south-facing cliff walls. During the summer, when the sun is higher in the sky, the cliff's shadow helped keep the buildings cool. In the winter, when the sun is lower in the sky, its light would strike the buildings directly and keep them warmer.

✘ A major disadvantage of the cliff pueblos was that the people had to climb up and down the steep cliff walls to tend their fields on the mesa top and in the canyon below. Perhaps, some archaeologists suggest, the Anasazi moved to the cliffs because pueblos there would be easier to defend in case of an enemy attack. During their final years at Mesa Verde, the Anasazi began to build towers, which may have been used for sending signals or watching for approaching enemies.

Daily Life

✔ The Anasazi planted and tended fields of corn, squash, and beans. They gathered wild plants—roots, berries, nuts, seeds, and fruits—and hunted deer, rabbits, and other animals.

This keyhole kiva, found near the Spruce Tree House at Mesa Verde, is typical of the kivas that the Anasazi built for community meetings and religious ceremonies.

They also raised turkeys, but not for food. Instead, the feathers were wrapped around fibers used to weave warm robes and blankets for the chilly nights and cold winters. Animal skins also provided coverings. Fibers from the yucca plant were twisted into cords to make baskets, sandals, ropes, and snares for catching small animals.

Although some tasks, such as harvesting crops, were shared by all the people, men and women generally had different roles in Anasazi society. Women were responsible for preparing and cooking food. They made cornmeal by grinding dried corn with a hand-held stone called a **mano** (MAH noh) against a flat stone slab called a **metate** (mə TAHT ee). Some Pueblo Indians of today still grind corn in this way. The coarse cornmeal was mixed with water and baked in flat cakes on a stone griddle or formed into small balls and boiled in soups or stews. Beans and squash were cooked alone or with meat. Foods were flavored with salt and wild plants, such as onion and mustard.

Women also cared for the young children. Babies were tucked snugly into cradleboards that their mothers wore on their backs or propped up nearby as they worked. Girls learned how to prepare food, weave baskets, and make clothing, while boys practiced hunting with smaller versions of the men's bows and arrows.

Men were responsible for clearing land and building houses and other structures. They cut logs with stone axes to make wooden supports for floors and roofs. The axes were also used to chip large sandstone chunks into rectangular blocks for building.

Desperate Times

By the 1200s, several thousand Anasazi were living in the cliff pueblos of Mesa Verde. All the available land was being used to grow crops, and nutrients in the soil were becoming depleted, or used up. As more land was cleared for fields, hunters had to search farther for game. It was also more difficult to find wood to use for building and fuel.

In 1276, a disastrous 23-year period of drought began. Year after year, crops failed because there was not enough rain. The climate also became cooler, which made the growing season shorter. Skeletons unearthed at Mesa Verde show evidence of malnutrition among the Anasazi people. Conflicts also arose as people competed for scarce food. As conditions worsened, groups of people began to move away. Some pueblos seemed to have been abandoned suddenly, with pots, baskets, and tools simply left behind. By the time the drought finally ended, no Anasazi remained at Mesa Verde.

What Happened to the Anasazi?

When they abandoned their pueblos at Mesa Verde and other locations in the Four Corners region, the Anasazi moved south and east. Some groups settled along the Rio Grande River in what is today northern New Mexico. Other groups joined the Hopi, Zuni, and Tewa peoples of Arizona and western New Mexico.

As the Anasazi merged with other peoples, they lost many of their old customs and adopted new ones. The present-day Pueblo Indians of the American Southwest are descendants of the Anasazi. However, it is difficult to tell which of their traditions are derived from the Anasazi and which are derived from other cultures.

Mesa Verde Today

After Wetherill discovered the Mesa Verde cliff pueblos, many people worked to convince the U.S. government to protect the ruins. Finally, in June 1906, President Theodore Roosevelt signed a bill establishing Mesa Verde as a national park. Today, more than 600,000 visitors tour the ruins every year. Mesa Verde is the only national park in the United States created specifically to preserve the works of an ancient people. This park is a monument to the skill of the Anasazi who built this early, authentically American architecture.

Recalling details

1. Match each word in the left column with a description in the right column.

___d___ adobe   **a.**   hand-held stone used to grind corn

___b___ pueblo   **b.**   community of connected homes

___a___ mano

___c___ kiva   **c.**   underground room used for meetings and ceremonies

        d.   sun-dried mud

Identifying sequence of events

2. Number the following events in the order in which they occur.

___4___ Small villages on top of the mesa joined to form large towns.

___1___ Small family groups lived in shallow rock alcoves.

___5___ The Anasazi built their pueblos in large alcoves in the canyon walls.

___3___ The Anasazi built connected houses with square rooms and vertical walls.

___2___ The Anasazi built permanent pithouses on top of the mesa.

Identifying the main idea

3. Reread the paragraph with an X next to it. Underline the sentence that states the main idea.

Using context clues

4. For each sentence below, circle the correct meaning of the underlined word.

a. Desert <u>nomads</u> herd their sheep and goats to find grass and water.

people who raise crops

(people who move from place to place)

people who eat meat

b. The bear <u>foraged</u> for berries as it roamed the forest.

(searched)   competed   dug down

c. <u>Alcoves</u> near the main entrance held statues of the library's founders.

(shallow recesses)   hallways   platforms

d. While he was unemployed, he <u>depleted</u> his savings account.

added to   (used up)   took out

INTERPRETING FACTS

Distinguishing fact from opinion

1. Identify each of the following statements as fact or opinion by writing *F* or *O* on the line.

___O___ The Anasazi built cliff pueblos to escape enemy attacks.

___F___ Pueblos in south-facing cliff walls were cooler in the summer and warmer in the winter.

___F___ Mesa Verde National Park is a popular tourist attraction.

___O___ Too many people visit Mesa Verde National Park every year.

Inferring comparisons and contrasts

2. Why were Anasazi girls' activities and boys' activities different?

The children were learning the different skills needed by adult women and men in the society.

Inferring the unstated main idea

3. Reread the paragraph with a check mark next to it. Write a sentence describing its main idea.

Answers may vary. The Anasazi obtained everything that they needed from their surroundings.

1. Use the items listed in the box to complete the cause-and-effect chains.

> Food became scarce.
> All the available land was being used to grow crops.
> The Anasazi abandoned Mesa Verde.
> The growing season became shorter.
> A 23-year drought began.
> People suffered from malnutrition.
> Nutrients in the soil were being depleted.

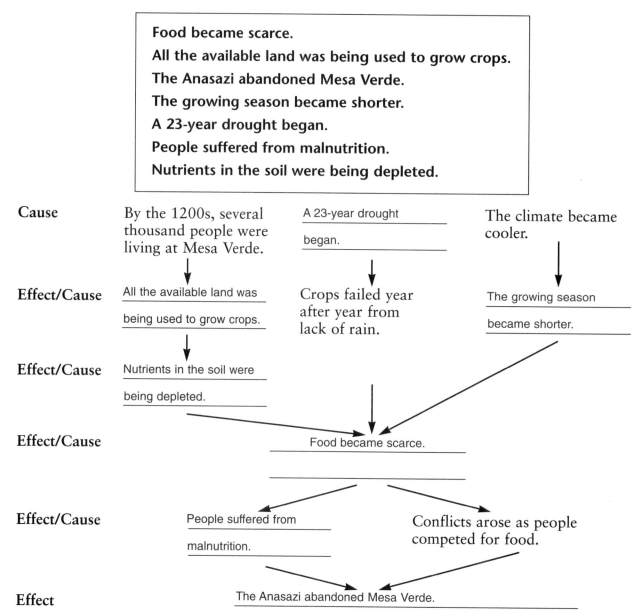

Cause

By the 1200s, several thousand people were living at Mesa Verde.

A 23-year drought began.

The climate became cooler.

Effect/Cause

All the available land was being used to grow crops.

Crops failed year after year from lack of rain.

The growing season became shorter.

Effect/Cause

Nutrients in the soil were being depleted.

Effect/Cause

Food became scarce.

Effect/Cause

People suffered from malnutrition.

Conflicts arose as people competed for food.

Effect

The Anasazi abandoned Mesa Verde.

2. Answer the following questions by inferring a cause or an effect.

  a. Why did the Anasazi leave belongings behind when they abandoned their pueblos?

Answers may vary. They left too quickly to pack their belongings. They wanted to travel lightly. They could make new pots, baskets, and tools when they settled in a new location.

  b. How did making Mesa Verde a national park help protect the ruins?

Answers may vary. Park rangers could stop people from disturbing the ruins and stealing baskets, pots, and other objects found in the pueblos.

▶ **Real Life Connections** Which aspects of the Anasazi culture would you like to learn more about? Tell why.

Diagrams

Reading a Science Selection

▶ Background Information

Radiation of all kinds surrounds us. Except for visible light, humans cannot see this radiation. In this selection, you will read about the electromagnetic spectrum, the visible spectrum, and waves.

▶ Skill Focus

Textbooks often contain **diagrams** to show what is being explained in the paragraphs. Diagrams can be best understood if you read the paragraphs first, then look at the diagram. A diagram can help you visualize the scientific material that has just been described.

Be sure to read the diagram's **captions** and the **labels**. They usually contain important information. As you study the diagram, think about the paragraphs that you have just read and how they relate to the diagram. It may be helpful to go back to the paragraphs again and try to visualize the diagram as you are reading the paragraphs.

Use the following steps for reading a selection with diagrams.

1. Read the paragraph or paragraphs before each diagram, and then study the diagram. Be sure to read the labels and captions with the diagram. The paragraph below the diagram may also explain what is pictured. Read that paragraph, too.
2. Read the rest of the paragraphs. Look back at the diagrams whenever you think they will help you.
3. After you have finished reading the paragraphs and studying the diagrams, look away from the selection. Try to picture what you have read and the details in the diagrams. If you are not able to do so, read the material again.
4. Follow this method until you understand all the ideas in the selection.

This method of study is especially useful when you are reading about a scientific subject. The different parts of a scientific process, or of the interconnected parts of something in nature, are frequently difficult to understand from reading alone. You may need both a diagram and a description in words to see the process clearly.

▶ Word Clues

Read the sentences below. Look for context clues to the underlined word.

> This movement forms alternating crests and troughs. Alternating means one coming after the other.

The word *alternating* is explained by the definition in the second sentence.

Use **definition** context clues to find the meanings of the three underlined words in the selection.

▶ Strategy Tip

While reading this selection, study the diagrams carefully. If necessary, go back and forth from the text to the diagrams. Do so until you understand the information presented about radiation.

The Electromagnetic Spectrum

If you have ever thrown a pebble into a pond, you have probably observed ripples, or waves, radiating out from the point where the rock entered the water. If you ever watched the tide come in, you have seen wave after wave of water crash onto the beach. Water and other liquids are the easiest media, or substances, in which to see the movement of waves. Yet waves can also occur in solids, including the earth, and in gases, including the air. In fact, the air around you is filled with invisible waves.

A number of different kinds of radiation, or waves, share common characteristics. These waves are grouped together in what is called the **electromagnetic spectrum**, shown in Figure 1. This name comes from the fact that either electricity or magnetism can produce these waves. The waves of the electromagnetic spectrum include radio waves, television waves, light, and X rays.

Characteristics of Waves

One characteristic of electromagnetic radiation is that all these waves travel at the same speed—about 300,000 kilometers per second, which is the speed of light.

All waves in the electromagnetic spectrum share another characteristic in that they are **transverse** waves. If you have ever watched a cork or a piece of wood bob up and down in water, you have watched transverse waves in action. The cork goes up and down at right angles to the movement of the wave over the surface of the water. See Figure 2. As the energy of the wave passes through a medium,

or substance, the medium moves up and down perpendicular to the wave movement. This movement forms alternating crests and troughs. Alternating means one coming after the other. The crests are formed by the upward movement of the water, and the troughs are formed by the downward movement of the water. The distance from the crest of one wave to that of the next wave is called the **wavelength**. See Figure 3.

The radiations, or waves, in the electromagnetic spectrum share some characteristics with all other waves. For example, different types of waves have different wavelengths. **Frequency** is the number of complete wavelengths that pass a given point in a specific amount of time. Frequency is measured in **hertz**, abbreviated Hz. One hertz is the passage of one complete wavelength per second. If a wave has a frequency of 1,000 Hz, then 1,000

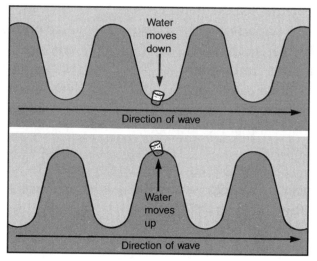

Figure 2. The water and the cork move up and down as the wave moves from left to right.

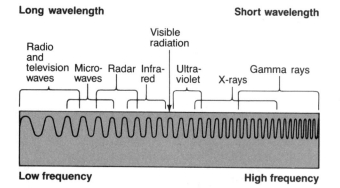

Long wavelength   **Short wavelength**

Radio and television waves | Microwaves | Radar | Infrared | Visible radiation | Ultraviolet | X-rays | Gamma rays

Low frequency   **High frequency**

Figure 1. The electromagnetic spectrum includes many forms of radiation, or waves.

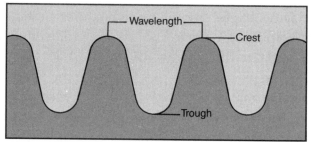

Figure 3. A wavelength is measured from crest to crest.

wavelengths pass a given point every second. The frequency of sound waves is also measured in hertz.

The frequency and the wavelength of a wave have an **inverse** relationship: The higher the frequency of a wave, the shorter its wavelength is, and vice versa. If, for example, the frequency is doubled, the wavelength is cut in half. The reverse is also true: The lower the frequency of a wave, the longer its wavelength is.

Types of Radiation

The shortest waves in the electromagnetic spectrum are **gamma rays**, which are <u>emitted</u> by the nuclei of certain atoms. *Emitted* means "given out." Because their wavelengths are so short, gamma rays have a very high frequency. They are so powerful that they can travel through 60 centimeters of concrete or 30 centimeters of steel. They can also pass through the bones and tissues of living organisms, which makes gamma rays <u>potentially</u> dangerous. *Potentially* means "having the possibility of doing or being something." Under controlled conditions, however, gamma rays can be used for the medical purpose of killing cancer tissue because this tissue is destroyed more easily than healthy tissues.

The next most powerful type of electromagnetic radiation is **X rays**. These waves are produced when high-speed electrons strike a heavy metal, such as tungsten. X rays can penetrate soft body tissues, but they do not pass through bones and teeth. As a result, when an X-ray picture is taken of the human body, the bones and teeth form a shadow on the film. Although X rays can be very useful, they can, like gamma rays, be dangerous. People who work around X rays often wear protective clothing, including lead aprons, to protect their bodies from this radiation.

Ultraviolet waves can cause sunburn. They can also be used to sterilize materials and to preserve food. Scientists can figure out the composition of certain rocks and minerals that glow when placed under ultraviolet light. There is evidence that certain insects have sense receptors for detecting ultraviolet light.

Visible light is the portion of the

Figure 4. Visible light forms a spectrum of color from red to violet.

electromagnetic spectrum whose waves produce the colors that humans can detect. Visible light forms a spectrum of color from red to violet. Humans see these colors because their eyes have special receptors that are sensitive to this part of the electromagnetic spectrum. Because visible light waves have less energy than other waves in the spectrum, they are not dangerous.

Ultraviolet waves can cause sunburn. They can also be used to sterilize materials and to preserve food.

Infrared radiation is made up of waves that carry heat. Most substances produce infrared waves, but hot objects produce more of these waves than do cold objects. One useful application of infrared radiation is heat-efficiency studies of houses. A picture can be taken of a house on film that is sensitive to infrared rays. The result is a picture showing the various temperatures of the structure, thereby identifying areas of heat loss.

Microwaves are used in radar to determine the speed and location of a distant object. They are also produced by microwave ovens to cook food and by transmitters that send messages between the earth and space. Satellite broadcasts of television programs are in part made possible by microwaves.

Television and radio transmissions also depend on radiation in the electromagnetic spectrum. Radio and television waves are among the longest waves in the spectrum. When you set a television or radio to a channel or station, you set that device's tuner to pick up only certain wave frequencies. These waves carry the sound and picture signals from the selected station.

The waves used in communication, such as radio and television broadcasts, are coded before they are transmitted. You may know that radio stations are either AM or FM, but do you know what these letters mean? Radio waves can be <u>modulated</u> in one of two ways: by varying the height, or amplitude, of the waves or by varying the frequency of the waves. To modulate something means to regulate or adjust it. AM stands for amplitude modulation, and FM stands for frequency modulation.

RECALLING FACTS

Recalling details
1. Name four types of radiation in the electromagnetic spectrum.

Answers may include four of the following: radio and

television waves, microwaves, radar, infrared radiation,

visible light, ultraviolet light, X rays, and gamma rays.

Recalling details
2. What two characteristics do all forms of electromagnetic radiation share?

They all travel at the speed of light, and they are all

transverse waves.

Recalling details
3. What does the word *frequency* mean when applied to radiation? What unit is used to measure it?

Frequency is the number of waves passing a given

point in a specific amount of time; hertz (Hz) is the unit

used to measure it.

Identifying cause and effect
4. What is the relationship between a wave's frequency and its energy?

The relationship is: the higher the frequency, the

greater the energy.

Identifying cause and effect
5. If the length of a wave is doubled, what happens to its frequency?

The frequency is reduced by one-half.

Using context clues
6. Draw a line to match each word with its explanation.

emitted   **a.** adjusted

potentially   **b.** given out

modulated   **c.** having the possibility of doing or being something

INTERPRETING FACTS

Circle the letter next to each correct answer.

Making inferences
1. Which wavelength has the greatest energy?
    a. 100,000 hertz
    b. 1,000,000 hertz
    (c.) 5,000,000 hertz

Making inferences
2. Suppose you want to see if a sealed cardboard box contained a hard metal object. Which kind of radiation would you use?
    (a.) X rays
    b. visible light
    c. radio waves

Making inferences
3. Which kind of radiation does your body produce?
    a. visible light
    (b.) infrared radiation
    c. ultraviolet light

Inferring cause and effect
4. The frequency of a wave 2 meters long is 10,000 hertz. If the wave's frequency is reduced to 5,000 hertz, what is its wavelength?
    a. 1 meter
    b. 2 meters
    (c.) 4 meters

1. Briefly describe Figure 1 in your own words.

The types of radiation in the electromagnetic spectrum are arranged by their wavelengths, from longest to shortest,

and by their frequencies, from lowest to highest.

2. Visible light is at about the center of the electromagnetic spectrum. On which side of visible light are the types of radiation with the lower amounts of energy? _____ on the left

3. Which has a longer wavelength—visible light or gamma rays? _____ visible light

4. Which has more energy—visible light or radio waves? _____ visible light

5. Explain how X rays are used to take X-ray pictures of the body.

The X rays can penetrate the soft tissues of the body but cannot pass through teeth and bones. As a result, in an

X-ray picture, bones and teeth show up as clear shadows on the film.

6. Explain Figure 2 in your own words.

As a transverse wave passes through a medium, the medium rises and falls. The movement of the medium is

perpendicular to the direction of the wave.

7. Explain Figure 3 in your own words.

The high point in a wave is its crest, and the low point is its trough. The distance from the crest of one wave to that

of the next wave is the wavelength.

8. Explain Figure 4 in your own words.

Visible light forms a spectrum of colors that humans can see; it ranges from red to violet.

▶ **Real Life Connections** What can you do to protect yourself from ultraviolet light?

Word Problems

__Reading a Mathematics Selection _____

▶ **Background Information**

Problem situations reflect the kind of mathematics that you encounter in everyday life. In real life, the questions arise naturally from the situation.

▶ **Skill Focus**

Use the following five steps to complete and solve word problems.

1. Read the problem. Sometimes the statement of the problem does not contain a question or direction. Instead, it might give a problem situation or group of facts. In such cases, you have to determine the problem yourself. To do so, you need to understand all the information given. Try to picture the information in your mind. Then read the situation described in the problem again to be sure that you know how the various facts are related.

2. Decide on a question to ask about the information provided and how to answer the question. In other words, you have to look at the different pieces of information in the situation and decide what you need to find out in order to solve the problem.

    Write a sentence about each fact. Then look for information that has not been given but that you can find using the information provided. Write down a question about the missing information that logically connects the facts.

    Then decide which operation or operations are necessary to answer your question. Write one or two mathematical sentences, or equations, that describe the operation or operations.

3. Estimate the answer to your question. The estimate is one way to be sure that the question can be answered using the information given in the problem situation.

4. Carry out the plan. Solve the mathematical sentence or sentences that you wrote in the second step.

5. Reread the problem situation and your question. Is the answer to the question logical? Is it close to your estimate?

▶ **Word Clues**

The problem situations in "Completing and Solving Word Problems" are about time zones. A *time zone* is a region in which all cities and towns operate on the same time standard. Before time zones were used, each city operated under its own time, based on the position of the sun in the sky. If you are not familiar with time zones, look up this term in a dictionary.

▶ **Strategy Tip**

In reading the problem situation in the following selection, you need to picture a real-life situation in your mind and think of a logical question to answer. After you have decided on the question, you can solve the problem.

Completing and Solving Word Problems

As you travel across a country as large as the United States, you pass from one time zone to another. When you make a long distance telephone call, you may also find that the person you are calling is in a different time zone. The change in time from one place to another across the globe results in many different problem situations.

When you read a problem situation, you must first determine the fact that you want to find from the information given and then how to find it. In other words, you make up a question before you solve the problem. The answer to the problem gives you the missing fact.

Use the following five steps to complete a problem and to solve it.

1. Read the problem situation.
2. Decide on a question to ask about the facts in the situation and how to find the answer.
3. Estimate the answer.
4. Carry out the plan.
5. Reread the problem situation and your question.

READ THE PROBLEM SITUATION

Longitude is measured from 0 degrees in Greenwich, England, to 180 degrees at the opposite point on Earth. It is measured in both directions, east and west. It takes 24 hours for Earth to complete one rotation. By agreement, the time is kept the same throughout a band near a particular longitude line. These bands are called time zones.

Carefully read the information in the problem situation. Think about what kind of problem you could solve with the information presented. Many practical problems concerning time zones are related to the basic facts in this description of longitude and the rotation of Earth.

DECIDE ON A QUESTION TO ASK AND HOW TO FIND THE ANSWER

The problem situation gives you information about longitude and about the number of hours that Earth takes to rotate. It may help to write the facts that include numbers as individual sentences.

1. Earth is divided into longitude lines that cover 180° east and 180° west.
2. There are 24 hours in one day.

You also know that, at any given time, the time in a single time zone is the same.

What can you determine from this information? You can find out the average number of degrees of longitude in one hour of time, that is, the number of degrees that Earth rotates in one hour. Because there are 24 hours in a day, you must divide the total number of longitude degrees by 24. Therefore, the question to ask is this: *What is the average number of degrees that Earth rotates in one hour of time?*

Write mathematical sentences, or equations, that show how to solve this problem. You first have to determine the total number of longitude degrees, t, for the entire globe. Then divide that figure by the number of hours in a day to find the average number of degrees rotated per hour, a.

$$180 + 180 = t$$
$$t \div 24 = a$$

ESTIMATE THE ANSWER

For the first equation, you can round to hundreds. For the second equation, you can round to tens.

$$200 + 200 = 400$$
$$400 \div 20 = 20$$

Your estimate is that the sun appears to move an average of about 20 degrees of longitude in an hour of time. Notice that, because 180 was rounded *up* twice, the estimate of 400 is rather high. Also, because the divisor, 24, was rounded *down*, the estimate for the quotient is also high. You therefore expect the answer to be less than the estimate of 20 degrees.

CARRY OUT THE PLAN

$$180 + 180 = 360$$
$$360 \div 24 = 15$$

REREAD THE PROBLEM SITUATION AND YOUR QUESTION

After rereading the problem situation, write the complete answer to the question asked in the second step.

The sun appears to move an average of 15 degrees of longitude in one hour.

This answer is, as you expected, somewhat less than the estimate of 20 degrees.

Complete and solve the following problem situation.

Read: When Kathleen telephones you at noon, she tells you that it is 9:00 A.M. in Los Angeles, where she is. You need to telephone Kathleen the next day when it is 11:00 A.M. in Los Angeles.

Make sure that you understand the problem situation. On the next day, Kathleen is still in Los Angeles, and you are still in your time zone. If one of you had traveled to a different time zone, you would need to know about that event to write a problem that you could solve.

Decide: What question does this information suggest? If you are required to call Kathleen at a particular time where she is, then you need to know what time it will be where you are. A logical question would be: *To speak with Kathleen at 11:00 A.M. her time, at what local time should you place your call?*

You need to determine the difference, d, in time between your time zone and that of Los Angeles. Then you need to use this information to find your local time, t, when it is 11:00 A.M. in Los Angeles.

The problem is complicated because the United States uses a 12-hour clock instead of a 24-hour clock. There are several ways to deal with the 12-hour clock. The easiest is probably to convert it to a 24-hour clock, solve the problem, then convert back to a 12-hour clock. To convert to a 24-hour clock, add 12 to any time that is given as P.M., or to midnight. To convert back to a 12-hour clock, subtract 12 from any answer that is greater than 12. The remainder is the local time, a, in terms of a 12-hour clock.

In this problem, all the times, are A.M. or before noon, so they are already the same as on a 24-hour clock. Therefore, if you get an answer that is greater than 12, you must subtract 12 from it. The problem is a two-step problem if you do not need to subtract 12, but it is a three-step problem if you need to subtract 12.

$$12 - 9 = d$$
$$11 + d = t$$

If t turns out to be greater than 12, the third equation is as follows:

$$t - 12 = a$$

Estimate: Because all the numbers are small, rounding is not necessary. Instead, estimate by looking at the problem logically. Kathleen's first call was later according to your local time than it was according to Los Angeles time. The answer will therefore also be later than 11:00 A.M. local time.

Carry Out:

$$12 - 9 = 3$$
$$11 + 3 = 14$$

Because 14 is greater than 12,

$$14 - 12 = 2$$

Reread: You should call Kathleen at 2:00 P.M. Because this answer is later than 11:00 A.M., it matches your estimate.

RECALLING FACTS

Recognizing sequence of events
1. Before you can write the equations that describe a problem for a given problem situation, what must you do? You must first decide on a question to be asked.

Recalling details
2. From what city is longitude measured? Greenwich, England

Recalling details

3. How do you change a time based on a 12-hour clock to a time based on a 24-hour clock?

If the time is P.M. or midnight, add 12 to the given time. If the time is A.M. or noon, it stays the same.

Recalling details

4. How is a problem situation different from a word problem?

Unlike a word problem, a problem situation does not provide the question.

Recalling details

5. What method of measuring Earth's surface is used in determining time zones?

longitude lines

INTERPRETING FACTS

Making inferences

1. Time zones were not used until after the railroads were built over long distances. Why were they not used earlier?

Before the railroads, travel was so slow that no one cared if each city operated on its own time. The railroads needed

uniform times so that they could set up and keep schedules.

Making inferences

2. If you estimate a division problem by rounding the divisor up, will the answer be less or

greater than the estimate? ————————— less —————————

Making inferences

3. If an army officer says that the time is 1900 hours, what time would this be on the usual

12-hour clock? ————— 7 P.M. —————

SKILL FOCUS

For each of the following problem situations, write the question that you think should be asked. Then write the equations as a plan, make an estimate, carry out your plan, and state the answer to the question in a complete sentence.

1. Read: Time zones are about 15 degrees longitude apart. When it is 9:00 A.M. in Washington, D.C., it is 5:00 P.M. in Moscow, Russia.

Decide: About how many degrees of longitude separate Washington and Moscow? $5 + 12 = t$; $t - 9 = h$;

$h \times 15 = a$

Estimate: $5 + 10 = 15$; $15 - 10 = 5$; $5 \times 15 = 75$

Carry Out: $5 + 12 = 17$; $17 - 9 = 8$; $8 \times 15 = 120$

Reread: There are about 120 degrees of longitude between Washington and Moscow.

2. **Read:** Time zones are about 15 degrees longitude apart. Buenos Aires, Argentina, is at 60 degrees west longitude, while Canberra, Australia, is 150 degrees east.

Decide: How many hours apart are the time zones in Buenos Aires and Canberra? $60 + 150 = d$; $d \div 15 = a$

Estimate: $60 + 150$ is about 200; $200 \div 15$ is about 15

Carry Out: $60 + 150 = 210$; $210 \div 15 = 14$

Reread: Buenos Aires and Canberra have time zones that are 14 hours apart.

3. **Read:** The 0 degree longitude line, called the prime meridian, passes through Greenwich, England, a suburb of London. You want to call Chicago, Illinois, from London at 4:00 P.M. London time. Chicago is at 90 degrees west longitude. As you travel west, the time becomes earlier.

Decide: What time is it in Chicago when it is 4:00 P.M. in London? $90 \div 15 = d$; $4 + 12 = t$; $t - d = a$

Estimate: $90 \div 15 = 6$; the time should be about 5 hours earlier than 4:00 P.M.

Carry Out: $90 \div 15 = 6$; $4 + 12 = 16$; $16 - 6 = 10$

Reread: When it is 4:00 P.M. in London, it is 10:00 A.M. in Chicago.

4. **Read:** Los Angeles is at 120 degrees west longitude. You need to call Mogadishu, Somalia, which is about 45 degrees east longitude. It is 9:00 A.M. in Los Angeles.

Decide: What time is it in Mogadishu? $120 + 45 = d$; $d \div 15 = e$; $9 + e = t$. If t is greater than 12, then you must find $t - 12$ to get P.M. time.

Estimate: $120 + 50 = 170$; $170 \div 15 =$ about 10; $9 + 10 = 19$. Because 19 is greater than 12, you must subtract 12 to get the P.M. time: $19 - 12 = 7$.

Carry Out: $120 + 45 = 165$; $165 \div 15 = 11$; $9 + 11 = 20$; $20 - 12 = 8$

Reread: When it is 9:00 A.M. in Los Angeles, it is 8:00 P.M. in Mogadishu.

5. **Read:** Someone in a town in Iceland that is about 15 degrees west longitude wants to call St. Petersburg, Russia. St. Petersburg is about 30 degrees east longitude. It is 6 a.m. in the town in Iceland.

Decide: What time is it in St. Petersburg? $30 + 15 = d$; $d \div 15 = e$; $6 + e = t$. If t is greater than 12, you must subtract 12 to get P.M. time.

Estimate: $30 + 15 = 45$; $45 \div 15 = 3$

Carry Out: $30 + 15 = 45$; $45 \div 15 = 3$; $6 + 3 = 9$

Reread: When it is 6 A.M. in the town in Iceland, it is 9 A.M. in St. Petersburg, Russia.

▶ **Real Life Connections** When it is noon in Chicago, Illinois, what time is it in your community?

Suffixes

A **suffix** is a word part that is added to the end of a word to change its meaning. If the root word ends in *y* or *e*, its spelling may have to be changed.

When a word ends in y preceded by a consonant, you change the *y* to *i* before adding a suffix. When the *y* is preceded by a vowel, you make no spelling change.

rely + able = reliable   pay + able = payable

When a word ends in *e* and the suffix begins with a vowel, you drop the final *e* before adding the suffix. You make no spelling change if the suffix begins with a consonant.

festive + al = festival   festive + ly = festively

Below are ten suffixes and their meanings. Study them carefully.

Suffix	Meaning	Suffix	Meaning
able	that can be	ful	full of
al	of or like	ive	having
ance	the act of	ly	like in manner
ant	a person or thing that	ness	quality or state of
ation	the condition of being	ous	characterized by

Write the correct suffix after each word below. If the word requires a spelling change before the suffix can be added, cross out the final e or y. The first one is done for you.

1. desire __able__   that can be desired
2. fame __ous__   characterized by fame
3. ordinary __ily__   in an ordinary manner
4. disinfect __ant__   a thing that disinfects
5. vary __iation__   the condition of being varied
6. pay __able__   that can be paid

7. territory __ial__   of territory
8. decorate __ive__   having to do with decoration
9. guide __ance__   the act of guiding
10. rude __ness__   the quality of being rude
11. grace __ful__   full of grace

Use one of the words above to complete each sentence below.

1. The Louisiana Purchase was a valuable __territorial__ addition to the United States.
2. The library is __ordinarily__ closed on Sundays.
3. The school clubs are under the __guidance__ of teachers.
4. The bill is __payable__ within 60 days.
5. Wallpaper gives a __decorative__ effect to the kitchen.
6. Being overworked was not an excuse for her __rudeness__.
7. The busy corner of Oak and Main is a __desirable__ location for a clothing store.

Federal Income Tax Form

In late December or early January, the government sends you a federal income tax form to fill out. By February 1, your employer must send you a W-2 form, which tells how much money you earned in the previous year and how much tax was withheld from your earnings. You must then fill out your income tax form and mail it in, with any payments due, no later than April 15.

Study the front of the completed Form 1040A on the next page.

A. Circle the letter in front of the phrase that correctly completes each sentence.

1. The person filing the return checked Head of Household on line 4 because
   a. her two children live with her.
   b. she is not married.
   c. she is married but filing a separate return.
   d. she has no dependents.

2. You know that the person filing the return is in favor of public financing of presidential election campaigns because
   a. she filled in the amount of money she wished to contribute to the fund.
   b. she checked "no" in the Presidential Election Campaign Fund box.
   c. she checked "yes" in the Presidential Election Campaign Fund box.
   d. she subtracted $3 in figuring her adjusted income.

3. Adjusted gross income is the amount of money received that you must pay tax on. On line 16, the adjusted gross income of the person filing this return is less than her total income on line 14 because
   a. she doesn't work full-time.
   b. she claims three exemptions.
   c. she received unemployment compensation.
   d. she contibuted money to an IRA (Individual Retirement Account).

B. Complete the following sentences.

1. The person filing this return checked Head of Household to identify her filing status
.

2. You can tell that the person filing the return was unemployed for part of the year because she filled in line 12
.

3. The person filing the return claimed three exemptions. They are herself and her two children living with her
.

4. The person filing the return entered $155.80 on line 8a because she received taxable interest income
.

Form 1040A	Department of the Treasury—Internal Revenue Service		
1040A	**U.S. Individual Income Tax Return** (0) 1994		IRS Use Only-Do not write or staple in this space.

Label
(See page 16.)

Use the IRS label. Otherwise, please print or type.

L A B E L   H E R E

Your first name and initial: Lois C.   Last name: Robinson

If a joint return, spouse's first name and initial   Last name

Home address (number and street). If you have a P.O. box, see page 17.
25 Hampton Lane   Apt. no.

City, town or post office, state, and ZIP code. If you have a foreign address, see page 17.
Athens, Ohio 45701

OMB No. 1545-0085

Your social security number: 212 ¦ 36 ¦ 7104

Spouses's social security number:

For Privacy Act and Paperwork Reduction Act Notice, see page 4

Presidential Election Campaign Fund (See page 17.)
Do you want $3 to go to this fund? . . . .   Yes ✓   No
If a joint return, does your spouse want $3 to go to this fund?

Note: Checking "Yes" will not change your tax or reduce your refund.

Check the box for your filing status
(See page 17.)
Check only one box

1 ☐ Single
2 ☐ Married filing joint return (even if only one had income)
3 ☐ Married filing separate return. Enter spouse's social security number above and full name here. ▶ _____
4 ☑ Head of household (with qualifying person). (See page 18.) If the qualifying person is a child but not your dependent, enter this child's name here. ▶ _____
5 ☐ Qualifying widow(er) with dependent child (year spouse died 19 ___).   (See page 19.)

Figure your exemptions
(See page 20.)

If more than seven dependents, see page 23.

6a ☑ **Yourself.** If your parent (or someone else) can claim you as a dependent on his or her tax return, **do not** check box 6a. But be sure to check the box on line 18b on page 2.

b ☐ **Spouse**

c **Dependents:** (1) Name (first, initial, and last name)	(2) Check if under age 1	(3) If age 1 or older, dependent's social security number	(4) Dependent's relationship to you	(5) No. of months lived in your home in 1994
Lisa Robinson		095 ¦ 83 ¦ 7622	daughter	12
Peter Robinson		404 ¦ 20 ¦ 1504	son	12

No. of boxes checked on 6a and 6b: 1

No. of your children on 6c who:
• lived with you: 2
• didn't live with you due to divorce or separation (see page 23): ___
Dependents on 6c not entered above: ___

d If your child didn't live with you but is claimed as your dependent under a pre-1985 agreement, check here. . . . . ▶ ☐

e Total number of exemptions claimed.

Add numbers entered on lines above: 3

Figure your total income
(See page 20.)

Attach Copy B of your Forms W-2 and 1099-R here.

If you didn't get a W-2, see page 25.

Enclose, but do not attach, any payment with your return.

7	Wages, salaries, tips, etc. This should be shown in box 1 of your W-2 form(s). Attach Form(s) W-2	7	28,742	75
8a	**Taxable** interest income (see page 25). If over $400, attach Schedule 1.	8a	155	80
b	**Tax-exempt** interest. DO NOT include on line 8a. 8b			
9	Dividends. If over $400, attach Schedule 1.	9		
10a	Total IRA distributions. 10a	10b Taxable amount (see page 26). 10b		
11a	Total pensions and annuities. 11a	11b Taxable amount (see page 27). 11b		
12	Unemployment compensation (see page 30).	12	1,482	00
13a	Social security benefits. 13a	13b Taxable amount (see page 31). 13b		
14	Add lines 7 through 13b (far right column). This is your **total income.** ▶	14	30,380	55

Figure your adjusted gross income

15a	Your IRA deduction (see page 34). 15a	1,500	00		
b	Spouse's IRA deduction (see page 34). 15b				
c	Add lines 15a and 15b. These are your **total adjustments.**		15c	1,500	00
16	Subtract line 15c from line 14. This is your **adjusted gross income.** If less than $25,296 and a child lived with you (less than $9,000 if a child didn't live with you), see "Earned income credit" on page 44. ▶		16	28,880	55

Cat. No. 11327A   1994 Form 1040A page 1

Lesson 16

Conflict and Resolution

Reading a Literature Selection

▶ Background Information

For many people, the first taste of adult responsibility comes with a driver's license. How to deal with this responsibility continues to be a matter of controversy. Many lawmakers have suggested that all new drivers be required to take a course in defensive driving.

▶ Skill Focus

Often the characters in a short story, play, or novel have a goal to achieve or a problem to solve. The struggle to achieve the goal or solve the problem is called **conflict**.

A character can face three main types of conflict.

Conflict with Self

A character may struggle with emotions or feelings within himself or herself. This struggle is an internal conflict. An example is the athlete who excels in all sports but must choose only one sport.

Conflict with Another Character

A character may struggle against another person. This struggle is an external conflict.

An example is two candidates competing against each other for the same class office.

Conflict with an Outside Force

A character may struggle against nature, society, technology, or a force over which he or she has no control. This struggle is also an external conflict. An example is a worker trying to decide which new skills are necessary to compete in a different job market.

In literature, the main character facing the conflict is called the **protagonist**. Often the protagonist is opposed by a rival or adversary; this character is called the **antagonist**. The antagonist can be a single character, an outside force, or a combination of both.

By the end of a story, the protagonist succeeds or fails in achieving the goal or solving the problem. The way a conflict is settled is called the **resolution**.

As you read a story, identify the protagonist and the antagonist. Be sure to identify the story's conflict and resolution.

▶ Word Clues

When you read a word that

you do not know, look for context clues to help you. Read the sentences below.

> He looked conceited, Curt thought, and <u>egotistical</u>, too. He sure wasn't modest.

If you don't know the meaning of the word *egotistical*, the word *modest* can help you. *Egotistical* and *modest* are antonyms, words that are opposite in meaning. *Egotistical* means "not modest."

Look for **antonym** context clues to find the meanings of the three underlined words in the selection.

▶ Strategy Tip

As you read "New Car, New Image," look for the conflicts that the protagonist faces. How is the antagonist different in each conflict? Are all the conflicts resolved? Answering these questions will help you understand the story's characters and action better.

New Car, New Image

Curt gave the sleek, green fender one last swipe with the chamois cloth before he opened the door on the driver's side and jumped into the car. As Curt pressed on the accelerator, the engine responded with a roar. Curt then looked into the rearview mirror. Was he imagining it, or did he somehow look more mature, more experienced, more sophisticated?

Heading for the beach, Curt couldn't wait to see Carmen's face. The car would have to impress her, and she wouldn't ignore him now.

Curt roared into the beach parking lot and came to a halt. He saw Carmen and her friends clustered around a new guy. They didn't turn around to check out Curt's car or Curt.

Curt was miffed that no one had seen him drive up. Who was that guy, soaking up all the attention and taking the spotlight away from him? He looked conceited, Curt thought, and egotistical, too. He sure wasn't modest.

"Hi, Curt," someone said, as he joined the group.

"This is Darrell Jackson. He's a race car driver." Ordinarily, Curt would have been thrilled to meet a race driver, but now he felt angry—cheated of his moment of glory. He felt like a <u>nonentity</u> again, instead of a somebody.

"I have my own car," Curt offered loudly, so Carmen would be sure to hear. "Fixed it up myself."

"That's great!" said Darrell heartily. Curt thought that he sounded false and patronizing. "That's how I started, too."

"Darrell was just telling us about a defensive driving course that he's teaching," Carmen said.

"Since you have a car, you should take the course, Curt," said Darrell.

Curt bridled. "I know how to drive. I have my license and my own car."

"Sure," said Darrell, "but you can never learn too much about driving, especially defensive driving. An automobile is the most dangerous instrument in everyday use. Every time you drive, you're taking a chance."

"Most worthwhile things involve some risk," Curt argued. "You're a race driver. That's risky."

"Yes, but I understand the risk that I'm taking, and I know what to do about it. Most drivers don't. Anyway, ordinary driving is far more dangerous than race driving."

"Yeah? Why?"

"Because of the other drivers. On a racetrack, all the drivers know what they're doing; they're competent and in control. That's not true on the highway. There are all sorts of irresponsible drivers on the road—people who are drunk, careless, or out to prove something."

"Prove something?" Carmen broke in.

"You mean people who always have to be the fastest?"

Darrell gave Carmen his brightest smile. What an operator this guy is, Curt thought.

Darrell answered Carmen. "Right. People like that are bad drivers who let themselves be manipulated by others and by their own emotions, instead of controlling the situation themselves. Good drivers don't need to prove they're good. They know that a car is a convenience and a pleasure, but also a potential danger."

"I'm a good driver," Curt grumbled. "I don't see any reason to take a defensive driving course." Curt was no longer calm. In fact, he was <u>seething</u>. Not only was this Darrell a racer, he was smart and self-confident. Look at the way he was talking to Carmen—so easily, so casually.

Curt was beginning to realize that just having a car wasn't going to turn him into Mr. Personality overnight. The realization hurt. Watching Darrell, he wondered how he could possibly compete. Again, he felt like a nonentity.

Darrell was directing all his attention to Carmen. "Defensive driving is essential, so that if an emergency comes up, you'll know exactly what to do. In an emergency, most drivers just press on the brake and brace their arms on the steering wheel, usually the worst things to do."

Carmen was listening raptly to Darrell's

> *Curt was beginning to realize that just having a car wasn't going to turn him into Mr. Personality overnight.*

every syllable. Curt was disgusted. "I've got to get going," he muttered.

"Here's my card," said Darrell. "Give me a call if you decide to take the course."

Curt dragged himself back to his car. He was furious; no one had even noticed his car! His big moment—and that Darrell Jackson had spoiled it. Once inside his car, he instantly felt better, more in control. He felt important.

"Curt!" It was Carmen, asking for a ride home. She slid in beside him.

"Wouldn't your friend Darrell give you a ride?" he asked casually.

"Oh, him . . . ," said Carmen. "He was nice, wasn't he—for an older man, anyway?"

Curt's heart soared. Here he was in his own car, with Carmen beside him! He turned the key, and the motor caught with a quick surge of power. Curt pulled out of the parking lot, driving quickly, surely. This was his chance to prove he was as good as that hotshot Darrell!

At the stoplight, a car pulled up alongside them, the driver gunning the motor. It was a red compact, almost the twin of his own. Curt glanced at the two boys in it, and they grinned back mockingly. Here was his chance to prove himself. Success with Carmen wouldn't <u>elude</u> him now; he would capture it and keep it within his grasp in one masterful move!

The light changed. Curt's foot came down hard on the gas. The car shot forward with a roar, tires screeching. They were off!

The other car moved with him, wheel to wheel. Curt was nosing ahead of the other car when they came to a bend. He pressed hard on the gas as he swept into the turn. The car wobbled under him. He wrestled with the wheel, almost losing control.

"Are you crazy?" Carmen screamed. "Stop!"

"I can beat him," Curt said through clenched teeth.

"So what? What are you trying to prove?"

Darrell's words came into Curt's mind: "Good drivers don't need to prove they're good." He lifted his foot from the accelerator, and the other car thundered past him and disappeared.

"Let's go get something to eat," Curt suggested, as casually as he could.

Two hours later, after taking Carmen home, Curt pulled up at his own house. He was thinking about Carmen. She was going out with him tomorrow!

"Thank goodness!" his mother greeted him. "It wasn't you!"

"What are you talking about?" Curt was jogged out of his daydreaming.

"It was broadcast on the radio. Two cars collided. Four teenagers were killed. Apparently, one of the cars was a red compact like yours, and I was terrified . . ."

A red compact? Was it the one he had raced? Suddenly, Curt realized that he and Carmen could have been the victims.

He dug into his windbreaker and pulled out a card.

"Where are you going?" his mother asked.

"I've got to make a phone call," Curt replied.

RECALLING FACTS

Indentifying cause and effect

1. Why didn't Carmen and her friends notice Curt's new car?

Carmen and her friends were talking to Darrell.

_____

_____

_____

Recalling details

2. According to Darrell, why is race car driving safer than everyday driving?

Race car drivers are aware of the dangers and take

precautions; on the track, the situation is controlled.

The same is not true of everyday driving.

_____

Recalling details

3. Darrell says that many drivers make two mistakes in an emergency. What are they?

They press on the brake and brace their arms on the

steering wheel.

_____

_____

Identifying plot

4. A story's climax marks the turning point in the plot. After the climax, the reader can predict the story's ending. Fill in the space between the lines next to the statement below that describes the climax in this story.

   ‖ a. Curt begins to race the other car, wheel to wheel.

   ‖ b. Darrell takes the spotlight away from Curt in the beach parking lot.

   ▊ c. Curt lifts his foot from the accelerator and lets the other car pass him.

   ‖ d. Carmen decides to go out with Curt.

Using context clues

5. Complete each statement with the correct word.

   elude   seething   nonentity

   a. Before being discovered, the dancer was a ___nonentity___ in the chorus line.

   b. The rabbit tried to ___elude___ its pursuers.

   c. The coach was ___seething___ because the team's carelessness cost them the game.

Inferring comparisons and contrasts

1. Why do you think Curt felt so different when he was in his car?

When he was with the others, Curt felt ordinary; however, his car gave him a sense of power, importance, and self-

esteem.

Inferring comparisons and contrasts

2. a. How are Curt and Darrell different?

Darrell is self-assured and easygoing. Curt is self-conscious and overly concerned about impressing others.

b. How are they alike?

Both Curt and Darrell like cars and know how to drive.

Understanding characters

3. How does Curt hope to become popular?

Curt hopes to impress people by using his car as an introduction.

Making inferences

4. At first, Curt assumes that Carmen is not interested in him. Is he correct? Explain.

Probably not. Insecure and shy, Curt thinks that no one could be interested in him. Yet, Carmen knows him well

enough to ask him for a ride home and to date him.

Making inferences

5. What happens to draw Curt and Carmen together?

Curt and Carmen face a dangerous situation together. Curt finally proves by his actions that he is a responsible and

mature person and driver.

Understanding character

6. From her reaction to Curt's reckless driving, what kind of driver do you think Carmen would be?

Carmen's reaction to Curt shows that she is a sensible, cautious person. She would probably be a very careful driver.

Drawing conclusions

7. Do you think Curt will take the defensive driving course? Explain.

Answers may vary. Yes. At the end of the story, Curt pulls out a card, which we infer is the card that Darrell gave

him. He says that he has to make a call, probably to sign up for Darrell's course.

Predicting outcomes

8. Suppose Curt ignored Carmen's outburst and decided to prove that he could outrace the other car. How might the story have ended?

Answers may vary. Students will probably conclude that an accident could have occurred, causing serious injury or

death to Curt and Carmen.

Think about the protagonist and the major and minor conflicts in this story. Use the information in the story to answer the following questions.

1. Who is the protagonist, the chief or leading character, in this story? _____ Curt _____

2. a. What internal conflict does the protagonist face?
Curt struggles with his own feelings of insecurity. He thinks that having his own car will make him popular.

   b. How is this conflict resolved?
Curt realizes that doing dangerous things to impress people, especially women, with his daring, is irresponsible and,

in fact, does not impress people who really care for him.

3. The protagonist also faces two external conflicts.
   a. Underline the statements that best describe these conflicts.
      Should Curt race the two boys in the green compact?
      How can Curt persuade Darrell that he doesn't need a defensive driving course?
      How can Curt win Carmen?
   b. Identify the antagonist in each of these two conflicts, and tell how the conflict is resolved.
The antagonist consists of the two boys in the other car. Curt resolves this conflict by deciding not to race them

recklessly on the curving road.

The antagonist is Darrell Jackson, who seems to have captured Carmen's attention. Curt resolves this conflict when

he wisely decides to stop racing the other car. This action so impresses Carmen that she agrees to go out with Curt

the next day.

4. How does the protagonist's internal conflict cause the external conflicts?
Curt's lack of self-confidence causes him to attempt to impress Carmen by driving recklessly.

5. Think about the protagonist's feelings and actions. Is the protagonist a static or dynamic character? Discuss.
Curt is a dynamic character. By the end of the story, he is more mature. He has realized that popularity is not based

on having things and that careful driving is very important. It is so important to him that he's even going to sign up for

the course in defensive driving that he thought was foolish and unnecessary at the beginning of the story.

▶ Real Life Connections To increase road safety in your county or state, what new driving law would you like to see enacted?

Reading a Map

Reading a Social Studies Selection

▶ **Background Information**

Many voters in the United States would be surprised to learn that they do not directly elect the President of the United States. Instead, they vote for a group of electors who support a particular political candidate. These electors become part of the electoral college, which officially elects the President at a later date.

As you will see in reading "The Electoral College," this system plays a controversial role in the U.S. government. Does it protect our democratic system by preventing the concentration of power in a few big states? Or is it fundamentally undemocratic, by preventing the direct election of the President?

▶ **Skill Focus**

A map often provides more than a picture of a geographic area. A map can show specific facts in such a way that they are easier to read and to locate than if they were presented in a paragraph or list.

For example, an **election map** indicates voting patterns in an area or region during a presidential election. When studying the results of an election, one finds that the number of votes cast in each state is as important as the number of votes cast throughout the nation.

Usually, an election map and a circle graph are used to show state-by-state voting patterns. The election map shows the voting patterns, and the graph shows the percentages of votes. From these two sources of information, the reader can infer, or figure out, the results of the election's returns.

The following questions will help you read election maps.
1. What is the title of the map?
2. What key is used to explain the colors on the map?
3. What geographic areas does the map show?
4. What does the accompanying graph represent?
5. What conclusions can you draw from the information that the map and graph present?

Knowing how to read this particular kind of map will enable you to follow elections more closely. You will understand why a close election came out the way that it did. You also will be able to read maps that show percentages state by state on many other subjects where popular opinion is measured in polls and surveys.

▶ **Word Clues**

When you read a word that you do not know, look for context clues to help you. Read the sentences below.

In every state, each political party chooses a <u>slate</u> of electors. In most states, this list of candidates is not put on the ballot that people see in their voting booths.

If you don't know the meaning of the word *slate*, the word *list* in the second sentence can help you. The words *slate* and *list* are synonyms.

Use **synonym** context clues to find the meanings of the three underlined words in the selection.

▶ **Strategy Tip**

The following selection describes how the electoral college system works. The maps and graphs that accompany the selection give specific information about three presidential elections.

The Electoral College

How to elect the President of the United States was a major problem at the Constitutional Convention of 1787. The convention members rejected the proposal that Congress elect the chief executive; they believed that the President would then be under control of the legislature. They also rejected the proposal that the people elect the President. Distance and limited mass communication made it impossible for every citizen to be personally acquainted with or thoroughly knowledgeable about each candidate. To solve this problem, the Constitutional Convention agreed to an indirect popular[1] election. The President would be chosen by a special body of electors, called the electoral college.

The candidate receiving a majority, at least 270 of the 538 electoral votes, is declared elected as President.

How the System Works

✗ Each state is <u>allotted</u> as many electors as the total number of its representatives and senators in Congress. Alaska, with its small population, is given three electoral votes— two for its senators and one for its representative. New York State, which is highly populous, has 33 electoral votes due to its large number of representatives. The legislature in each state has the power to appoint or elect its presidential electors. There is a total of 538 presidential electors today.

The framers of the Constitution thought of the electors as enlightened citizens who would freely deliberate as they chose the persons best qualified to fill the nation's two highest offices, the presidency and vice-presidency. With the emergence of political parties, however, the electors became "rubber stamps," pledging to vote for their party's nominees instead of for the candidates they personally thought best qualified.

The principle of the electoral college system is "winner take all." In each state, the presidential candidate who gets the most votes on election day gets *all* that state's electoral votes. For example, if a state has ten electoral votes, all ten votes are cast for the winner of the popular vote.

A Second Election

The winner in a presidential election is usually proclaimed by midnight of election day. However, the formal vote of the electoral college does not take place until the Monday after the second Wednesday in December. On that day, electors from each state and the District of Columbia convene in their capitals to cast one ballot each for President and Vice President.

✔ The ballots are then signed, sealed, and sent by registered mail to the President of the Senate in Washington, D.C. On January 6, a special meeting of both houses is called. The electoral votes are opened, and four tellers, along with one Democrat and one Republican from each house, count the votes in the presence of both houses of Congress. The candidate receiving a majority, at least 270 of the 538 electoral votes, is declared elected as President. The person receiving a majority of vice-presidential votes becomes the Vice President. If no candidate receives a majority, the House of Representatives chooses the President from the three candidates having the highest number of electoral votes. If no candidate receives a majority of electoral votes for Vice President, the Senate votes for the Vice President from the two candidates having the most votes.

Criticism of the System

Ever since the framers of the Constitution devised the electoral college, its shortcomings have been criticized. Critics are primarily worried about the possibility that the electoral college vote can go against the popular vote. Under the present system, a candidate can receive fewer popular votes than his or her opponents and still receive a

---

[1] popular: of or carried on by the people

majority of electoral votes. There are three reasons for this.

First, the winner-take-all feature of the system gives the winning candidate all of a state's electoral votes. Even though the other major party candidates receive popular votes, the votes count for nothing in the final outcome.

Second, the electoral votes are distributed among the states so as to ensure that each state has two electors because of its Senate seats, regardless of the size of its population. As a result, the distribution of electoral votes may or may not match the distribution of population and voters. The Senate-based electors can therefore seriously distort the picture. In fact, three Presidents—John Quincy Adams in 1824, Rutherford B. Hayes in 1876, and Benjamin Harrison in 1888—were elected without winning the popular vote.

In 1824, Andrew Jackson won the largest share of the popular vote—151,174, or 40.3 percent of the total. His nearest rival, John Quincy Adams, received 113,122 votes, or 30.9 percent. Ninety-nine of the 261 electors then voted for Jackson—far short of the constitutionally required majority. The election thus went to the House of Representatives and, early in 1825, it elected Adams to the presidency.

Although the system has not produced a distorted vote since 1888, it has come close several times. The most recent election in which this occurred was 1976, when Jimmy Carter defeated Gerald Ford by only 1,678,069 popular votes. If only a small number of voters in a few strategic states had voted for Ford instead of Carter, Ford could have won in the electoral college vote and been elected President.

The third major problem with the system is that it is not <u>obligatory</u> for the electors to vote for the candidate who wins the popular vote in their states. While electors are expected to follow the choice of the popular vote, they sometimes do not. This happened in eight elections—1796, 1820, 1948, 1956, 1960, 1968, 1972, and 1976. In no instance did the departure from custom have a bearing on the outcome of the election. Nevertheless, the potential is there.

Proposals for Reform

Proposals to reform the electoral college system have been introduced in every term of Congress since 1789. The strongest current proposal is to <u>revoke</u> the college and to elect the President directly by popular vote. The idea to eliminate the college is based on the democratic principle that the vote of each citizen would count equally in the election of a President. However, such a change in the voting system would require a constitutional amendment. This complicated process would encounter several stumbling blocks. For example, representatives from smaller states would certainly oppose a change because they benefit from the present system.

Despite its defects, the electoral college is likely to remain a part of the election process. A change would probably occur only in the event of a crisis. If the electoral college vote should ever go against the popular vote, reform would be inevitable. The very close elections of 1960, 1968, and 1976 make such an event a real possibility.

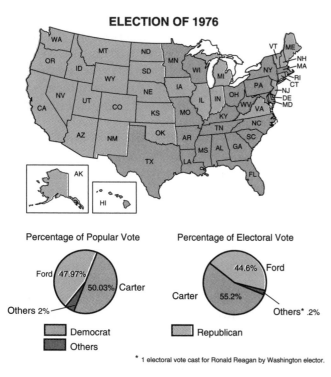

ELECTION OF 1976

Percentage of Popular Vote

Ford 47.97%
Carter 50.03%
Others 2%

Democrat
Others

Percentage of Electoral Vote

Ford 44.6%
Carter 55.2%
Others* .2%

Republican

* 1 electoral vote cast for Ronald Reagan by Washington elector.

Recalling details

1. Complete the sentence below.

A state is allotted ___2___ Electoral vote(s) for its senators and ___1___ electoral vote(s) for each of its representatives.

Identifying cause and effect

2. In the sentence below, draw a box around the word that tells you that there is a cause and effect relationship. Then underline the cause, and circle the effect.

> Representatives of smaller states would certainly oppose a change in the electoral college because they benefit from the present system.

Identifying the main idea and supporting details

3. Reread the paragraph with an X next to it. Circle the sentence that states the paragraph's main idea. Then write two details that support the main idea.

a. Alaska has three electoral votes.

b. New York has 33 electoral votes.

Using context clues

4. Use the words below to complete the following sentences.

allotted   obligatory   revoke

a. The school board decided to _____revoke_____ an earlier ruling against secret clubs.

b. Each school was _____allotted_____ ten new computers.

c. In most states, drivers' education is _____obligatory_____ if one wants to drive at sixteen.

Inferring the unstated main idea

1. Reread the paragraph with a check mark next to it. Write a sentence stating the paragraph's main idea.

The President is officially declared elected after the electoral votes are counted in the Senate.

Inferring details

2. If a state has 10 representatives in the House of Representatives, how many electoral votes would it have? It would have 12—2 for each senator, 10 for each member of Congress.

Distinguishing fact from opinion

3. Identify each statement as fact or opinion by writing O or F on the line provided.

___O___ The President of the United States should be elected by popular vote.

___F___ The electoral college was created by the framers of the Constitution.

Making generalizations

4. Write a generalization based on the following facts.

Facts The popular vote winner could fail to win the presidency.
Electors in various states represent different numbers of voters.
Electors are not required to follow the choice of the popular vote.

Generalization The electoral college system has several major defects or flaws.

5. When a political party in a state chooses its slate of electors, what considerations influence its choice?

The individual's loyalty to and work for the party are the most important considerations.

Inferring comparisons and contrasts

6. Describe the attitudes of the two groups below on this issue: The President should be elected by the strictly democratic method of giving each person one vote.

The framers of the Constitution   They did not support a strictly democratic election system.

Supporters of a popular vote election   They believe that the people should elect a president directly.

Predicting outcomes

7. How might the public react if, in the next election, the electoral college elected a candidate different from the winner of the popular vote?

There might be controversy, leading to a demand for reform of the system.

Making inferences

8. What would the presidency be like today if the Constitutional Convention had maintained its early position that the President be elected by Congress?

Answers may vary. The President would not be as independent as today's chief executive. Also, the concept of

separation of powers between the legislative and executive branches would be nonexistent.

SKILL FOCUS

Use the maps and graphs below and on page 68 to answer the following questions.

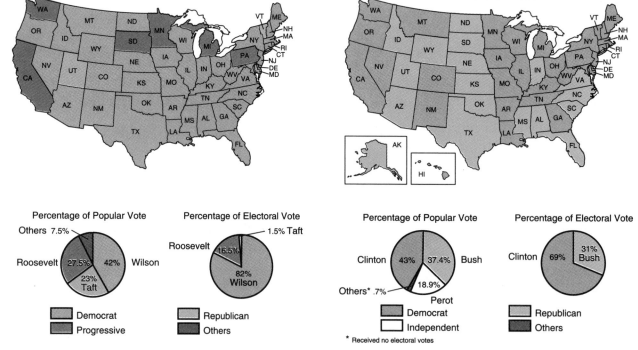

ELECTION OF 1912

ELECTION OF 1992

Percentage of Popular Vote
Others 7.5%
Roosevelt 27.5%   42% Wilson
23% Taft

Percentage of Electoral Vote
1.5% Taft
Roosevelt 16.5%
82% Wilson

■ Democrat   ■ Republican
■ Progressive   ■ Others

Percentage of Popular Vote
Clinton 43%   37.4% Bush
Others* .7%
18.9% Perot

Percentage of Electoral Vote
Clinton 69%   31% Bush

■ Democrat   ■ Republican
☐ Independent   ■ Others

* Received no electoral votes

1. What is the title of each map, in chronological order?

Election of 1912

Election of 1976

Election of 1992

2. On each map, a key explains the colors used. List the labels used in all three keys.

☐ Democrat   ☐ Republican   ☐ Independent

☐ Progressive   ☐ Others

3. What do the colors on the map represent?

Each state bears the color of the party that it carried in the popular vote and to whom it gave its electoral votes.

4. What geographic area is shown on the map? the United States

5. How is the area divided? state by state

6. What do the circle graphs accompanying each map represent?

The first graph shows the percentage of the popular vote cast for each candidate. The second graph shows the

percentage of the electoral vote given to each candidate.

7. What conclusions can you draw from the information presented on the maps and graphs?

Election of 1912

a. Which candidate won the election? _____Wilson_____

b. How large was his popular vote? __42%__ Electoral vote? __82%__

c. What can you infer about the results of this election?

Both the popular and electoral votes showed the nation supported Woodrow Wilson for President over Roosevelt, the

ex-Republican president, and Taft, the Republican president. However, if Roosevelt had not run, enough Republicans

might have voted for Taft to elect him.

Election of 1976

a. Which candidate won the election of 1976? _____Carter_____

b. How large was his popular vote? __50%__ Electoral vote? __55%__

c. What can you infer about the results of this election?

Neither Carter nor Ford was a national favorite; it was a very close election.

Election of 1992

a. Which candidate won the election of 1992? _____Clinton_____

b. How large was his popular vote? __43%__ Electoral vote? __69%__

c. What can you infer about the results of this election?

The popular vote was fairly close, but the electoral vote was heavily for Clinton—more than 2 to 1.

▶ **Real Life Connections** Would you like to keep the electoral college or do away with it? State your reasons. Be persuasive.

Main Idea and Supporting Details

___Reading a Science Selection ___

▶ **Background Information**

Preview the following selection before you read it. Read the boldfaced section headings, and look at the diagrams. Four sections describe how the science of genetics developed. Each section heading describes an important aspect of genetics: experiments, laws, concepts, and traits.

▶ **Skill Focus**

Many paragraphs that you read are packed with information. To understand how ideas in a paragraph are related and which ideas are important, you look for the **main idea** and **supporting details**.

Sometimes you need to read more than one paragraph to understand how ideas are related. For example, the chapters in many textbooks are divided into sections. Each section usually begins with a heading in boldfaced type. Think of this heading as the main idea of the entire section; it tells you the subject of the paragraphs in that section. You can then find the major and minor details about that subject by reading all the

paragraphs in the section. This is one way of summarizing or taking notes on the key ideas in a section.

The following diagram shows how the key ideas in a section are related.

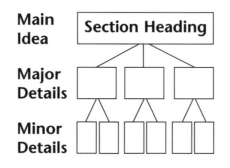

Main Idea | **Section Heading**

Major Details

Minor Details

When you read a section that is packed with information, use the following steps.
1. Use the heading of each section as the main idea.
2. Within each section, find at least two major details that develop or support the main idea.
3. Look for minor details that give more information about the major details.
4. Arrange the major and minor details to show how they are related. An outline and a diagram are two ways to organize information.

▶ **Word Clues**

Read the following sentence. Look for context

clues that explain the underlined word.

> Scientist have long known that offspring resemble, or look like, their parents.

If you do not know the meaning of the word *resemble*, the phrase *or look like* can help you. The phrase *or look like* is an appositive phrase. An appositive phrase explains a word coming before it and is set off from the word by commas or dashes.

Use **appositive phrases** to find the meaning of the three underlined words in the selection.

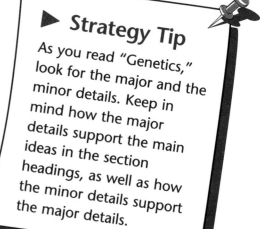

▶ **Strategy Tip**

As you read "Genetics," look for the major and the minor details. Keep in mind how the major details support the main ideas in the section headings, as well as how the minor details support the major details.

Genetics

Scientists have long known that offspring resemble, or look like, their parents. This resemblance applies to the several million different kinds of plants and animals living today. All organisms, or living things, possess certain characteristics that they pass on from one generation to the next. The passing on of traits from parents to offspring is called **heredity.**

The study of heredity is a relatively new science. For centuries, people applied the principles of heredity to improve their animals and plants, but they did not understand the patterns and processes involved. Not until the work of Gregor Mendel, an Austrian monk, was recognized in the early 1900s did **genetics,** the study of heredity, begin.

Mendel's Experiments

Mendel's interest in the mechanism of **inheritance,** or the passing on of traits from one generation to the next, led him to conduct experiments with pea plants. He chose pea plants because they grow rapidly, produce many seeds, and have contrasting traits that are easy to observe. His experiments involved over ten thousand pea plants.

Mendel chose several plant characteristics to study, including seed shape, seed color, and stem length. The traits occurred in contrasting pairs. For example, seeds were either round or wrinkled and either green or yellow; plants were either tall or short.

Mendel's first step was to grow purebred plants by allowing them to self-pollinate. Self-pollination occurs when the male and female reproductive organs are on the same plant. The seeds of such plants always produce other plants with identical traits, generation after generation. For example, a purebred tall plant produces tall offspring. Purebred plants with yellow seeds produce offspring with yellow seeds.

Mendel wondered what would happen if two purebred plants with contrasting traits were cross-pollinated. Cross-pollination occurs when the male and female reproductive organs are on different plants. If a purebred tall plant and a purebred short plant were cross-pollinated, would a plant of medium height result?

Calling the two plants with contrasting traits the **parental generation,** or P_1, Mendel crossbred for all observable traits. The offspring of these crosses were designated, or referred to as, the **first filial generation,** or F_1. In all the crosses, the F_1 generation showed only one of the two traits of the P_1 generation! For instance, a tall plant and a short plant produced only tall offspring. It seemed that the traits of one parent had disappeared in the F_1 generation.

Next Mendel allowed the plants of the F_1 generation to self-pollinate and produce a **second filial generation,** or F_2. To his surprise, some of the offspring showed the "lost" trait. Among the offspring of the tall plants, there were about three times as many tall plants as short plants. See Figure 1.

Mendel believed that hereditary factors, or units, carried the traits that he was studying. A pair of factors was responsible for each trait. Because the offspring of contrasting purebred parents exhibited only one trait, that trait must be stronger than the other. Mendel called this trait the **dominant** trait. He called the trait that seemed to disappear the **recessive** trait.

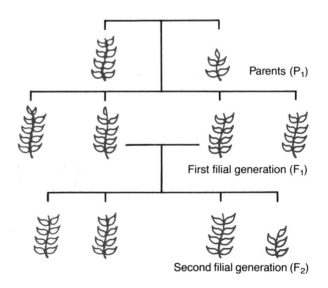

Figure 1. The F_1 generation shows only the trait of one parent. Some of the F_2 generation show the "lost" trait.

Mendel's Laws of Heredity

Mendel conducted the same experiments repeatedly, each time obtaining the same results. He tried to explain his observations by developing hypotheses, or logical explanations, for what he saw. For nearly 35 years, Mendel's work was ignored. Finally, supported by the results of other experiments, Mendel's conclusions were accepted as laws.

The Law of Dominance states that of two contrasting traits, one trait is dominant over the other. The dominant trait appears in the offspring; the recessive trait does not appear. In pea plants, tallness is dominant over shortness; round seed shape is dominant over wrinkled seed shape.

The Law of Segregation states that hereditary factors occur in pairs. These pairs are <u>segregated</u>, or separated, during the formation of reproductive cells. A parent hands down only one factor of every pair to each of its offspring.

The Law of Independent Assortment states that each pair of hereditary factors is inherited independently of the other pairs. For example, a tall pea plant can have round or wrinkled seeds. This law is not always followed in nature.

Since Mendel's time, scientists have discovered exceptions to Mendel's laws. For example, some traits are determined not by one pair of hereditary factors but by several pairs in combination. However, Mendel's theories in general have been repeatedly proven.

Concepts of Heredity

Today scientists know that Mendel's factors of heredity are **genes**. An organism that has two identical genes for a given trait is called a **purebred**: It can be pure dominant or pure recessive. An organism that carries different genes for a trait is called a **hybrid**: It carries one dominant gene and one recessive gene for that trait.

Geneticists use symbols to indicate dominant and recessive forms of a trait. Capital letters are used for dominant traits. For example, Y stands for yellow seeds, R for round seeds, and T for tall plants. All these traits are dominant. The same letter in lower case represents the recessive trait. Green seeds are represented by y, wrinkled seeds by r, and

short plants by t. For a purebred tall plant that has two dominant genes, the genetic symbol is TT. For a purebred short plant with two recessive genes, the symbol is tt. For a plant with one dominant and one recessive gene, the symbol is Tt.

Geneticists use Mendel's laws and the principles of probability to predict possible offspring types. They also use a special chart, called a **Punnett square**, to show the possible combinations resulting from a cross of two organisms. The two genes of one parent are identified at the top of the square; the genes of the other parent are identified on the left side of the square. Each box within the square represents the possible combination of genes that one offspring could have. (See Figure 2.)

Some gene pairs contain neither a dominant nor a recessive gene. In such cases, the offspring exhibit a blending of the traits of the parents. The genes exhibit **incomplete dominance**. For example, when red four o'clock flowers are crossed with white four o'clock flowers, the offspring are pink.

Inherited Traits

Traits that an organism inherits from its parents can be both physical and mental. In pea plants, seed color, seed shape, and plant height are physical traits. Some common physical traits in humans are eye color, hair color and texture, skin color, general body shape and size, and blood type. Many abnormal conditions and diseases are inherited, including hemophilia, muscular dystrophy, color blindness, and sickle cell anemia.

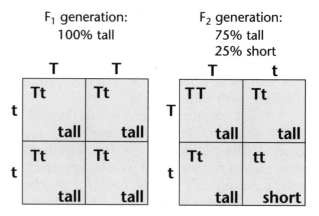

Figure 2. The Punnett square shows possible genetic combinations.

Mental traits include general intelligence—a basic mental ability that influences the capacity to learn—and aptitudes in art, music, mathematics, languages, and other fields. Obviously, people are born with certain mental traits. However, scientists do not agree on whether such traits are entirely inherited or are partly the result of other factors that we do not yet understand.

Inherited physical and mental traits alone do not determine what an organism becomes. A person's <u>environment</u>, or surroundings, affects his or her hereditary traits, strongly influencing whether and how these traits develop. For example, research has shown that mental stimulation can raise a child's intelligence level.

R ECALLING FACTS

Recalling details

1. If two purebred plants with contrasting traits were crossed, what would the offspring be like?

They would probably all show only the dominant trait.

Recalling details

2. What does the Law of Dominance state?

Of two contrasting traits, one trait is dominant over the

other and expresses itself in the offspring. The

recessive trait does not appear.

Identifying cause and effect

3. How can you explain the existence of tall pea plants with smooth seeds and tall pea plants with wrinkled seeds?

The Law of Independent Assortment states that each

pair of hereditary traits is inherited independently of

other pairs.

Identifying cause and effect

4. A tall pea plant is crossed with a short pea plant. About one-quarter of the offspring are short. What is probably true of the tall parent plant?

It is a hybrid with one dominant gene and one

recessive gene.

Recalling details

5. In addition to inherited physical and mental traits, what other factor influences how an organism develops?

Environment also influences development.

Using context clues

6. Draw a line to match each word with its explanation.

segregated   referred to

designated   separated

environment ——— surroundings

I NTERPRETING FACTS

Making inferences

1. Incomplete dominance occurs in shorthorn cattle. If red shorthorn cattle are crossed with white shorthorn cattle, the offspring are _____.

   a. red

   b. white

   c. roan, or reddish brown

2. If a purebred tall pea plant (TT) is crossed with a purebred short pea plant (tt),
the offspring are _____.

   || **a.** all tall purebred

   || **b.** half tall purebred, half short purebred

   |▌   **c.** all tall hybrid

Inferring cause and effect

3. How could the laws of heredity be used to improve farm animals?

   |▌   **a.** Farmers could cross-breed animals that have the traits they want.

   || **b.** Farmers could feed animals the kind of food that makes them grow larger.

   || **c.** Farmers could know in advance how many offspring an animal will have.

S KILL FOCUS

The diagram below shows how the major and minor details are related in the section on Mendel's experiments. Using this model, complete the diagram on the next page for two of the remaining three sections in the selection. For each diagram, write the heading of the section in the main idea box. Then reread the paragraphs in each section. Write a sentence in each of the three "Major Details" boxes. To complete the diagram for each section, write at least two minor details, using phrases instead of sentences.

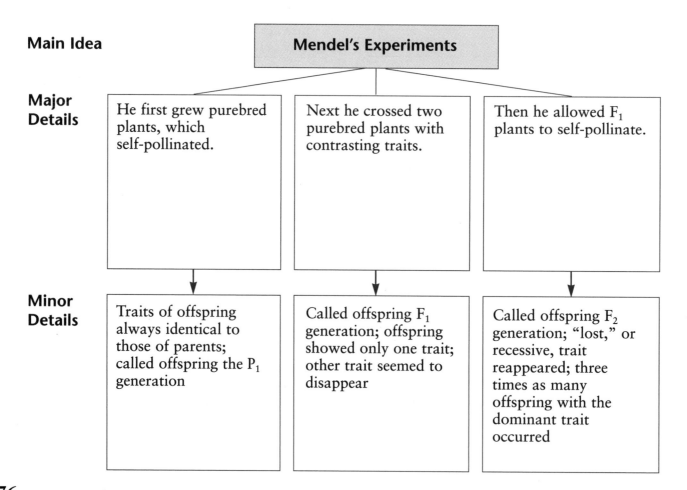

Main Idea — Mendel's Experiments

Major Details
- He first grew purebred plants, which self-pollinated.
- Next he crossed two purebred plants with contrasting traits.
- Then he allowed F_1 plants to self-pollinate.

Minor Details
- Traits of offspring always identical to those of parents; called offspring the P_1 generation
- Called offspring F_1 generation; offspring showed only one trait; other trait seemed to disappear
- Called offspring F_2 generation; "lost," or recessive, trait reappeared; three times as many offspring with the dominant trait occurred

Main Idea

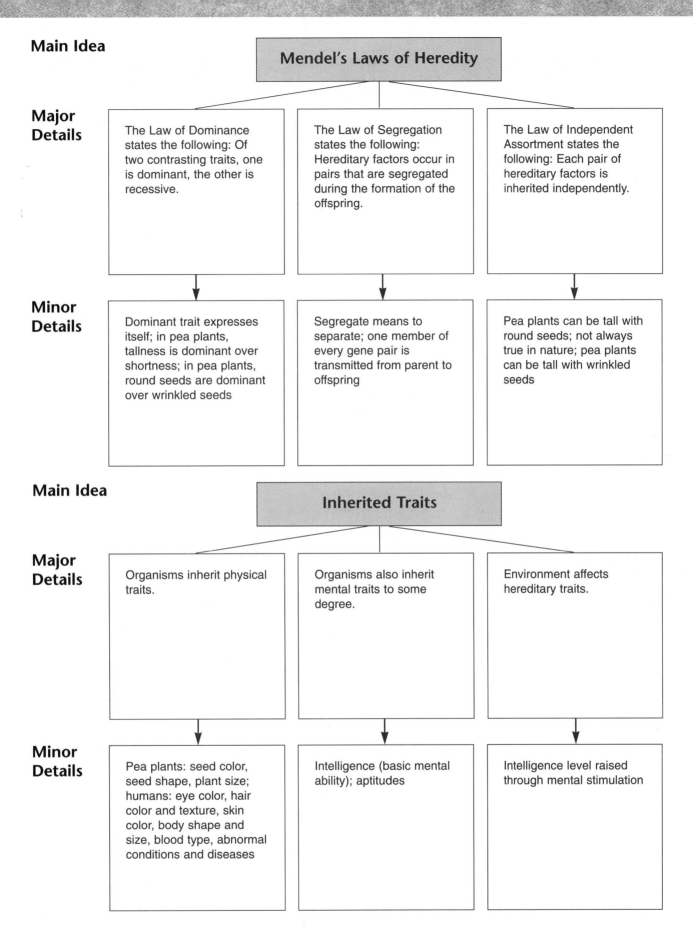

Mendel's Laws of Heredity

Major Details

The Law of Dominance states the following: Of two contrasting traits, one is dominant, the other is recessive.

The Law of Segregation states the following: Hereditary factors occur in pairs that are segregated during the formation of the offspring.

The Law of Independent Assortment states the following: Each pair of hereditary factors is inherited independently.

Minor Details

Dominant trait expresses itself; in pea plants, tallness is dominant over shortness; in pea plants, round seeds are dominant over wrinkled seeds

Segregate means to separate; one member of every gene pair is transmitted from parent to offspring

Pea plants can be tall with round seeds; not always true in nature; pea plants can be tall with wrinkled seeds

Main Idea

Inherited Traits

Major Details

Organisms inherit physical traits.

Organisms also inherit mental traits to some degree.

Environment affects hereditary traits.

Minor Details

Pea plants: seed color, seed shape, plant size; humans: eye color, hair color and texture, skin color, body shape and size, blood type, abnormal conditions and diseases

Intelligence (basic mental ability); aptitudes

Intelligence level raised through mental stimulation

▶ **Real Life Connections** Imagine that you are a breeder of championship show dogs. How would knowledge of genetics help you in your work?

Similar and Congruent Triangles

— Reading a Mathematics Selection

▶ **Background Information**

Geometry is the branch of mathematics that is concerned with the properties of figures. The study of similar and congruent shapes is an important part of geometry.

Mathematicians have developed rules for proving which figures are congruent and which are not. The simplest and most important of these rules applies to triangles—figures with three straight sides. All figures with more than three straight sides can be divided into a number of triangles. Therefore, if you can prove that triangles are congruent, you can also find out whether other figures are congruent.

In this selection, you will learn how figures can be identified as similar or congruent. You must not rely on the appearance of the diagrams. Two figures that look congruent may be slightly different.

▶ **Skill Focus**

When two geometric figures are exactly the same shape, the figures are called **similar**. If two geometric figures are not only exactly

the same shape, like similar figures, but are also exactly the same size, the figures are said to be **congruent**. The relationships between similar figures can be used to find the measurements of an object that is too tall or too distant to measure.

Suppose you need to find out the height of a building in your community. You obviously cannot measure the building's height, but you can calculate the building's height by making it correspond to the height of something that you can measure. For example, you know that the height of a nearby flagpole is 18 feet. You measure its shadow and find that it is 12 feet. You measure the shadow of the building and find it is 48 feet. The height and the shadow of the flagpole are related to each other in the same way that the height and the shadow of the building are related to each other. This is true because the heights and shadow-lengths for the two objects make them similar shapes. They are, in fact, similar triangles.

You can set up these two relationships in a mathematical form called a

proportion. By working out the proportion, you can find the height of the building.

$$\frac{\text{flagpole's height}}{\text{flagpole's shadow}} = \frac{\text{building's height}}{\text{building' shadow}}$$

$$\frac{18}{12} = \frac{n}{48}$$

$$12n = 864$$

$$n = 72 \text{ feet (height of building)}$$

▶ **Word Clues**

When reading the following selection, you will find words whose parts come from Latin or Greek. You will understand geometry better if you know that *tri* is a prefix meaning "three," *poly* is a prefix meaning "many," *penta* is a prefix meaning "five," *hexa* is a prefix meaning "six," and *gon* is a root meaning "angle."

▶ **Strategy Tip**

Use the rules to show that the figures are congruent or similar. Symbols on the figures indicate when sides or angles are equal. Check all descriptions against the figures to make sure that you understand the text.

Similar and Congruent Figures

While any two geometric figures can be similar or congruent, geometric figures with straight sides are the simplest to study. The most important of straight-sided figures is the closed figure whose sides are all straight line segments that meet but do not cross. This type of figure is called a **polygon** (POL i gahn).

The polygon below has five straight sides: *AB, BC, CD, DE,* and *EA.* The sides are named by the points at the ends of the line segments. This polygon also has five angles: *A, B, C, D,* and *E.* An angle is named by the point where the two sides meet, called the **vertex** of the angle. Angles can also be named by using three letters. The vertex of the angle is the middle letter of the three-letter name, while the other two letters are the names of points on the sides. For example, angle *A* could also be called angle *EAB.*

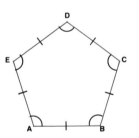

Notice the short lines marked on the five sides of the polygon. These short lines mean that the sides are all equal. Short arcs are also used to show that the five angles are equal. Because this polygon has *five* angles, it is called a **pentagon** (PEN tə gahn). The figure is a **regular** pentagon because all the sides and angles are equal.

If the figure had *six* angles (and therefore also six sides), it would be a **hexagon** (HEK sə gahn). If all the angles and sides were equal, it would be a regular hexagon.

A polygon with three sides is known as a **triangle**. A regular triangle is called an **equilateral triangle** because all its sides and angles are equal. An **isosceles** (eye SAHS ə leez) triangle is a triangle that has two equal sides. A **scalene** (skay LEEN) triangle has no equal sides. A **right** triangle has one angle equal to 90 degrees, called a **right angle**.

Any plamoon can be separated into triangles. Here is one way to separate a regular hexagon into triangles.

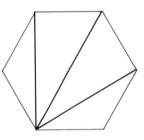

Any polygon can be separated into triangles. The rules for showing that two triangles are congruent can be used for showing that other polygons are congruent. Following are four of those rules. Notice that the rules for congruence all have abbreviations.

1. **SSS:** Two triangles are congruent if all three sides of one have the same lengths as all three sides of the other.
2. **SAS:** Two triangles are congruent if two sides of one have the same lengths as two sides of the other and the angle between the matching sides is the same size in both triangles.
3. **ASA:** Two triangles are congruent if two angles of one are the same sizes as two angles of the other and the side between these matching angles has the same length in both triangles.
4. **HL:** Two right triangles are congruent if the longest side of each triangle has the same length and a shorter side of each has the same length.

The abbreviation *HL* for rule 4 may not be clear. The longest side of a right triangle is called the **hypotenuse** *(H)* (hy PAHT ən yoos), while the shorter sides are called **legs** *(L)*. The abbreviation *HL* stands for hypotenuse-leg.

With these rules, you do not have to measure all the sides and angles of two triangles to find out if they are congruent. For example, look at the following triangles.

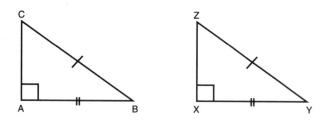

Right triangle *ABC* is congruent to right triangle *XYZ* by *HL*. This relationship can be expressed as follows.

$$\triangle ABC \cong \triangle XYZ$$

The marks on the sides of the two triangles indicate equalities: The sides with single marks have the same length, and those with double marks have the same length. The sides with single marks are the hypotenuses of the two triangles. The hypotenuse of a right triangle is always opposite the right angle, which is marked with the symbol for a right angle. The sides with double marks are both legs.

If two triangles are neither similar nor congruent, their relationship can be expressed as follows.

$$\triangle ABC \not\cong \triangle XYZ$$

In the following diagram, two pentagons have been separated into triangles. The five pairs of matching sides are marked with short lines to indicate which ones are the same lengths. The three pairs of matching angles are marked with arcs to show which ones are the same sizes. Using the rules for congruence, you can show that all three pairs of matching triangles are congruent.

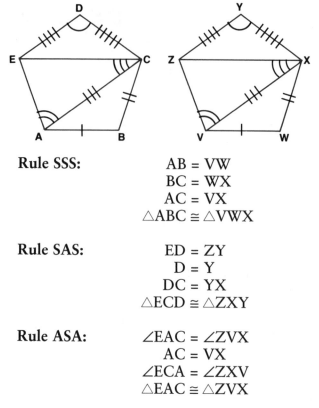

Rule SSS:	AB = VW
	BC = WX
	AC = VX
	$\triangle$ABC $\cong$ $\triangle$VWX

Rule SAS:	ED = ZY
	D = Y
	DC = YX
	$\triangle$ECD $\cong$ $\triangle$ZXY

Rule ASA:	$\angle$EAC = $\angle$ZVX
	AC = VX
	$\angle$ECA = $\angle$ZXV
	$\triangle$EAC $\cong$ $\triangle$ZVX

Because all the triangles are congruent, and because they completely describe the two pentagons, you know that the two pentagons are congruent. This conclusion is true because any polygon can be separated into triangles.

In triangles *MNO* and *PQR* below, two pairs of angles are marked with arcs. Angles *M* and *P* in triangles *MNO* and *PQR* are each marked with a single arc, which indicates that they are the same size. Similarly, angles *N* and *Q* are each marked with double arcs, which indicates that they are the same size. The two triangles are similar, since they have two pairs of angles that are the same sizes. This can be expressed as follows.

$$\triangle MNO \sim \triangle PQR$$

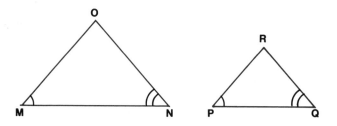

Recalling details

1. What makes two figures congruent?

They have the same shape and the same size.

Recalling details

2. What makes two figures similar?

They have exactly the same shape.

Recalling details

3. What is a polygon?

It is a closed figure whose sides are all straight line

segments that do not cross.

Recalling details

4. What do you call a polygon whose sides and angles are all equal?

It is called regular.

Recalling details

5. What do you call the longest side of a right triangle?

It is called the hypotenuse.

Recalling details

6. If two angles of a triangle have the same sizes as two angles of another triangle, what can you say about the triangles?

They are similar.

INTERPRETING FACTS

Making inferences

1. Write the letter of the true statement on the line provided. __a__

   a. All congruent polygons are similar.

   b. All similar polygons are congruent.

Making inferences

2. How many sides would you expect to find on a polygon with seven angles? __7__

Making inferences

3. In triangles *ABC* and *XYZ*, angle *A* equals angle *X*, angle *B* equals angle *Y*, and side *AB* equals side *XY*. What can you conclude about the two triangles?

They are congruent.

SKILL FOCUS

A. For each of the following diagrams or descriptions, decide whether the two triangles indicated are similar, congruent, or not necessarily similar or congruent. Write the mathematical expression that describes the figures on the short line provided to the right of the diagram. Do not label congruent triangles as similar. If the triangles are either similar or congruent, write the reason on the line provided below the diagram.

1.

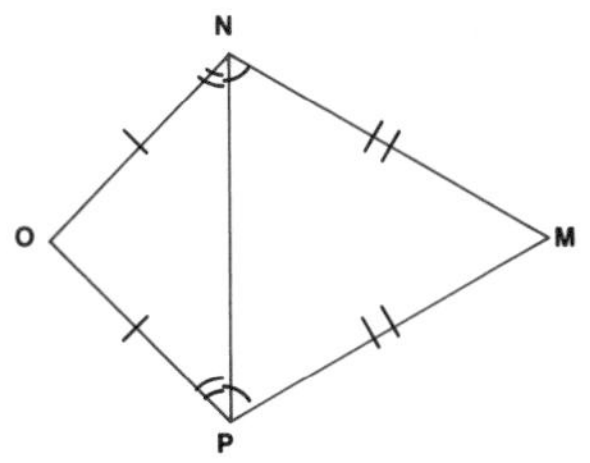

$\triangle PMN \not\cong \triangle PNO$

$\triangle PMN$ and $\triangle PNO$

2.

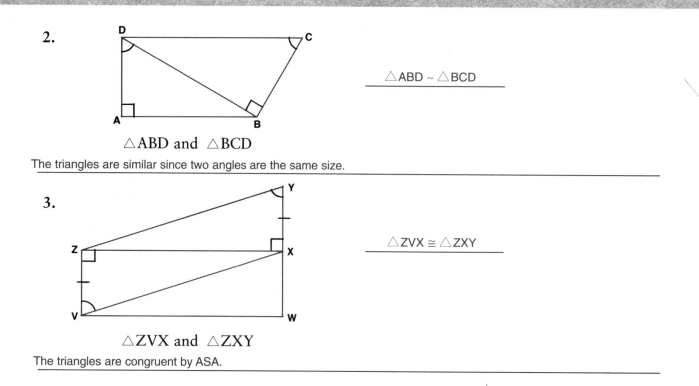

$\triangle ABD \sim \triangle BCD$

$\triangle ABD$ and $\triangle BCD$

The triangles are similar since two angles are the same size.

3.

$\triangle ZVX \cong \triangle ZXY$

$\triangle ZVX$ and $\triangle ZXY$

The triangles are congruent by ASA.

4. Regular pentagon *ABCDE* is separated into triangles by drawing line segments *AD* and *BD*, forming three triangles. Line segments *AD* and *BD* are equal. Which two triangles are congruent and why?

$\triangle ADE$ is congruent to $\triangle BDC$ by either of two rules. SSS: AE = BC and ED = CD by the definition of *regular;*

AD = BD. SAS: $\angle E = \angle C$ by the definition of *regular.*

5. Regular hexagon *MNOPQR* is separated into triangles by drawing line segments *RN*, *RO*, and *QO*. Show that triangle *MNR* is congruent to triangle *PQO*.

From the definition of *regular*, MN=PQ, MR=PO, and $\angle M = \angle P$. The triangles are congruent by SAS.

B. Answer each question by writing the answer on the line provided.

1. A surveyor measures a triangle as having two sides of 250 meters each, with the angle between them being 60 degrees. The third side of the triangle she measures as 300 meters. She then lays out another triangle that has two sides of 250 meters each, with the angle between the sides being 60 degrees. What is the length of the third side of the second triangle? Why?

The third side measures 300 meters because the two triangles are congruent by SAS.

2. In triangles *FGH* and *IJK*, sides *FH* and *IK* are equal. Angle *F* equals angle *I*, and angle *H* equals angle *K*. Does angle *G* equal angle *J*? Why or why not?

Yes. The triangles are congruent by ASA.

▶ **Real Life Connections** Explain how knowing about similar and congruent triangles could help someone design a patchwork quilt.

Multiple Meanings

Some words have entirely different meanings when used in different subject areas. Examples of such words are listed below.

cone	**date**	**force**	**organ**	**plant**
current	**figure**	**note**	**plane**	**scale**

Read the two definitions for each word below. Write the word from the list that fits the two definitions on the line before the first definition.

1. _____ organ _____

Music: a large wind instrument consisting of various sets of pipes

Science: a body part made up of specialized tissues and having a special purpose

2. _____ plant _____

Science: a living organism that cannot move from place to place by itself and can make its own food

Social Studies: the buildings, machinery, and other fixtures of a factory

3. _____ cone _____

Mathematics: a solid with a circular base and a curved surface tapering evenly to a point

Science: the seed-containing fruit of some evergreen trees

4. _____ figure _____

Art: the outline or shape of something

Mathematics: the symbol for a number

5. _____ scale _____

Mathematics: a regularly spaced series of marks along a line, used for measuring

Science: any of the thin, flat, hard plates forming the outer covering of many fish and reptiles

6. _____ current _____

Social Studies: now in progress; now going on

Science: a flow of liquid or gas in a specific direction

7. _____ force _____

Science: a push or a pull on an object

Social Studies: fighting strength or military organization of a nation

8. _____ note _____

Literature: a statement added to a book, at the back or at the bottom of a page, to explain something or to give more information

Music: a tone of definite pitch; also, a symbol for a tone indicating pitch and duration

9. _____ date _____

Social Studies: the time at which a thing happens or is done

Science: the sweet, fleshy fruit of a cultivated palm

10. _____ plane _____

Mathematics: a surface that wholly contains every straight line joining any two points lying on it

Science: to rise partly out of the water while moving at a high speed

Main Idea and Supporting Details

Many paragraphs that you read are packed with information. Knowing how to find the main ideas and the supporting details helps you understand the information in a paragraph. The **main idea** expresses the subject of a paragraph. A **major detail** is a supporting idea that is often an important example or a fact about the main idea.

The major details of a paragraph help develop or complete the thought expressed by the main idea. The main idea and major details work together as a unit to support one another. You could say that the main idea depends on major details.

Not all details in a paragraph are major details. Paragraphs often contain details that are not important to the main idea. They are called **minor details**, and they explain or tell more about the major details. While the minor details may add interest to the main idea, the main idea does not depend on them.

The following selection is about the training of Seeing Eye guide dogs at Seeing Eye Headquarters in Morristown, New Jersey. As you read, look first for the main idea. Then try to determine which of the details are major and which are minor.

The Seeing Eye Team

1. Before being given to a blind person as a Seeing Eye guide, a dog goes through a special process. After the puppy comes to the Seeing Eye Headquarters from an independent breeder or the Seeing Eye breeding station, it goes to live with a 4-H family for 14 months. The dog stays in this loving home and is taught basic obedience. The children in the family might take their puppy on buses, on trains, or into stores, introducing it to situations that it will meet as a guide dog. Next, the dog spends a month in a holding kennel. There, strenuous physical exams show if the dog could serve a blind master well. Then the dog is assigned with nine other dogs to a qualified instructor for three months of rigorous training.

2. The training period with the instructor is the most important and demanding. During training, the instructor walks many miles a day with the eager dog. The dog thus encounters typical outdoor situations of the average American town. Then, while blindfolded, the instructor takes the dog out for obedience exercises and traffic tests. With the instructor holding the harness, the dog must avoid such hazards as traffic and low-hanging tree branches. In this unique way, the instructor acts as a stand-in for the blind member of the future Seeing Eye team.

3. The ultimate meeting of the two team members is well-planned and emotional. The dog has been vigorously trained to be a faithful, responsible, and hard-working companion. The blind person has answered many questions about his or her lifestyle and home environment. When the blind person reaches out to his or her new friend, a stirring relationship of interdependence begins. The blind person will always know a new kind of freedom. The dog will always know a new kind of responsibility. They both will learn a new kind of love.

For each paragraph, complete the diagram. In the box labeled "Main Idea," write the sentence from the paragraph that states the main idea as it appears in the paragraph. When filling in the boxes labeled "Major Details" and "Minor Details," use your own words. Use the completed boxes to guide you. Not all major details have minor details.

Paragraph 1

Main Idea

Before being given to a blind person as a Seeing Eye guide, a dog goes through a special process.

Major Details

| The puppy is sent to a 4-H family to live for 14 months. | The dog spends a month in a holding kennel. | The dog is assigned to an instructor for three months of training. |

Minor Details

| It learns basic obedience there. | It meets situations it will encounter later in life. | The dog is examined to see if it will make a good guide dog. |

Paragraph 2

Main Idea

The training period with the instructor is the most important and demanding.

Major Details

| The instructor walks many miles a day with the dog. | The instructor, blindfolded, takes the dog out for obedience exercises and traffic tests. |

Minor Details

| In this way, the dog meets many typical outdoor situations. | The instructor holds the harness as the dog learns to avoid traffic and tree branches. | The instructor acts as a stand-in for the blind person. |

Paragraph 3

Main Idea

The ultimate meeting of the two team members is well planned and emotional.

Major Details

| The dog has been vigorously trained. | The blind person has answered many questions. | A stirring relationship begins when the student reaches out to the dog. |

Minor Details

| The blind person gets a new kind of freedom. | The dog gets a new kind of responsibility. | They learn to love each other. |

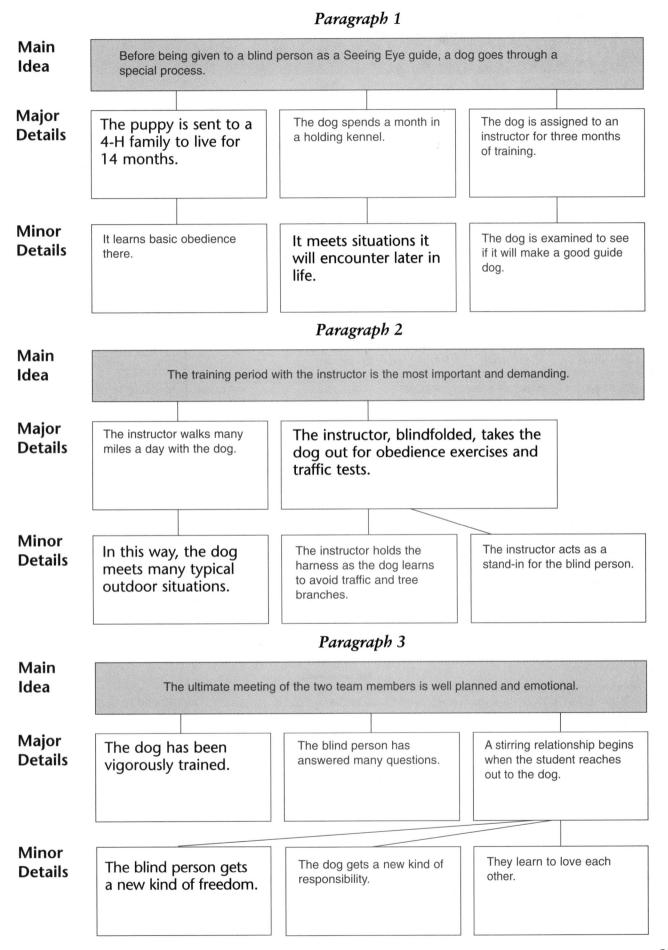

Voter Registration Form

To vote in a local or federal election, you must first register, that is, officially enroll your name. Any U.S. citizen who will be 18 years old before the next election can register to vote. You register to vote in the county where you live. Once your registration form is approved, the Board of Elections sends you a voter notification card. After you are registered, you may vote in your county for as long as you live there and vote once every five years.

Although voter registration forms differ from one county to the next, they all ask for the same kinds of information. When you fill out the form, you can decide if you want to join a political party.

Study the completed voter registration form below.

BOULDER COUNTY — REGISTRATION OF VOTERS

				FOR OFFICE USE ONLY		
				DIST.	PREC.	AFFIL.

LAST NAME	FIRST NAME	MIDDLE NAME OR INITIAL		
Torres	Marcos	Juan		

HOUSE NO.	NAME OF STREET OR ROAD	APT.NO.	ZIP CODE	DATE OF REGISTRATION		
				MO.	DAY	YEAR
503	39th Street	3B	80302			

PLACE OF BIRTH— STATE OR FOREIGN COUNTRY	TERM OF RESIDENCE IN COLORADO	SEX	AGE	DATE OF BIRTH		
	YEARS			MO.	DAY	YEAR
Mexico	1	M	21	2	20	74

I AM A CITIZEN OF THE UNITED STATES AND A RESIDENT OF BOULDER COUNTY, COLORADO. I HAVE NOT BEEN CONVICTED MORE THAN ONCE OF AN INFAMOUS CRIME NOR AM I CURRENTLY UNDER THE SENTENCE IMPOSED PURSUANT TO A CONVICTION OF AN INFAMOUS CRIME. I AM NOT UNDER GUARDIANSHIP FOR MENTAL DISABILITY.

I DO SOLEMNLY SWEAR (OR AFFIRM) THAT THE INFORMATION SET FORTH HEREON ABOUT MY PLACE OF RESIDENCE, NAME, PLACE OF BIRTH, CRIMINAL OFFENSES, QUALIFICATIONS AS A VOTER AND MY RIGHT TO REGISTER AND VOTE UNDER THE LAWS OF THIS STATE IS TRUE.

☞ *Marcos Juan Torres*

SIGN NAME IN FULL

GIVING FALSE INFORMATION TO PROCURE VOTER REGISTRATION IS PERJURY AND IS PUNISHABLE BY IMPRISONMENT FOR NOT MORE THAN 10 YEARS.

PARTY AFFILIATION CHOICE   (ONE MUST BE CHECKED)
PARTY AFFILIATION. Only voters affiliated with the Democratic or Republican Party vote in the primary election of their party. All voters vote in a general election.

DEMOCRAT _____ REPUBLICAN _____

OTHER (SPECIFY) _____

DECLINES TO AFFILIATE _____ ✓

FOR OFFICE USE ONLY	I.D. NUMBER

- - - - - - - - - - - - - - - - - - Fold here for mailing - - - - - - - - - - - - - - - - - -

PRIOR REGISTRATION Have you ever registered to vote before? *yes* _____ APPROXIMATE YEAR *1992*

If yes, complete the following:
Name on last registration ___ *Marcos Juan Torres*

Address on last registration ___ *9 Mulberry Avenue*

La Cruces		*New Mexico*	*88001*
(Post Office)	(County)	(State)	(Zip)

Party affiliation on last registration _____ Date of Birth ___ *2/20/74*

SIGN YOUR NAME BELOW AND AFTER HAND SYMBOL ABOVE

Date ___ *9/20/95* ___ Signature of Voter *Marcos Juan Torres*

RESIDENCE: Registering to vote in this county is declaration of residence in this county and state, and authorization to cancel any prior registration in another Colorado locality or another state.
DISQUALIFYING CRIME: Contact Boulder County Board of Supervisors of Elections, 494-3161, if you have been convicted of a crime.

Telephone Number (In event we need clarifying information) ___ *555-2282*

Answer each question by underlining the correct phrase or sentence.

1. What is the name of the person registering to vote?
   a. Torres Marcos Juan
   b. <u>Marcos Juan Torres</u>
   c. Juan Marcos Torres
   d. Marcos Torres Juan

2. How is it determined where this applicant is supposed to register?
   a. He is registering in the state in which he was born.
   b. He may register in any county as long as he registers in the state in which he lives.
   c. He may register in any state in the United States.
   d. <u>He is registering in the county where he lives.</u>

3. What could be the result if the applicant did not fill out the voter registration form honestly?
   a. He could have to pay a costly fine.
   b. He could lose his party affiliation.
   c. <u>He could be jailed for up to ten years.</u>
   d. He could never vote in an election.

4. The two major parties are required to choose their candidates for a general election by holding a primary election. Would this applicant be allowed to vote in a primary election?
   a. Yes, he is affiliated with the Democratic party.
   b. Yes, he is affiliated with the Republican party.
   c. <u>No, he is not affiliated with any political party.</u>
   d. No, he would not be at least 18 years old on or before the election.

5. Once each party chooses its candidate, a general election is held. According to this application, who is permitted to vote in general elections?
   a. <u>all voters, regardless of party affiliation</u>
   b. voters with no party affiliations
   c. voters affiliated with the Universal party
   d. voters who have voted before

6. How do you know that the applicant has registered to vote before?
   a. He is 21 years old, and an 18-year-old can register to vote.
   b. This application is only for applicants who have registered before.
   c. <u>He completed the "Prior Registration" section of the application.</u>
   d. He has lived in Boulder for only one year, so he probably voted elsewhere in the last election.

7. What is the result of registering to vote in one county or state?
   a. You can vote in any other state in the country.
   b. <u>You cannot vote in another county or state.</u>
   c. You can vote in any county in the state.
   d. You must register there again next year.

8. When was this voter registration form filled out?
   a. February 20, 1974
   b. February 20, 1994
   c. February 20, 1992
   d. <u>September 20, 1995</u>

Lesson 23

Theme

Reading a Literature Selection

▶ **Background Information**

How does the education of a young woman today compare with that of her forebears? How have attitudes about women's roles in society changed over the centuries? This play helps to answer these questions.

▶ **Skill Focus**

A writer usually does not directly state the **theme**. Instead, the reader must infer a story or play's message from clues in the plot, setting, dialogue, and title of the work. The thoughts, feelings, and actions of the characters also offer clues to the theme. In a play, the stage directions signal the characters' attitudes and feelings.

The following questions may help you to infer the theme in a play:

1. What words, especially in the stage directions, suggest each character's feelings and attitude?

2. How does your attitude toward the subject compare with each character's attitude?

3. How do the characters' attitudes help you infer the theme?

▶ **Word Clues**

When you read, you may come across a word that names a person, place, or thing. If the paragraph has no context clues to explain the word, there may be clues elsewhere. Read the sentences below.

> Lady Arabella appears suddenly beside Kay. Arabella is 18 and dressed in the stylish Elizabethan upper-class fashion of 1598—a starched ruff, a farthingale,[1] an undergown, and an overgown.

Notice that there is a raised number after the word *farthingale*. The raised number is a signal to you to look at the bottom of the page for a footnote with the same number. A footnote gives a brief definition or explanation of the word. The footnote for *farthingale* tells you what it is.

> [1]farthingale (FAR thin gayl): a hoop or series of hoops worn beneath a woman's skirt in the sixteenth and seventeenth centuries.

The footnotes in the play are like entries in a dictionary; they help you pronounce and define words.

Use **footnote** context clues to find the meanings of the six other numbered words in the selection.

▶ **Strategy Tip**

As you read "Other Times, Other Customs," notice how the stage directions help to suggest the characters' feelings and attitudes. How does each character's feelings and attitude help you to understand the theme? Reading plays requires active reading.

Other Times, Other Customs

Cast

Kay, 17, a high school senior
Lady Arabella, 18, a noblewoman of
   Elizabethan times

The Scene

The open, airy library of Cornelia Seton High School. It has glass window-walls, modern upholstered seating, and carpeting. Kay is sitting at a desk in an alcove, preparing an assignment for English IV.

Kay (*reading*): "Studies serve for delight, for ornament, and for ability. Their chief use for delight is in privateness and retiring; for ornament, is in discourse; and for ability, is in the judgment and disposition of business." (*to herself, skeptically*) Yes, that's great, Sir Francis Bacon, but in your day men took care of all the business. So what did young women study? Tell me that.

Lady Arabella appears suddenly beside Kay. Arabella is 18 and dressed in the stylish Elizabethan upper-class fashion of 1598—a starched ruff, a farthingale,[1] an undergown, and an overgown. She is also wearing a gold pomander[2] on a chain around her neck. Her blonde hair is frizzed and her face painted.

Arabella: Why, we had to attend to our own business, to be sure. You have a chair for me, of course?

Kay reluctantly gets out of her chair and offers it to Arabella with an ironic, sweeping gesture.

Kay (*challenging*): Who are you, anyway? Lady Macbeth? The Lady of the Lake?

Arabella (*with great dignity*): I am Lady Arabella Mayne, and my business is to manage my husband's household, which I can assure you is a considerable task.

Kay: I don't see why. Anybody can keep house.

Arabella: Perhaps you have married too young, my dear, and have come to rely too heavily on your housekeeper. Believe me, that is a serious mistake.

Kay: I'm not married.

Arabella (*sympathetically*): Not married! Oh, my poor dear!

Kay: Nowadays, women don't have to get married; they can have careers. Even if I marry, I'll still have a career. (*proudly*) I'm going to be a veterinarian. (*Arabella looks puzzled.*) A veterinarian, you know, an animal doctor.

Arabella (*disapprovingly*): Will, our groom, does that. (*graciously*) But, of course, a lady must know how to make medicines.

---

[1] farthingale (FAR thin gayl): a hoop or series of hoops worn beneath a woman's skirt in the sixteenth and seventeenth centuries.

[2] pomander (PAH man dər): an apple-shaped case or box containing perfume, spices, and other aromatic substances; worn as a protection against odor and infection.

Kay: Is that what you learned at school?

Arabella: Oh, my dear, I wouldn't go to school. That would hardly be suitable for a woman of my station. I was taught at home by a governess. (*sentimentally*) Dear Dame Willoughby! She taught me to read and write. I can also do the household ciphers[3] (*noticing that Kay is not impressed*), but then I see that you can read, too. (*patronizingly*) Can you write?

Kay (*insulted*): Of course! Have you taken leave of your senses, m'lady? (*Kay is beginning to take on some of Arabella's condescending airs as if to put her down a bit.*)

Arabella (*not even hearing Kay's remarks*): But it was Mother who taught me to make medicine. Why, Sir Barnaby never would have married me if I hadn't known how to make elixirs[4] or other helpful nostrums.[5] After all, I have to keep the servants—all 28 of them—healthy. (*sighs importantly*) If that were the worst of it, I'd be grateful, but, no, I have to oversee all their labors—spinning, baking, tending cattle, and so forth, and, of course, I must discipline the maids and servants. So that is my business, and I studied hard to learn it. Fortunately, Mother was an excellent teacher. (*sighs again, importantly*) Having so many maids and servants is such a responsibility, isn't it?

Kay (*irritated*): How do you imagine I would know? Do you believe we're millionaires? My father's a carpenter, and my mother sells shoes.

Arabella (*amazed*): A carpenter! (*severely*) Why should a carpenter's daughter want to be educated? And your mother sells . . .

Kay: Naturally, they work and so will I. Today, social class is unimportant. Education is a great equalizer. Everyone goes to school nowadays.

Arabella: Why?

Kay: Well . . .

Arabella (*disapprovingly*): What do you learn in your school?

Kay: In economics we're learning about marketing in developing countries, in physics we're studying nuclear technology, and last year in biochemistry we studied genetics.

Arabella: Who manages your households?

Kay: Well, it isn't that hard. We have machines to do the work—dishwashers, vacuum cleaners, refrigerators, microwave ovens, home computers . . .

Arabella (*firmly*): These things mean nothing to me, and your education sounds very peculiar. It seems to be all about things you will never see and places where you are not likely to go.

Kay (*huffily*): Well, your education sounds pretty peculiar to me. Wouldn't you rather learn something besides how to keep house?

Arabella (*with great pride*): But oh, my dear, I *did*. I play the dulcimer[6] and lute. I sing. I dance. I am fluent in French—my Norman heritage, of course. I speak some Italian and German. My business—is that what you mean by career? My career, then, is to be Sir Barnaby's capable wife. Your career, well, that is different. Each of us has been educated for the life she expects to lead. Forgive me if I prefer my own.

Kay (*earnestly*): Wouldn't you really rather be in my shoes if you could?

Arabella (*amused*): Absolutely not! (*as if to a child or an underling*) Permit me to

---

[3] ciphers (SY fərz): numbers used in accounting or budgeting.

[4] elixirs (i LIK sərz): a medicinal solution thought to have curative or restorative powers.

[5] nostrums (NAHS trəmz): household remedies.

[6] dulcimer (DUL sə mər): a musical instrument with wire strings stretched over a sound box, played with two padded hammers or by plucking.

explain: Your life, my dear, sounds just a little bit dull—dull and not very responsible. Sincerely, now, don't you envy me?

Kay (*firmly*): Not a whit, m'lady!

Arabella (*shrugging elegantly*): Well, *Autres temps, autres moeurs.*[7] I must go now.

[7] *Autres temps, autres moeurs:* A French saying meaning "Other times, other customs."

This has all been most educational. (*She vanishes.*)

Kay: I'll say. (*She picks up her book again but sits contemplating for a moment before she opens it. She then speaks thoughtfully.*) Well, there's no accounting for tastes. (*She opens her book and proceeds to read.*) "Studies serve . . ."

Curtain

RECALLING FACTS

Identifying setting

1. What is the actual setting of this play?

The actual setting is the present, in the Cornelia Seton High School library.

Comparing and contrasting

2. a. How are Kay and Arabella alike?

Kay and Arabella are both intelligent, young women.

Each is well-educated according to the custom of her day.

b. How are they different?

Arabella is a responsible, married noblewoman who is somewhat arrogant. In contrast, Kay is a typical teenager still in school. Arabella is the head of her household; Kay wants to become a veterinarian.

Comparing and contrasting

3. a. How is Arabella's education different from Kay's?

Arabella was taught household skills at home by her

mother, and she learned reading and writing from her

governess, Mistress Willoughby. Kay is learning much

broader skills from teachers.

_____

b. Why does Arabella say that Kay's education sounds peculiar to her?

Arabella thinks that Kay is learning about things she

will never see and about places she will never visit.

_____

_____

Using context clues

4. Fill in the space next to the word that completes each sentence.

a. The _____ gave off an aroma that permeated the hall.

‖ pomander ‖ farthingale ‖ elixirs

b. Arabella prepared helpful _____ to keep her servants healthy.

‖ pomander ‖ ciphers ▌ elixirs

c. Today, an accountant might do Arabella's household _____.

‖ nostrums ‖ dulcimer ▌ ciphers

d. The _____ gained widespread popularity during the American folk music movement of the 1960s.

‖ nostrums ▌ dulcimer ‖ farthingale

INTERPRETING FACTS

Inferring setting

1. There is an implied setting in the play as well as the actual one. Describe the implied setting.

Arabella's home is an Elizabethan country estate in

1598. It is self-sufficient, with cattle, farming, and

many servants.

_____

_____

Understanding character

2. In what ways do Arabella's manner and attitude reflect her time?

Arabella comes from a very class-conscious society

containing nobles and servants. She belongs to the

nobility, or ruling class. Her authoritative manner

reflects her role as the manager, or overseer, of

servants.

Making inferences

3. Why does Arabella say Kay's life is irresponsible compared to hers?

Answers may vary. Kay's responsibilities do not seem

clear-cut, concrete, or meaningful. She can't relate to

them.

_____

Making inferences

4. Kay says, "Everyone goes to school nowadays," and Arabella asks, "Why?" How would you answer Arabella?

Answers may vary. In the modern world, things

change very quickly, and one must keep up with them

in order to be a responsible citizen.

_____

_____

Inferring comparisons and contrasts

5. How is the purpose of education in the 1590s different from the purpose of education in the 1990s?

In the 1590s, a woman like Arabella was educated to

be responsible for the world of her own household.

She had to run it well and be responsible for the

people in it. In the 1990s, a woman like Kay is

educated to be responsible in the world of her

community, country, and the like. She learns to be

independent.

_____

6. In the England of Arabella's day, only about 30 percent of all adults could read and write. Most of these were men. How would these two facts have made the lives of Elizabethan men and women different from yours?

Answers will vary. Possible answers include:

Communication would depend more on speech than

on print; fewer women could hold responsible

positions in society and government.

7. This play opens with a quotation that describes three different uses for study. The rest of the story is about the third use. Give examples of the first two uses from your own experience.

Answers will vary. Possible answers: Studies for delight

might include reading for relaxation, for personal reasons,

for curiosity. Studies for ornament might include use in

one's daily conversation and showing how

knowledgeable one is.

SKILL FOCUS

1. Kay and Arabella share the same opinion about education.
   a. Circle the word below that best describes their opinion.

   comic   sentimental   ironic   (serious)

   b. Explain your choice.

   Kay and Arabella both feel education is important and serious because it prepares a person for responsibilities in

   the world.

2. a. Underline the two words below that best identify Kay's attitude.

   <u>earnest</u>   bitter   <u>sincere</u>   cautious   sad

   b. Go back to the play. Underline the words and phrases in the stage directions and dialogue that reveal Kay's attitude.

3. a. Circle the three words that best identify Arabella's attitude.

   bitter   (boastful)   (arrogant)   (dignified)   carefree

   b. Go back to the play. Circle the words and phrases in the stage directions and dialogue that reveal Arabella's attitude.

4. What does Kay learn from her encounter with Arabella?

   Kay learns that education serves many purposes depending on the time and place. While women have always

   sought learning, their approach to it has been influenced by the customs of their times.

5. Despite the differences in the two women's tones of voice, the author's attitude about the education of women is clear, and it can be expressed as the theme of the play. In a few lines, write what you believe to be the theme of the play.

   Answers will vary, but students should include reference to the fact that the education of women is important

   regardless of when, where, or how they are educated.

▶ **Real Life Connections** In your opinion, what is the biggest change in education since the late 1500s?

Comparing and Contrasting

Reading a Social Studies Selection

▶ **Background Information**

Shifts in the United States population and increased use of technology have accelerated the ongoing change in the U.S. job market. Economists study occupational trends to predict future job availability.

▶ **Skill Focus**

When reading, you will often need to compare and contrast information about people, places, or trends. To **compare**, look for similarities. To **contrast**, look for differences.

One way to compare and contrast information about two or more topics is to put it into visual form. For example, statistics, or numerical facts, are sometimes presented in the form of graphs and tables.

When shown in visual form, statistics can help people to understand quantitative information—that is, information that tells how many or how much. Because statistics can show important trends, or patterns, people often use them to draw conclusions or to make predictions. Comparing and contrasting graphs and tables

showing labor statistics can be useful in predicting occupational trends.

While statistics give important information, they present only a partial picture of developing trends. By studying the text as well as the graphs and tables, you can make comparisons and contrasts. From these similarities and differences, you can draw conclusions and make projections.

Use these steps when looking for comparisons and contrasts in graphs and tables.

1. Preview the graphs and tables before reading.
2. Read the selection carefully to understand the topics being compared and contrasted.
3. Identify the type of statistical information given on the graph or table.
4. Study the graph to find relationships among numbers.
5. Use the statistical similarities and differences to draw conclusions and to make projections about trends.

▶ **Word Clues**

Read the following sentence. Look for context clues that explain the underlined word.

By analyzing the changing nature of the economy and the factors causing these changes, a person can <u>forecast</u>, or predict, future trends in employment.

If you do not know the meaning of the word *forecast*, the phrase following the word *or* can help you. To *forecast* means to predict. The word *forecast* is explained in an appositive phrase set off by commas and the word *or*. Appositive phrases may be set off by commas, dashes, or the word *or*.

Use **appositive phrases** to find the meanings of the three underlined words in the selection.

▶ **Strategy Tip**

Before reading, preview the graphs and tables. As you read, compare and contrast the information in the text with the statistics in the graphs and the table. Both sources of information will help you draw conclusions about job trends.

Jobs of the Future

A person planning for a career today must look carefully at the expected occupational trends and changes in the job market. Affecting the economy are changes in the size, age, and distribution of the population, as well as developments in technology. These changes also affect employment opportunities. For example, an aging population has increased the need for medical care and other health services. Computer technology has not only eliminated or changed the nature of many jobs but also created new occupations. By analyzing the changing economy and the factors causing these changes, a person can forecast, or predict, future trends in employment.

A New Labor Force

The United States <u>labor force</u>—the total number of people over the age of 16 who are employed or are actively seeking work—totaled 127 million in 1992. By the year 2005, the labor force is expected to reach 151 million, an increase of 19%. This increase represents a slight slowdown in the growth of the labor force compared with growth during the previous 13-year period, 1979–1992. The slowdown is largely due to slower population growth in the United States.

✗ ✗ <u>The U.S. labor force will become more diverse by 2005.</u> White non-Hispanic men will make up a slightly smaller proportion of the labor force than in 1992, while women and minority group members will make up a larger share. Between 1992 and 2005, blacks, Hispanics, Asians, and other ethnic groups will account for roughly 35% of all people entering the work force. In addition, women will continue to join the labor force in growing numbers. In 1979, women made up 42% of the labor force. By 2005, their share is expected to be 48%.

The age make-up of the U.S. population will change from 1992 to 2005. There will be a smaller proportion of children and teenagers and a larger proportion of middle-aged and older people. The decline in the proportion of children and teenagers reflects the lower birth rates of the 1980s and 1990s. The large increase in the middle-aged population reflects the aging of the baby boom generation—

Age Distribution of Labor Force

Source: Bureau of Labor Statistics

Figure 1.

people born between 1946 and 1964. The rapid growth of the older population reflects both the high birth rates before the 1930s and improvements in medical technology that are allowing Americans to live longer.

The changing age make-up of the U.S. population will directly affect tomorrow's work force. Young people age 16 to 24 are expected to make up roughly the same percentage of the labor force in 2005 as they did in 1992. However, the percentage of workers age 25 to 34 will decline dramatically, from 28% to 21%. The baby boom generation will continue to add members to the work force, but their share will decline slightly. The most striking change will be a large increase in the percentage of workers between the ages of 45 and 54. These workers will account for 24% of the labor force in 2005, up from 18% in 1992. Workers in this age group usually have more employment experience than younger workers. Thus, employers will be able to choose from a larger pool of experienced <u>applicants</u>, people seeking jobs, in coming years.

Education: A Prerequisite for Employment

The education level of the labor force has

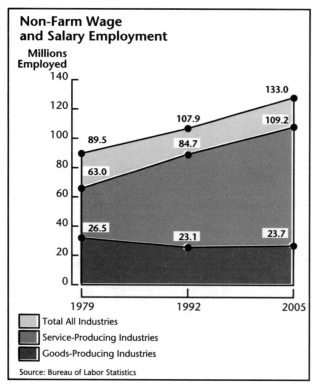

Non-Farm Wage and Salary Employment

Millions Employed

133.0
120
107.9
109.2
100
89.5
84.7
80
63.0
60
40
26.5
23.1
23.7
20
0

1979   1992   2005

□ Total All Industries
■ Service-Producing Industries
■ Goods-Producing Industries

Source: Bureau of Labor Statistics

Figure 2.

Fastest Growing Occupations 1992–2005

	Number of Jobs		Change
	1992	2005	1992–2005
Home health aides	347,000	827,000	+138.1%
Human services workers	189,000	445,000	+135.9%
Personal and home care aides	127,000	293,000	+129.8%
Computer engineers and scientists	211,000	447,000	+111.9%
Systems analysts	455,000	956,000	+110.1%
Physical and corrective therapy assistants and aides	61,000	118,000	+92.7%
Physical therapists	90,000	170,000	+88.0%
Paralegals	95,000	176,000	+86.1%
Occupational therapy assistants and aides	12,000	21,000	+78.1%
Electronic pagination systems workers	18,000	32,000	+77.9%
Special education teachers	358,000	625,000	+74.4%
Medical assistants	181,000	308,000	+70.5%
Private detectives	59,000	100,000	+70.2%
Corrections officers	282,000	479,000	+69.9%
Child care workers	684,000	1,135,000	+65.8%
Travel agents	115,000	191,000	+65.7%
Radiology technologists and technicians	162,000	264,000	+62.7%
Nursery farm workers	72,000	116,000	+62.0%
Medical records technicians	76,000	123,000	+61.5%

Source: Bureau of Labor Statistics

Figure 3.

risen dramatically in recent years. In 1980, for example, 19% of all workers age 25 and older had completed four years of college. In 1992, 27% had a bachelor's degree or higher. The trend toward higher educational achievement is expected to continue.

From 1992 to 2005, employment growth will be faster for occupations requiring higher levels of education or training than for those requiring less. Managerial, professional, and technical positions will make up an increasing proportion of new jobs that become available. Many of the occupations projected to grow most rapidly are those with higher earnings.

Office and factory automation, changes in consumer demand, and the movement of factories overseas will continue to affect job opportunities. Employment in jobs requiring little formal education may decline. They may also <u>stagnate</u>, or stay the same, making job opportunities for people who have not finished high school increasingly limited. In addition, those workers will be more likely to have low paying jobs with little opportunity for advancement.

> *By 2005, service jobs are expected to make up 82% of the job market.*

Goods Versus Services

 Today industries providing services employ more people than those providing goods. Currently, about 21% of the labor force is employed in goods-producing industries, such as mining, manufacturing, and construction. About 79% of United States workers are employed in service-producing industries, such as health care, education, transportation, communications, and banking. Economists forecast a continued increase in the number of jobs in service-producing industries. By 2005, service jobs are expected to make up 82% of the job market.

Employment Trends in Service Industries

Health services will continue to be one of the fastest growing industries in the U.S. economy from 1992 to 2005. For example, home health care is the second most rapidly growing industry today. The increased demand for health services is due to improvements in medical technology, the growing size of the U.S. population, and the increasing proportion of older people in the population.

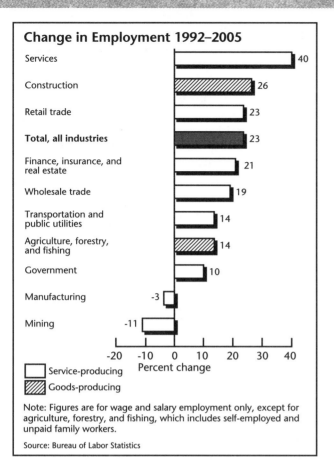

Change in Employment 1992–2005

Industry	Percent change
Services	40
Construction	26
Retail trade	23
Total, all industries	23
Finance, insurance, and real estate	21
Wholesale trade	19
Transportation and public utilities	14
Agriculture, forestry, and fishing	14
Government	10
Manufacturing	-3
Mining	-11

Percent change

☐ Service-producing
▨ Goods-producing

Note: Figures are for wage and salary employment only, except for agriculture, forestry, and fishing, which includes self-employed and unpaid family workers.

Source: Bureau of Labor Statistics

Figure 4.

Business services also will generate many jobs by 2005. However, this industry will grow more slowly than it did from 1979 to 1992. Business services includes one of the fastest growing industries in the U.S. economy: computer and data processing services. This industry's rapid growth is due to advances in technology, worldwide trends toward office and factory automation, and increased demand by companies, government agencies, and individuals.

Other service industries also will experience growth from 1992 to 2005. Education, for example, is expected to add 2.8 million jobs due to population growth and rising school enrollments. Employment in social services is expected to increase by 1.7 million. In fact, the most rapidly growing industry in the U.S. economy today is residential care. The economy will also see strong job growth in the passenger transportation industry, including travel agencies. Employment in the communications industry, however, is expected to decline by 12%. This decline is due to labor-saving technology and increased competition among companies.

Employment Trends in Goods-Producing Industries

Overall employment in goods-producing industries is expected to show little change between 1992 and 2005. However, growth will vary among industries, with some industries experiencing an increase in jobs and others experiencing a decrease.

Employment in the construction industry, for example, is expected to increase 26%, from 4.5 million in 1992 to 5.6 million in 2005. The need to improve the nation's roads, bridges, and tunnels will offset the declining demand for new homes and office buildings. Also, after declining for many years, overall employment in farming, forestry, and fishing is projected to grow by 14%, from 1.7 million to 2 million jobs.

Jobs in other goods-producing industries will continue to decline. For example, employment in manufacturing is expected to decrease by 3% from its 1992 level of 18 million jobs. Most of the jobs that will disappear will be production jobs, as machines continue to replace people. However, the number of professional and technical positions in manufacturing will increase. Mining employment, which includes the petroleum industry, is expected to decline 11% by 2005, from 631,000 to 562,000 jobs.

Retraining for New Jobs

In the past, people would remain in the same career—and perhaps even with the same employer—throughout their entire working lives. Today, most workers change employers several times, and it is not at all unusual to change careers entirely. The trend toward changing careers is caused by several factors.

Computers, word processors, assembly line robots, and other innovations have eliminated many types of jobs. At the same time, however, technology has created new jobs that require technically trained workers. In recent years, downsizing—reductions in the number of full-time employees on staff—and company mergers have resulted in an increasing number of experienced workers among the unemployed. For many workers, continued employment will depend on retraining for a new career. The only constant in the job market of the future will be constant change.

RECALLING FACTS

Identifying cause and effect

1. Read the following pairs of sentences. On the lines provided, write either *cause* or *effect*.

a. _____cause_____ The changing make-up of the U.S. population will directly affect tomorrow's work force.

_____effect_____ The percentage of workers age 25 to 34 will decline dramatically.

b. _____effect_____ Demand for health services will increase between 1992 and 2005.

_____cause_____ The proportion of older people in the U.S. population will increase from 1992 to 2005.

c. _____cause_____ Technology has eliminated many types of jobs and created new ones.

_____effect_____ For many workers, continued employment will require retraining for a new career.

Identifying the main idea

2. Reread the paragraph that has an X next to it. Then circle the sentence that states its main idea.

Identifying the main idea and supporting details

3. Reread the paragraph marked with XX. Underline the sentence that states its main idea. Then circle three details in the paragraph that support the main idea.

Using context clues

4. Complete the following sentences with one of the words or phrases below.

stagnate   labor force   applicants

a. Economists expect employment in factory jobs in the United States to _____stagnate_____.

b. Workers of every type make up the population of the _____labor force_____.

c. Too many _____applicants_____ for the available jobs causes unemployment.

INTERPRETING FACTS

Making inferences

1. Put check marks next to the three groups of people who are more likely to face unemployment in the next decade.

✔ a. high school dropouts   ___ c. nurses   ✔ e. factory assembly line workers

___ b. computer repair technicians   ✔ d. coal miners

Inferring cause and effect

2. Write one cause for the following effect.

Cause Machines will continue to replace people.

Effect Most of the manufacturing jobs that are lost will be production jobs.

Inferring cause and effect

3. What will be the effect of having more 45- to 54-year-olds in the labor force?

Employers will be able to choose from a large pool of experienced applicants.

Making generalizations

4. Read the facts listed below. Then write a generalization based on these facts.

a. Technology creates new jobs.

b. Future technology will eliminate many present-day jobs.

c. New technical jobs will require new skills.

Generalization Changes in technology will demand new skills for new types of jobs.

98 Lesson 24 *Comparing and contrasting*

Use the selection, the graphs, and the table to answer the following questions.

1. Identify the information given.

Figure 1: What do the bars on the graph compare?

The age distribution of the work force in 1979, 1992, and 2005.

What do the numbers in the bar sections represent?

The percentage of each age group in each of the three years.

Figure 2: What two types of industries does this graph compare?

The two types are goods-producing and service-producing industries.

Which type will account for most of the total growth in employment between 1992 and 2005?

Service-producing industries will grow the most from 1992 to 2005.

Figure 3: What information is given for each of the occupations listed in the table?

The number of jobs in 1992 and 2005 and the percentage of change in the number of jobs from 1992–2005

What does + represent in the right column? The + sign indicates that the percentage represents

an increase.

Figure 4: What type of information is presented in this graph?

The information concerns changes in employment 1992–2005 in various service-producing and goods-producing

industries.

2. Find relationships between statistics.

Figure 1: Describe the change in the proportion of workers age 35 to 44 in the labor force.

The change is an increase from 19% to 27% and then a decrease to 25%, but an overall increase.

Figure 2:

By 2005, how many jobs will there be in goods-producing industries? 23,700,000

Since 1979, has there been much growth in job availability in this category? no

By 2005, how many jobs will there be in service-producing industries? 109,200,000

Since 1979, has there been much growth in job availability in this category? yes

In which industry has there been continuous growth? service-producing industries

Figure 3: In which three occupations are at least 800,000 jobs expected by the year 2005?

home health aides, systems analysts, child care workers

Which of those occupations will have the largest number of workers? child care workers

Figure 4: Why do the bars for manufacturing and mining extend to the left of the vertical line?

The bars for these two types of industry show decreases in employment from 1992–2005.

▶ **Real Life Connections** Write a paragraph describing your thoughts on a job or career that interests you.

Classifying

___ Reading a Science Selection ___

▶ **Background Information**

Hundreds of careers in science require varying amounts of formal education. The following selection, "Careers in the Sciences," briefly describes a number of these science careers. Some of these careers may be of interest to you. If you look up information about any of these fields, you will find many more careers than are covered here.

▶ **Skill Focus**

Sometimes information is organized by **classifying** similar objects or ideas into groups. Classifying makes it easier to see similarities and differences among the groups. People who work with a great number of objects, as scientists do, group them according to their characteristics. The members of each group share the same characteristics.

When scientists classify plants, for example, they use their knowledge of the characteristics of plants to separate them into groups. The members of each group are similar in some specific way.

In addition to plants and animals, scientists classify the branches of scientific study into groups. Three major categories are the life sciences, the earth sciences, and the physical sciences. Many different types of scientists work in each category.

As you read a selection that describes many groups, ask yourself such questions as the following.

1. What characteristics do the members in the same group share?
2. How are the members of one group different from those of another group?

▶ **Word Clues**

Knowing how to use definition context clues can be very helpful to you in reading scientific material. In writings about science, you will come across words that you do not know. When you read an article about a possible cure for a deadly disease, such as AIDS, scientific terms will be used that you probably have never seen before. Names for new drugs or techniques will be strange to you. Even articles about nutrition or dieting in newspapers and magazines may contain new words.

Read the following sentences. Look for the context clues that explain the underlined word.

> When people think of careers in science, they often picture a person in a white coat working in a laboratory and doing underlined esoteric experiments. Something that is esoteric is understood by very few people.

If you do not know the meaning of the word *esoteric* in the first sentence, read on. The second sentence states what the word *esoteric* means. A word meaning that is stated directly can often be found before or after a new word.

Use **definition** context clues to find the meanings of the three underlined words in the selection.

▶ **Strategy Tip**

Preview the selection, "Careers in the Sciences," by reading the headings, boldfaced terms, captions, and introductory paragraphs. As you read, think about how careers in science are classified.

Careers in the Sciences

When people think of careers in science, they often picture a person in a white coat working in a laboratory and doing esoteric experiments. Something that is esoteric is understood by very few people. Another science career with which people are familiar is medicine, which includes doctors, nurses, technicians, and aides. In many other professions, often not identified as science careers, a strong background in one or more of the sciences is <u>imperative</u>. Something that is imperative is absolutely necessary. The following paragraphs describe some of the many careers in science, the requirements for these careers, and some of the specialists who work in science professions.

The Life Sciences

Careers in the life sciences can be divided into two major groups: the biology professions and the health professions. The professions in biology include many kinds of specialists who are involved in research and teaching. In general, entrance into these careers requires many years of college training plus original research.

Most biologists who study animals specialize in one group. For example, scientists called **ichthyologists** (ik thee AHL ə jists) study fish, **entomologists** (en tə MAHL ə jists) study insects, and **herpetologists** (her pə TAHL ə jists) study reptiles and amphibians. **Anatomists** and **physiologists** (fiz ee AHL ə jists) study the structure of living organisms and the functioning of their bodies. **Cytologists** (sy TAHL ə jists) are biologists who study cells.

Plant biologists, or **botanists**, may also specialize. **Bryologists** (bry AHL ə jists) study mosses and liverworts, while **lichenologists** (ly kə NAHL ə jists) specialize in the study of lichens. Some botanists specialize in plant

(*above*) A Paleontologist—a scientist who studies fossils—works on the bones of a Tyrannosaurus Rex, a huge, two-footed, flesh-eating dinosaur. (*right*) Two students at the Stevens Institute in Hoboken, New Jersey, conduct experiments in a chemistry lab.

pathology, the study of plant diseases. Others specialize in plant genetics, the study of how plant characteristics are transmitted from one generation to the next. The word *transmitted* means "passed along."

Many other careers depend on a knowledge of plants or animals but require less formal education. **Landscapers**, for example, know which plants grow best under specific conditions, and they select and artistically arrange plants around a home or building. **Animal keepers** in a zoo must have a knowledge of the animals under their care in order to keep them healthy. Certain **technicians** in sewage treatment plants use their knowledge of microscopic organisms to monitor the safe, effective operation of this essential community facility. Such careers require on-the-job training or one- or two-year specialized college courses or training programs.

While doctors and nurses treat people who are ill, there are many other challenging career opportunities in the health field. **Physical therapists** work with people who have various physical problems and help them regain or improve their ability to move. **Speech/language pathologists** help people who have lost their ability to speak or understand speech due to an accident or illness, or who have other speech and language problems. **Laboratory technicians** perform the numerous tests used to ascertain if a person is healthy. The word *ascertain* means "to find out." **Genetic counselors** provide information to people who have a family history of an inherited disease or disorder. All these careers require college training.

The Earth Sciences

People who work in the earth sciences are often fascinated with the way the oceans move, with the unpredictability of weather, or with the mysteries of outer space. Earth scientists include **meteorologists**, who monitor weather patterns and predict future weather conditions, and **astronomers**, who study the objects and events in space. **Seismologists** (syz MAHL ə jists) study earthquakes. **Geologists** study the rocks of the earth, using them as clues to the earth's past. **Paleontologists** (pay lee ahn TAHL ə jists) study fossils to reconstruct the earth's history. These careers require college preparation and original research.

(*above*) An Aquarist—a person who studies and works with fish and mammals at an aquarium—works with a dolphin, one of the smartest water-dwelling mammals. (*right*) A medical researcher conducts an experiment.

Gem cutters and stonemasons work with rocks. They must have an intimate knowledge of the composition of stones in order to cut and shape them with precision. Surveyors take precise measurements of the size, shape, and elevation of parts of the earth's surface, and cartographers, or map makers, use these measurements to make accurate drawings of part or all of Earth. Many of these careers are learned through apprenticeships and on-the-job training.

The Physical Sciences

The physical sciences deal with the study of the chemical and physical properties of matter in the universe, and they can be roughly divided into two areas: chemistry and physics.

Careers in chemistry include **organic chemistry**, which is the study of chemical compounds made primarily of carbon, such as gasoline and plastics. **Research chemists** analyze existing substances and create new ones for a variety of uses. **Assayers** (as SAY ərz) analyze the composition of ores and scrap metal and determine their value. **Pharmacologists** (far mə KAHL ə jists) understand the chemistry of medicines and study the effects of drugs. Some **criminologists** are chemists, too; they chemically analyze evidence from a crime scene, such as drugs, explosives, and paints. Their findings can help in the apprehension of criminals.

The field of physics includes many professions. **Nuclear physicists** (FIZ ə sists) study the structure and behavior of atoms. **Astrophysicists** study the chemical and physical properties of objects in space. Knowledge of the physical sciences is important to **aeronautical** (er ə NAW tic əl) engineers, as well as to nautical engineers. **Structural engineers** understand the properties of construction materials and the forces that act on a completed structure. These careers require four or more years of college education.

Other careers in the physical sciences require less formal education. Computer **repair technicians** must have a knowledge of electronics. **Opticians** grind and polish lenses for eyeglasses according to prescription requirements. **Automotive engineers** apply their knowledge of physical principles to the design and manufacture of safe, efficient, and comfortable vehicles.

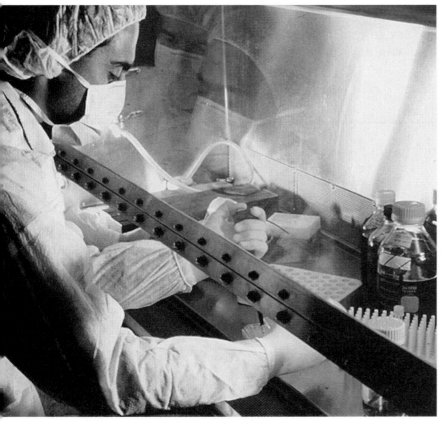

(*above*) An engineer surveys a location for a construction site. A surveyor measures the size, shape, and elevation of a section of land. (*left*) A medical researcher wears sterile clothing and works beneath a glass hood to conduct experiments for AIDS research.

Recalling details
1. What does a plant pathologist do?

studies plant diseases

Recalling details
2. Name a specialist who helps people with physical problems regain or improve their ability to move.

a physical therapist

Recalling details
3. What does a meteorologist do?

studies and predicts weather

Recalling details
4. Name two careers in earth science that usually require on-the-job training rather than a college education.

Possible answers: gem cutter, stonemason, surveyor,

cartographer

Recalling details
5. What does a pharmacologist do?

studies the effects of drugs

Recalling details
6. What does an optician do?

grinds and polishes eyeglass lenses to prescription

requirements

Recalling details
7. Why does a structural engineer need to understand physics?

to know the characteristics of construction materials

and the forces acting on completed structures

Using context clues
8. Draw a line to match each word with its explanation.

imperative   find out

transmitted   absolutely necessary

ascertain   passed along

INTERPRETING FACTS

Making inferences
1. Both families of a couple have a history of diabetes. Whom should the couple consult to find out the chances that a child of theirs will have diabetes?
- **(a.)** a genetic counselor
- **b.** a speech/language pathologist
- **c.** a paleontologist

Making inferences
2. What career might a person with an interest in rocks and mining find enjoyable?
- **a.** entomologist
- **b.** seismologist
- **(c.)** geologist

Making inferences
3. A ———————— would analyze samples of soil and fibers left behind by a burglar.
- **(a.)** a criminologist
- **b.** a meteorologist
- **c.** a lichenologist

Making inferences
4. To do their work accurately, cartographers depend on the work of ————————.
- **a.** astrophysicists
- **b.** oceanographers
- **(c.)** surveyors

Complete the following chart.
Possible answers include:

Careers in Science

		Specialty	Description	Education
Life Sciences	Biology	lichenologist entomologist cytologist plant geneticist	studies lichens studies insects studies cells studies inheritance in plants	college training plus original research
		landscaper animal keeper	selects and arranges plants around a house or other building cares for animals in a zoo	on-the-job training or one- or two-year college courses or training programs
	Health	doctor	treats illnesses	college training plus medical school
		physical therapist speech/language pathologist	helps people with bone or muscle problems helps people overcome speech and language difficulties	college training
Earth Sciences		geologist oceanographer meteorologist seismologist	studies rocks studies the ocean studies and predicts weather studies earthquakes	college preparation and original research
		gem cutter surveyor cartographer	cuts precious stones takes precise measurements of the earth draws maps using surveyors' measurements	on-the-job training
Physical Sciences	Chemistry	organic chemist pharmacologist criminologist	studies carbon compounds studies the effects of drugs analyzes evidence from crimes	four or more years of college
	Physics	nuclear physicist astrophysicist	studies the structure and behavior of atoms studies the properties of objects in space	four or more years of college
		computer repair technician automotive engineer	repairs computers designs automobiles	less formal education

▶ **Real Life Connections** Which field of science appeals to you most—the life sciences, the earth sciences, or the physical sciences? Tell why.

Understanding Probability

___ Reading a Mathematics Selection ___

▶ Background Information

Almost every day we think and talk about probability. We ask each other "what the odds are" that something will happen—that our favorite team will win, that our favorite actor will win the Oscar, or that we will get a good grade or do well on a test.

This selection presents the most basic rule of probability. This rule tells you how to find the number of possibilities when, for example, one thing can happen two ways, another can happen three ways, and still a third can happen four ways. Using this rule, you do not have to make a list. In fact, the answer turns out to be simply the product of 2 x 3 x 4.

▶ Skill Focus

Sometimes a mathematical problem states that two or more different things must be combined according to a given set of rules. The problem then asks how many different results can occur from the combination. For example, a committee of three persons representing both females and males has to be selected from a group of three females and two males. How many combinations of females and males can there be on the committee?

Sometimes the number of possibilities to be counted can be very large. Fortunately, mathematicians have developed rules for arriving at the different kinds of possible arrangements without counting.

One reason for knowing the number of possibilities is to find out the chance of one (or more) of the possibilities happening. You know that, if you toss a coin, it can land either heads (H) or tails (T). If you toss the coin a great many times, it will land H about half the time, since H and T are equally likely. In other words, each of the two events is equally likely. In mathematics, this idea is expressed by saying that the **probability** of either H or T is $\frac{1}{2}$.

Knowing how to use numbers to state probabilities can clarify "the odds" of something happening. Using fractions, such as $\frac{1}{2}$ and $\frac{1}{4}$, can help you see more clearly the difference between the odds of "two to one" and "one out of four."

▶ Word Clues

Knowing the meanings of the following words will help you to understand this selection: *Chance* is any measure of the likelihood that something will happen or not happen; *possibility* is anything that could happen; *probability* is a mathematical measure of chance.

Making distinctions between the meanings of key words is an important skill. Interpretations of any text can go astray if you are not alert to such distinctions. If someone writes that there is "a chance" something will happen, ask yourself: Does that mean a possibility or a probability?

▶ Strategy Tip

As you read "Understanding Probability," study the diagrams. Think about how they relate to the mathematical ideas presented in the paragraphs.

Understanding Probability

Probability is the chance that some event will happen or not happen. To find out the chance that a particular arrangement of objects or events will happen or not, you can use methods of computing probability. Determining the possible arrangements of objects or events involves special techniques because the number of possible arrangements of even a few things can be very high. Read the following problem.

Sara is planning her college program. In addition to her required courses, she can take two other courses. One must be a humanities course (H), and the other must be a science course (S). She has decided that she will take two of the following courses: Music Appreciation (H), European History (H), Introduction to Physics (S), Advanced Algebra (S), or Computer Programming (S). How many different combinations of courses can Sara take?

If Sara chooses one of the humanities courses, she cannot choose the other one. For example, suppose Sara decides to take the course in Music Appreciation; then she cannot take European History as the other course. However, she still has three courses from which to choose, since she can take any one of the three science courses.

You can show this arrangement in the following **tree diagram.**

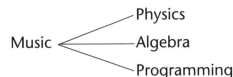

The number of possibilities, or "branches," represented in this tree diagram is three. If Sara had not decided on music and was still considering history, she would have more possibilities. In that case, another tree would start with history and branch to the three science courses. The total number of possibilities would be 6.

The Multiplication Rule

There is another way to look at this problem. Picking one of the science courses first is one possibility that can happen two ways: It can be paired with one of the two humanities courses. The other possibility, picking a humanities course first, can happen three ways: It can be matched with one of the three science courses. Either way, the total number of ways is therefore 2 × 3, or 6. This method, called the multiplication rule, is easier to use with large numbers.

The multiplication rule can also be used when several different things are being combined. For example, an automobile company might offer a car in six different colors, in four different body styles, and with either an automatic or standard transmission. One part of the tree diagram for this problem follows.

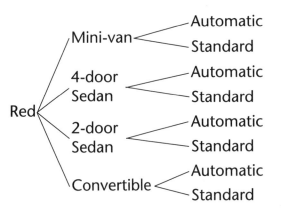

To arrive at the total number of possibilities, it would be necessary to do a total of six such diagrams, one for each color. It is easier, however, to use the multiplication rule:

6 (colors) × 4 (body styles) × 2 (transmission types) = 48

You get the same answer with either the multiplication rule or the tree diagram. In the part of the tree diagram shown for this problem, there are eight possibilities. (You always count the smallest branches to get the number of possibilities.) This diagram, however, represents the possibilities for just one color. For all six colors, there are 6 × 8 = 48 of the smallest branches, or possibilities.

One way to think about probability problems is to picture a number of marbles in a bag. Think of a bag that contains four marbles—a red, a green, a white, and a blue one. If you take one marble from the bag without seeing its color, there is a probability of one out of four that the marble will be red. The same probability applies to the other three marbles. Mathematically, this probability is expressed as $\frac{1}{4}$. The fraction indicates the chance that something will happen.

A probability is always expressed as a fraction between 0 (no choice) and 1 (certainty). For example, if all four marbles in the bag were red and you were to take one of them, the probability that it will be red is 1. The probability of red is a certainty. The probability of a green marble is 0—no chance.

Now consider a bag with two red and two blue marbles. If you remove one marble from the bag, what is the probability that it will be red? What is the probability that it will be blue? There are equal chances of getting either a red or a blue marble.

> A probability does not guarantee that an event will actually occur; it only indicates the chance that something will occur.

Suppose you replaced the first marble and picked again from the four marbles. The chance of getting one marble of each color is 2 out of 4, or $\frac{2}{4} = \frac{1}{2}$.

A probability does not guarantee that an event will actually occur; it only indicates the chance that something will occur. For example, suppose that you draw a marble from the bag, replace it, and repeat the experiment several times. The chance that you will get a red marble is $\frac{1}{2}$ for each repetition. In actuality, you may draw the blue marble much more often than the red, or vice versa. For a very large number of repetitions, however, you will draw the red about half the time and the blue about half the time.

There is a connection between counting and probability. If you can count the total number of equally likely events, then you can use that number to find the probability. As an example, consider the problem about the different kinds of automobiles. The chance of selling any one color, body style, or transmission is the same. For any particular car, such as a red convertible with automatic transmission, the probability of selling that combination is therefore $\frac{1}{48}$.

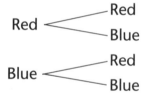

Red — Red
Red — Blue
Blue — Red
Blue — Blue

RECALLING FACTS

Recalling details
1. One event can happen in four ways, and another event can happen in five ways. What operation can be used to find the number of ways that both events can happen?

_____ multiply 4 by 5 _____

Recalling details
2. What is the lowest number that a probability can be? _____ 0 _____

Recalling details
3. What is the highest number that a probability can be? _____ 1 _____

INTERPRETING FACTS

Making inferences
1. In the first problem in the selection, Sara must choose one humanities course and one science course. If she could take any two of the five courses she wanted, would the number of possibilities go up, go down, or stay the same? Why?

The number of possibilities would go up. She would have 5 possible choices for the first course and 4 possible

choices for the second course, for a total number of 20 choices.

Making inferences

2. If you have two red marbles and three blue marbles in a bag, is the probability of drawing one red marble $\frac{1}{5}$? Why or why not?

No, it is $\frac{2}{5}$. While the probability of drawing any marble is $\frac{1}{5}$, the event of drawing a red marble is not equally likely for

a single draw.

A. For each problem, write the number of possible arrangements on the line provided. You may draw tree diagrams on another piece of paper.

   1. To mix batter, a cook can use a mixer with two bowl sizes and six speeds. ___12___

   2. To install a faucet, a plumber can use one of three wrenches and one of five fixtures.

      ___15___

   3. An airline inspector is going to make a round trip between two cities. She wants to be on different airlines going and returning. She has a choice of four different airlines each way. ___12___

B. A bag contains one red, one blue, and one green marble. You draw a marble from the bag, replace it, and draw another for a total of three draws. The tree diagram below shows the different arrangements possible. Use the diagram to solve each of the following problems.

   1. What is the probability of drawing one red marble each time in the three draws?

      ___$\frac{1}{27}$___

   2. What is the probability of getting a red marble on the second draw? ___$\frac{1}{3}$___

   3. What is the probability of getting a red, a blue, and a green marble in the three draws in that order? ___$\frac{1}{27}$___

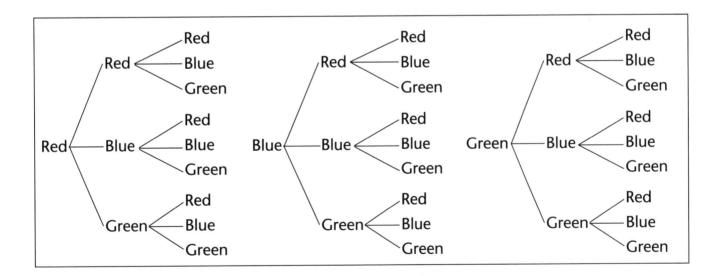

▶ **Real Life Connections** Create your own probability problem about the options available on a product that you would like to buy. Exchange problems with a partner and solve each other's problem.

Word Parts

When you are trying to figure out the meaning of an unknown word, knowing the meanings of the word's parts can be helpful. Roots, prefixes, and suffixes are word parts. Many of the words you know are made up of roots with prefixes and suffixes added to them.

The word *interject* is formed by combining the prefix *inter* and the root *ject*. The prefix *inter* means between, and the root *ject* means to throw. If you know these meanings, you can figure out that *interject* means to throw between or to insert.

Look at the following roots, prefixes, suffix, and their meanings. Notice that some of the roots have more than one spelling.

Roots		Prefixes		Suffix	
ject	to throw	con	with, together	ion	the act of
scrib (script)	to write	in	in, into, on		
ten (tain)	to hold	inter	between		
ven (vent)	to come	pre	before		
		re	back		

Read each word below. Use the meanings of the word parts to decide which meaning is correct. Write the letter of the meaning next to the word it defines.

_g_ rejection   **a.** the act of writing on

_e_ contain   **b.** to hold back

_a_ inscription   **c.** to write before

_f_ intervene   **d.** to keep from happening

_d_ prevention   **e.** to hold together

_h_ convene   **f.** to come between

_b_ retain   **g.** the act of throwing back

_c_ prescribe   **h.** to come together

Use one of the words above to complete each sentence below.

1. The blue pitcher will _____contain_____ a quart of milk.

2. The meeting will _____convene_____ promptly at 4:00.

3. The weakened dam could not _____retain_____ the water.

4. The inspector ordered the _____rejection_____ of the faulty parts.

5. The President was asked to _____intervene_____ in the dispute between the two countries.

6. The _____inscription_____ on his class ring included the date of his graduation.

Syllables

When dividing words of three or more syllables, you use the same guides that you use with two-syllable words. The only difference is that you have to use two or more guides.

In dividing the word *recovery*, for example, you use three guides.

1. Divide between the prefix and the rest of the word: re covery.

2. In words with one consonant between two sounded vowels with the first vowel short, divide after the consonant: re cov ery.

3. Divide between the rest of the word and the suffix: re cov er y.

Here is a summary of some guides to help you divide words into syllables.

Guide 1. In a compound word, divide between the two smaller words.
Guide 2. In words with double consonants, divide between the double consonants.
Guide 3. In words with a prefix or suffix, divide between a root word and its prefix or suffix.
Guide 4. In words with two consonants between two sounded vowels, divide between the two consonants.
Guide 5a. In words with one consonant between two sounded vowels with the first vowel long, you usually divide before the consonant.
Guide 5b. In words with one consonant between two sounded vowels with the first vowel short, you usually divide after the consonant.
Guide 6. Do not divide between a consonant blend or consonant and -le.

Divide each of the words below into syllables. Write the syllables separately on the line to the right of the word. Then write the numbers of the guides you used on the line to the left of the word. The first word is done for you.

1. __3, 2__ disapprove — dis ap prove
2. __4, 5a__ Bermuda — Ber mu da
3. __5b, 4__ cylinder — cyl in der
4. __4, 4__ astringent — as trin gent
5. __4, 3__ culturist — cul tur ist
6. __2, 3__ acceptance — ac cept ance
7. __5b, 3, 3__ limitedness — lim it ed ness
8. __5b, 6__ tapestry — tap es try
9. __3, 4__ uncertain — un cer tain
10. __2, 1__ buttermilk — but ter milk
11. __5b, 3__ frolicsome — frol ic some
12. __5a, 3__ legalize — le gal ize
13. __5a, 4__ romantic — ro man tic
14. __4, 6__ Kentucky — Ken tuck y
15. __4, 1__ fingerprint — fin ger print
16. __5b, 2__ Philippine — Phil ip pine
17. __4, 5a__ tornado — tor na do
18. __4, 5a__ curvaceous — cur va ceous
19. __2, 6__ syllable — syl la ble
20. __4, 5a__ singular — sin gu lar
21. __2, 4, 3__ essentially — es sen tial ly
22. __4, 3, 3__ fictionalize — fic tion al ize
23. __3, 6__ subentry — sub en try
24. __5b, 2__ parallel — par al lel

Outlining

A good way to understand and remember something you read is to make an **outline**. An outline can be written quickly and read easily. A good outline shows how the main idea and supporting details in a selection are organized.

In a paragraph, the most important idea is the main idea. In an outline of a selection or a chapter, the main idea of each paragraph is restated in a few words and written next to a Roman numeral: I, II, III, and so on.

The details that give important supporting information about the main idea are the major details. The major details are written next to capital letters: A, B, C, and so on. These letters are indented, or moved a little to the right, underneath the Roman numerals. By positioning them this way, you can see how the main idea and major details are related.

The details that give information about the major details are minor details. The minor details are written next to numbers: 1, 2, 3, and so on. These numbers are indented underneath the capital letters. This positioning shows you how the minor details are related to the major details.

Read the following paragraph. Then look at the outline next to it.

The Gray Panthers

How the Gray Panthers started is an interesting story. The group was founded by Margaret E. (Maggie) Kuhn and a few of her friends in 1970 when they were forced to retire from their jobs. From the beginning, Maggie and her friends organized for educational and charitable purposes. The Gray Panthers' members are people of all ages, dedicated to the cause of equal rights for all, regardless of age. The actual name of the group was given to it by the producer of a television talk show.

Gray Panthers

I. Background
   A. Founded by Maggie Kuhn and friends
      1. In 1970
      2. Forced to retire from jobs
   B. Organized for educational and charitable purposes
   C. Made up of people of all ages
   D. Dedicated to equal rights, regardless of age
   E. TV producer gave group name

Notice that *Background*, the main idea of the paragraph, is written next to Roman numeral I. *Founded by Maggie Kuhn and friends*, written next to capital letter A, is the first major detail about the group. *In 1970*, written next to number 1, tells a minor detail about when the group was founded. Notice the outline uses only words and phrases instead of full sentences.

Several other things are important to know about outlining. Every outline should have a title. An outline should always include at least two main ideas; it can never have a Roman numeral I without a II. There should be at least two major details under each main idea and at least two minor details under each major detail.

Read the two paragraphs about the Gray Panthers on the next page. Use the information in them to complete the outline.

The Gray Panthers have been very active since their beginning. They work on the "network principle" to get things done. Gray Panther chapters are in communities all over the country. There are 45,000 members in 60 local groups. The groups are involved directly with local issues. They are also involved in national concerns. The Gray Panthers have used three major methods to achieve their goals. Advocacy, education, and model projects to help changes happen have all been effective. The Panthers have brought several issues to the people's attention. They have published findings of an investigation of unfair practices in the hearing aid industry. They were the first to organize for nursing home reform. They've lobbied for an end to mandatory retirement. They've addressed the special problems of older women and the minority aged.

Although Maggie Kuhn died in 1995, the future looks bright for the Gray Panthers. They have a number of short-term goals. They want "patient's rights" for people living in nursing homes. They want the media to show older people in a more realistic, less negative way. The Panthers' long-term goals are less specific. They want the rigid separations between youth, adulthood, and old age to be broken down. They want workday alternatives that will let more people be productive for a longer time. They want learning to be a lifelong process. Finally, they believe first-rate health care should be available to all.

II. Achievements

  A. Network principle

    1. In communities nationwide

    2. Involved in local issues

    3. Involved in national concerns

  B. Methods to achieve goals

    1. Advocacy

    2. Education

    3. Model projects

  C. Issues brought to the public

    1. Unfair practices in hearing aid industry

    2. Reform of nursing homes

    3. End of mandatory retirement

    4. Problems of older women and minority aged

III. Future

  A. Short-term goals

    1. Patients' rights in nursing homes

    2. Fairness in media treatment

  B. Long-term goals

    1. Breakdown in age separations

    2. Workday alternatives

    3. Lifelong education

    4. First-rate health care

Reading a Résumé

Résumé (REZ oo may) is a French word that means "summary." A **résumé** is a summary of your job qualifications. It contains a brief but complete account of your job objective, or goal, personal history, education, job experience, and hobbies.

An interesting and well prepared résumé can help you stand out from other applicants in the eyes of a possible employer. A résumé should be neatly typed and should contain no spelling errors.

Read the sample résumé on the next page.

A. Match the parts of a résumé listed in the left column to the descriptions in the right column. Write the letter of each correct description on the line provided.

1. __b__ Job Objective
2. __d__ Education
3. __a__ References
4. __e__ Employment
5. __f__ Personal Data
6. __c__ Extracurricular Activities

a. people who know about you and your abilities
b. what kind of work you want to do
c. things you do after school hours
d. schools you went to and graduated from
e. work you have done that paid a salary
f. name, address, and telephone number

B. Answer the following questions using the information on the sample résumé.

1. To whom does this résumé belong? Sharon Waskiewicz
2. What is her current address? 92401 Woodley Street, Fresno, California
3. Why did she write this résumé? to find a summer job at a plant store or greenhouse
4. What high school did she graduate from? Fresno Senior High School
5. What school team was she captain of? volleyball
6. Which club relates to her interest in plants? Fresno Garden Club
7. In which three sports does Sharon participate? volleyball, gymnastics, swimming
8. How do you know that she excelled in gymnastics? She won the City Gymnastic award.
9. Notice that Sharon's places of employment are listed with her last job first. This is the correct way to list job experience on a résumé. Where was Sharon's first job?
   at the Plant Shed

10. How can you tell that she did not work full-time at her first job? Give two reasons.
   She didn't graduate until 1996, and she specified "Saturdays" on the dates.

11. Which reference could give a prospective employer information about Sharon's school work? Mr. Lowell, the principal of her high school

12. Why might a preschool have interest in hiring Sharon as an assistant?
   She has experience as a counselor and could teach tumbling and nature study.

Sharon Waskiewicz
92401 Woodley Street
Fresno, California 93711
(209) 487-9371

JOB OBJECTIVE

Summer job with plant store or greenhouse growing and caring for plants, with potential for returning each summer

EDUCATION

Fresno Senior High School
4000 E. Dunbar
Fresno, California 93740
Received academic diploma – June, 1984   B+ average
Plan to major in horticulture in college

EXTRACURRICULAR ACTIVITIES

Sports: volleyball team (1994–1996, captain), gymnastics club
School Organizations: glee club, Spanish club, yearbook editor
Honors: National Honor Society, City Gymnastic award (1996)
Special Interests: plants, swimming, dancing, writing poetry
Civic Organizations: Fresno Garden Club, church choir, library volunteer

EMPLOYMENT

1/96 – 6/96 (after school)	California State University, Department of Horticulture Fresno, California Assistant to Professor Timothy Lee. Grew and cared for ornamental plants in greenhouse.
6/95 – 8/95	Camp Wonderwood 1099 E. Greenstone, Fresno, California Counselor. Led nature walks and taught tumbling classes.
12/94 – 6/95 (Saturdays)	The Plant Shed 4234 E. Rogers, Fresno, California Stockperson. Cared for ornamental plants and flowers. Sold merchandise, operated cash register.

REFERENCES

Prof. Timothy Lee
Department of Horticulture
California State University at Fresno
5011 E. Calby
Fresno, California 93740
(209) 555-2107

Lorna Alvarez, M.D.
4645 W. Hawthorne
Fresno, California 93740
(209) 555-6200

Ms. Janet Lord
Director
Camp Wonderwood
1099 E. Greenstone
Fresno, California 93711
(209) 555-1349

Mr. Brandon Lowell
Principal
Fresno Senior High School
4000 E. Dunbar
Fresno, California 93740
(209) 555-0100

Lesson 31

Point of View

Reading a Literature Selection

▶ Background Information

What happens when standing up for a principle means the possibility of losing a friendship? In "The Chance of a Lifetime," a young man's need for friendship is balanced against his integrity.

▶ Skill Focus

Before writing, an author must decide who is going to narrate the story. If the author wants the narrator to reveal the thoughts and feelings of all the characters in the story, the author must use an omniscient, or all-knowing, narrator. In a story told from a third-person **omniscient point of view**, the narrator is not identifiable.

The omniscient narrator can reveal as much or as little about the characters as is necessary for the story's development. By choosing an omniscient point of view, the author does not limit the story to the thoughts and feelings of only one character. Yet, the omniscient narrator often reveals more about one character than about other characters.

Read the following paragraph.

> Katherine was enraged. She could hardly speak. Rachel, on the other hand, was delighted with events and could hardly conceal her joy. Donna, caught between two friends, wisely did not betray her emotions.

The narrator reveals the feelings of not just one character but of all of them. Thus, the narrator is all-knowing.

When you examine the point of view in a story, think about the following questions.

1. Is the narrator an outsider or a participant in the events?
2. Does the narrator reveal what one or all of the characters in the story are thinking or feeling?
3. Why might the author have chosen this point of view?

▶ Word Clues

When you read a word that you do not know, look for context clues to help you understand it. Read the sentences that follow.

> Rafael gazed down the long corridor towards his locker. Every time he walked the length of the hallway between classes, he felt as if he were running the <u>gauntlet</u> through a hostile crowd.

Sometimes there are no context clues to help you clearly understand the meaning of a new word. You will need a dictionary to help you. You may find it convenient to finish what you are reading before looking up the word.

Use a **dictionary** to find the meanings of the four underlined words in the selection.

▶ Strategy Tip

As you read "The Chance of a Lifetime," notice how effectively the author uses the narrator to give clues to the personality of the characters by revealing their thoughts and feelings. Why is the omniscient point of view effective in telling this story?

The Chance of a Lifetime

Rafael gazed down the long corridor towards his locker. Every time he walked the length of the hallway between classes, he felt as if he were running the gauntlet through a hostile crowd.

It wasn't that people were <u>overtly</u> nasty; in fact, no one had been unpleasant in the two months since he had transferred to Seneca High. It was just that no one had particularly welcomed him, either. So Rafael couldn't help feeling that the absence of a warm welcome was actively excluding him, too.

Rafael was shy and something of a computer whiz, but not at ease talking to others. He was at his best when he was tinkering with a program or playing a computer game.

As Rafael walked down the hall, he noted anxiously that Rick and a couple of other guys were clustered around his locker. Rafael admired them—the easy way they stood, the way they dressed, the laughing, casual way they had with everyone. They were the Club, and Rafael thought they must be the most popular group in school.

Since coming to Seneca High, Rafael had done his <u>utmost</u> to impress Rick and the rest of the Club. He tried to be funny and acted as though he was not too serious about his classes. He didn't think, however, that his act was working. Until this moment, he hadn't believed that the Club even knew he existed. Now it seemed they were waiting for him. Rafael tried to remain calm; he tried not to fumble with the lock on his locker.

Rick was watching every move Rafael made—sizing him up and estimating his chances of success; he decided Rafael was just the person they needed. He sidled over to Rafael. "What's up? You getting adjusted to the new school, or what?"

Rafael turned abruptly, surprised at the friendly overture from Rick. "Uh, things are okay. I'm getting along . . ."

Rick nodded. "We've heard you know a lot about computers. Maybe you could help us. We've got a proposition for you. If you agree to it, you'll have it made. You'll be a member of the Club—we might even make you an officer or something."

Rafael couldn't believe he was being offered a chance to join the Club. It seemed too good to be true.

"What do you say?" Rick asked.

To hide his excitement, Rafael turned and opened his locker. "Sure," he said, as <u>nonchalantly</u> as possible. "What do you want me to do?"

Rick leaned closer, lowering his voice. "We want you to get us a copy of the chemistry exam out of the school computer. Your aunt works in the office. It should be simple for you to strike up a conversation with her and then dawdle around until you can check out this week's password into the computer system. Then you could log onto the school computer with your own terminal and get us a copy of next week's exam. Can you do it?"

Rafael began slowly, "I can do it. The question is . . ."

"Don't worry," Rick said reassuringly and with an edge of challenge, "nobody'll suspect you. They'll never know! Besides, you're not even taking chemistry."

With a grin and a wave, Rick and his pals sauntered off. Rick was delighted. He thought Rafael would never really fit in, but, if he could get the job done, they might make him a sort of unofficial member of the Club—keep him happy until they needed him again.

Rafael stared after them, stunned. He felt slightly nauseous. All morning, Rafael was oblivious to all the others around him. Rick's words kept echoing in his mind. I could never do it, he thought; I'd be too terrified.

Rafael was aware, however, that Rick was correct. No one would ever suspect him, least of all his aunt who trusted him implicitly. She probably kept the password near her terminal. It would be a simple matter to tap into the school computer and get a readout of the exam. No one would ever know, and he would have the friends he so desperately wanted.

The only problem was that it was outright theft. A voice kept nagging Rafael—"you don't want to do this; you know it's wrong." He tried not to listen to that voice, but it wouldn't go away.

By lunchtime, his temples were throbbing. The last thing he wanted was his tuna sandwich. Unable to eat, Rafael opened his notebook and began to write. Writing down his thoughts often helped him to sort them out.

"What do you do," he wrote, "if you have to choose between friendship and honesty? Aren't friends the most important thing? Why does integrity have to rear its righteous head and get in the way? What good is it to be right but alone?"

Rafael wrote through lunchtime. When he closed his notebook, he knew what had to be done. Suddenly famished, he gulped down his sandwich on the way to English class, but, when he walked into the room, his stomach knotted again. He'd forgotten to complete the essay that was due today. There was only one thing to do. Rafael scrawled his name on the notes he'd composed during lunch and handed them in.

Rafael put the whole thing out of his mind until English class the next day. Ms. Grady started the class by saying, "I'd like to read one extraordinary essay."

To his dismay, Rafael recognized his paper. How awful to have his innermost thoughts on display! The class would

> "What do you do if you have to choose between friendship and honesty?"

disdain him; for sure they'd think he was a loser.

The class stirred restlessly as Ms. Grady began, but the room was absolutely still by the time she read Rafael's last paragraph: "There is something more important than having friends. You can't have friends until you have self-respect."

Silence hung over the room for a long moment before students began to applaud. (Ms. Grady felt relieved. The students had responded to Rafael's essay as positively as she had hoped.) A wave of relief swept over Rafael, too. They hadn't laughed; they had understood. Indeed, many of the students were relieved that someone had spoken up for honesty. Rafael was particularly pleased when Nancy approached him after class. She'd never spoken to him before. "What a terrific essay!" she said warmly. "It was so honest." {Nancy was surprised at Rafael's candor and courage; she had thought him to be a lot different. She had the wrong impression because she had noticed he was around the Club.}

Rafael smiled at her; he'd always liked her, but he'd thought he wouldn't have a chance unless he were a member of the Club.

"I guess this is the first time I ever let anyone know my real feelings," he said.

Just then, Rick interrupted them. His face made it evident that he hadn't appreciated Rafael's essay. He was enraged; in fact, furious. He felt betrayed. "So," he sneered, "you're not going to do it!"

"No, I'm not," Rafael agreed.

"I thought you had guts! I sure had you figured wrong."

"I guess you did," responded Rafael. I never really respected Rick at all, Rafael realized. He pivoted abruptly on his heel and addressed Nancy: "You know, I was so thrilled about becoming a member of the Club that I was willing to abandon my own integrity. But that's really not what I wanted at all. I realize now what I really wanted was to be respected, not because I belonged to a certain exclusive clique, but because of my own worth."

"I imagine that's what we all want," Nancy said, "but it takes forever for the majority of us to realize it."

They walked down the corridor together. Rafael felt Rick's eyes boring into him, but he was no longer concerned with Rick's opinion of him.

RECALLING FACTS

Recalling details
1. Why would no one suspect Rafael of stealing the chemistry exam?

Rafael was not a chemistry student. If the exam were

stolen through the computer, no one would even know

it was gone.

Identifying cause and effect
2. Why did Rafael become anxious and ill-at-ease during morning classes?

Rafael was faced with a difficult decision: whether or

not to steal the chemistry exam.

Identifying plot
3. A story's climax marks the turning point in the plot. After the climax, the reader is able to predict how the story will end.

Fill in the space between the lines next to the statement that describes the turning point in this story.

‖ Rafael decides to turn in his notes.

▌ The class responds to Ms. Grady's reading of Rafael's essay.

‖ Rafael realizes that he could get away with stealing the chemistry exam.

Identifying conflict and resolution

4. What conflict does Rafael face? How does he resolve it?

Rafael must decide whether he will sacrifice his own

integrity to steal an exam so he can join a club. He

resolves the conflict by deciding not to steal the exam.

Using context clues

5. Write the letter of the correct meaning on the line next to each word.

b overtly   **a.** the maximum amount

c nonchalantly   **b.** outwardly, in the open

d candor   **c.** casually, indifferent

a utmost   **d.** sincerity, frankness

INTERPRETING FACTS

Inferring details

1. How did Rick learn that Rafael wouldn't steal the chemistry exam?

Rick heard Rafael's essay read aloud in class and immediately understood Rafael's feelings about cheating and

stealing the exam.

Making inferences

2. a. Why did Nancy assume that Rafael was like Rick?

Nancy noticed Rafael hanging around with members of the club and assumed that he must hold the same values—

values she did not like.

b. How did Nancy feel about Rick?

Nancy did not like Rick.

Drawing conclusions

3. At the beginning of the story, Rafael believes that Rick and the rest of the Club must be the most popular group in the school. Is he correct? Support your answer.

No. From the response to Rafael's essay, the other students are apparently tired of the Club's dishonesty.

Understanding character

4. a. Is Rafael a static or dynamic character? Explain. Rafael is a dynamic character. By the end of

the story, he is no longer in awe of the Club. He realizes that there are other more important things in life than

belonging to the Club.

b. Is Rick a static or dynamic character? Explain. Rick is a static character. He is the same at the

end of the story as he was at the beginning.

Making inferences

5. Who was given "the chance of a lifetime"? Was it really "the chance of a lifetime"? Explain.

Rafael was given the opportunity to join the Club, but he turned it down. What he had to do to join the Club went

against his beliefs. For him, it was not the chance of a lifetime that Rick had hoped it would be.

Identifying theme

6. Fill in the space between the lines next to the statement that best describes the story's theme, or message.

|| Friendship must come first.

▌| The principle of honesty must be upheld, no matter how difficult it is to do so.

|| If you're honest, everyone will respect you.

In a story told from the third-person omniscient point of view, the narrator is an all-knowing storyteller, aware of the thoughts and feelings of all the characters.

1. a. Does the author of the story tell you who the narrator is? <u>no</u>

   b. Is the narrator an outsider or a participant in the story? <u>an outsider</u>

   c. Whose thoughts and feelings does the narrator reveal? <u>Rafael's, Rick's, Ms. Grady's, and Nancy's</u>
   _____

2. Go back to the story, and do the following.
   a. Circle phrases and sentences that reveal Rafael's thoughts and feelings about the Club and about Nancy.
   b. Underline phrases and sentences that reveal Rick's thoughts and feelings about Rafael.
   c. Put brackets around phrases and sentences that reveal Nancy's thoughts and feelings about Rafael.
   d. Put parentheses around phrases and sentences that reveal Ms. Grady's thoughts about reading Rafael's essay aloud to the class.

3. Does the narrator look into the mind of Rafael's aunt? Explain. <u>No. The narrator does not reveal</u>
<u>her thoughts and feelings because she is not a character in the story.</u>

4. Why is the omniscient point of view suitable for this story? <u>The omniscient point of view permits</u>
<u>the narrator to reveal the thoughts and feelings of all the main characters, not just those of one character.</u>

5. Read the following paragraph. It does not reveal the thoughts and feelings of any of the characters.
   The toddler grinned, looked around, and pushed his cup over the edge of the highchair. Immediately, his mother leaped up, grabbed a sponge, and began mopping up the mess. Alison, his seven-year-old sister, began chanting, "Billy made a mess! Billy made a mess!"
   a. Rewrite the paragraph using the omniscient point of view.
   <u>Answers will vary. However, students should be encouraged to use words and phrases that reveal the thoughts and</u>

   <u>feelings of each character.</u>
   _____
   _____
   _____
   _____

   b. Circle phrases or sentences in your paragraph that reveal the mother's thoughts and feelings.
   c. Underline phrases or sentences that reveal Alison's thoughts and feelings.
   d. Put brackets around phrases or sentences that reveal Billy's thoughts and feelings.

▶ **Real Life Connections** What would you do if you saw your best friend cheating on an exam? State your response and your reasons for this response.

Reading a Flow Chart

Reading a Social Studies Selection

▶ **Background Information**

Citizens of the United States are governed by a code of laws. Congress, the legislative branch of the government, adds to and amends these laws. To do so, Congress goes through a number of steps in a process by which proposed legislation, known as a bill, becomes a law. This selection traces that process.

▶ **Skill Focus**

A **flow chart** shows the important stages, or steps, in an intricate process. Information explaining these stages is presented in boxes. Arrows or lines connect the boxes to show the flow or movement from one stage to another.

When reading a flow chart, first become familiar with the information inside the boxes. Be sure you know the meanings of all the words. Then read the flow chart by following the arrows. Sometimes color is used to show different parts of the same process.

The flow chart above shows three of the stages in the process by which a bill becomes a law.

As you read and study a flow chart, ask yourself the

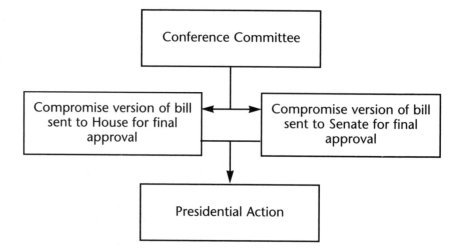

following questions.

1. What process does the chart describe?
2. What groups are part of the process described in the chart?
3. How does the chart show the order and movement of events?
4. How are the events in the chart related to each other?

▶ **Word Clues**

Read the following sentence. Look for context clues that explain the underlined word.

> In the House, a representative drops the proposed bill into the hopper, a large box hanging at the edge of the clerk's desk.

If you do not know the meaning of the word *hopper* in the first part of the sentence, read the rest

of the sentence, which states its meaning. A word meaning that is stated directly can often be found before or after a new word.

Use **definition** context clues to find the meanings of the three underlined words in the selection.

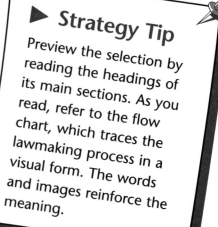

▶ **Strategy Tip**

Preview the selection by reading the headings of its main sections. As you read, refer to the flow chart, which traces the lawmaking process in a visual form. The words and images reinforce the meaning.

How a Bill Becomes a Law

Citizens of the United States are governed and protected by the laws set forth in the Constitution. Congress, the legislative, or lawmaking, branch of the federal government, processes over 20,000 bills, or proposed laws, during one Congressional session. Of this huge number of bills, fewer than 10 percent actually become laws. Where do these bills originate? How does Congress decide which bills should be passed into law? What steps are involved in the process? The legislative procedure is an intricate one filled with rules, regulations, and human drama.

To understand how a bill becomes a law, we will follow a fictional bill through Congress. The bill is titled Jobs for Young Americans. If passed into law, it would provide full-time or part-time employment opportunities and job training programs for citizens between the ages of 16 and 18.

> The legislative procedure is an intricate one filled with rules, regulations, and human drama.

The Introduction of a Bill

The idea for a bill may come from various sources—a member of Congress, the executive branch of the government, an interest group, or even a private citizen.

✗ However, only an official member of the House of Representatives or the Senate may formally introduce a bill. In the House, a representative drops the proposed bill into the hopper, a large box hanging at the edge of the clerk's desk. In the Senate, a senator formally presents a proposed bill to the members of the Senate.

Our Jobs for Young Americans bill is introduced in the House of Representatives. It is assigned a number and a title, and it is entered in the *House Journal* and the *Congressional Record.*

House Committee Action

Both houses of Congress have a number of standing committees with responsibility for bills on certain subjects. After a bill is introduced, the speaker of the House assigns it to the appropriate committee. The Jobs for Young Americans bill is handed over to the House Committee on Employment Opportunities. It is at this stage that most bills die. Members of the House committee decide if the bill has merit and if it is politically acceptable.

If the committee majority decides against a bill, it is pigeonholed, or put aside to be forgotten. If the bill survives, the chair of the House Committee on Employment Opportunities assigns it to a subcommittee, a committee within a committee. During this stage, the subcommittee conducts public hearings, at which testimonies are given for and against passage of the bill.

Finally, the members of the subcommittee "mark up" the bill, that is, they go through it line by line, making changes that they believe are necessary. The subcommittee recommends to the full committee that the "marked-up" version of the bill be approved. The Committee on Employment Opportunities can decide either to kill the bill by not acting on it or to report it to the House floor. During the committee stage, the procedure for handling a bill introduced in the Senate is similar.

The House Rules Committee

In the next stage, a House bill is sent to the House Rules Committee, sometimes referred to as the "traffic cop of the House." Members of this committee hold a hearing to decide how and when to schedule a bill for action on the floor of the House. By majority vote, the Rules Committee can handle the bill in several ways. It can prevent a bill from reaching the floor for political reasons, rush it through for immediate consideration, or schedule it on one of the House calendars. A Senate bill does not go through this stage; instead, it goes directly from the appropriate committee to floor action at the discretion of the majority floor leader.

The Rules Committee decides by a majority vote to report the Jobs for Young Americans bill to the House for consideration with the possibility of amending it. The speaker of the House and the majority leader confer with influential House members about scheduling the bill for debate.

Floor Action

On the House floor, the bill is read to the representatives, so that they can propose and vote on amendments. Once it is in its final form, the bill is opened up for House debate. Because the House is such a large body, strict regulations limit the time allowed for debating a bill.

Finally, our Jobs for Young Americans bill is put to a vote in the House. In the past, this was done by a time-consuming roll call; today, a computer-operated electronic voting system is used. A personal computer card identifies each representative's vote.

If the bill is defeated by the floor vote, the process has to begin all over again. However, most bills that come this far pass at this stage. Our House bill on jobs for young Americans is sent to the Senate for consideration.

Senate Action

✗ To become a law, a bill must be passed by a majority vote in both houses of Congress and presented to the President for approval or disapproval. Our Jobs for Young Americans bill was introduced in the House and passed; it now goes on to the Senate. If the bill had been introduced and passed in the Senate, it would then proceed to the House.

The Senate follows the same basic steps as the House except that the Senate does not have a rules committee. When a floor debate is finished on a bill, senators vote on it using the

How A Bill Becomes A Law

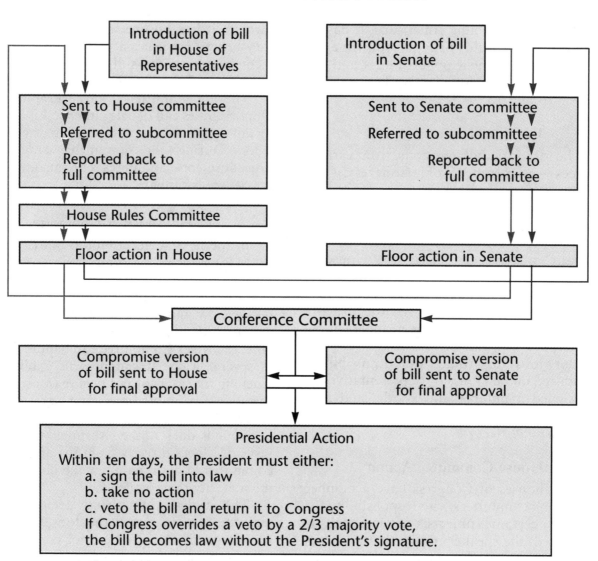

traditional roll-call system. The Senate passes our Jobs for Young Americans bill, but in a slightly altered form. As a result of the debate, some wording changes may have to be made before a majority will pass a bill.

The Conference Committee

✔ Before the Jobs for Young Americans bill is sent to the President, the House and the Senate must agree on a single version of it. The Conference Committee, the next group that the bill must pass through, arrives at this version. The party leadership of each house appoints a few senators and representatives to the committee. In arriving at an agreeable version of the bill, the members of this committee do some of the toughest bargaining in Congress. The members work out a compromise, which is then considered by the whole Congress.

Finally, majorities in both the House and the Senate agree upon our Jobs for Young Americans bill. It has successfully passed through the legislative branch of the government, but it is not yet a law.

Presidential Action

For a bill to become law, it must be presented to the President of the United States. This final stage of the lawmaking process can be a dramatic one. The President may veto, or give a negative response to the bill. Then the bill is returned to the house in which it originated. In some cases, the Congress may choose to override the Presidential veto by a two-thirds vote in each house. If the President supports the bill, he or she will sign it into law. The President may also choose not to act on the bill and let it become law without the presidential signature. This occurs ten days after he or she has received it from Congress.

With the President's approval, our fictional Jobs for Young Americans bill becomes a law of the United States. The American democratic system of government serves the idea of law expressed long ago by the Latin poet Ovid:

For this reason the laws are made: that the strong shall not have power to do all that they please.

RECALLING FACTS

Identifying sequence of events
1. Number in correct sequence the stages that a bill in the House goes through to become a law.

__4__ Floor action

__6__ Conference Committee

__1__ Introduction of a bill in House

__5__ Senate action

__3__ Rules Committee

__8__ Presidential action

__2__ Committee stage

__7__ Congressional vote on compromise bill

Identifying cause and effect
2. On the lines provided, write the cause for the effect below.

Cause   The House and the Senate may pass

different versions of the bill.

___

Effect The bill must pass through the Conference Committee.

Comparing and contrasting
3. a. In which house of Congress is debate limited in time by strict rules and regulations?

House of Representatives

b. In which house of Congress is debate freer and less limited in time?

Senate

4. Reread the two paragraphs that are marked with Xs. In each paragraph, underline the sentence that best states its main idea. Then circle two details that support the main idea.

Using context clues

5. Complete each of the following sentences by filling in one of the words below on the line provided.

   pigeonholed   subcommittee   veto

   a. There were enough votes in Congress to override the President's ____veto____.

   b. A group was chosen from the committee to serve on a ____subcommittee____ discussing endangered animals.

   c. The unpopular bill was rejected by the House committee and ____pigeonholed____ without further consideration.

INTERPRETING FACTS

Making inferences

1. Why would a President choose to let a bill become a law without his or her signature?

Possible answers include: The President wouldn't want to lose the support of certain people by signing an unpopular

bill into law. The President might be opposed to the contents of the bill while certain people are in favor of it.

Inferring comparisons and contrasts

2. The House of Representatives uses a computer voting system because ____it is so large____.

   In contrast, the Senate still uses a roll-call vote because ____has fewer members____.

Inferring cause and effect

3. On the lines below, write the effect for the cause below.

   Cause The United States Constitution set up a system of checks and balances among the various branches of the government.

   Effect Both the President and the Congress are involved in the lawmaking process.

Making inferences

4. Why would a political party like to have the most power in the House Rules Committee?

The Rules Committee can determine when a bill comes up for floor action.

Inferring the unstated main idea

5. Reread the paragraph with a check mark next to it. Write a sentence describing its main idea.

In the Conference Committee stage, members of the House and Senate work out a compromise version of a bill.

Making generalizations

6. Identify each of the following generalizations as True or False.

____False____ The President plays the most important role in the lawmaking process.

____True____ The committee stage is the most difficult period for a bill to survive.

____False____ The President's decision on a bill is final.

126 Lesson 32 *Reading a flow chart*

To answer the questions below, use the selection and the flow chart on page 124.

1. What process does the flow chart describe? How a bill becomes a law

2. a. What are the two different starting points on the flow chart? Introduction of a bill in the House of Representatives, Introduction of a bill in the Senate

    b. How are they distinguished on the chart? Their paths follow different colored arrows.

    c. What is the last stage shown on the flow chart? Presidential Action

3. What three major areas of the government are represented on the chart?
House of Representatives, Senate, President

4. How does the chart show the order and movement of the stages in the process?
with lines, arrows, and different colors

5. a. If a bill is introduced in the House, where does it go after its passage there?
to the Senate

    b. If a bill is introduced in the Senate, where does it go after its passage there?
to the House

    c. At what point do the two different paths of the flow chart come together?
Conference Committee

6. a. How are the events on the chart related to each other?
All the stages are related to the passage of a bill.

    b. For a bill introduced in the House, what stage must it go through between committee consideration and floor action? House Rules Committee

    c. The Conference Committee consists of members from which two groups?
House of Representatives and the Senate

    d. For what reason would the bill go back to the House and Senate after receiving Presidential action? if the President vetoed the bill

7. In your opinion, how helpful is a flow chart in following the stages of a complex process?
Answers will vary, but they should include the idea that a flow chart makes it visually easier to follow the steps in a complicated procedure. A flow chart also summarizes information related to a process.

▶ **Real Life Connections** Think of a process that takes place in stages over time, such as applying to get into a school or going through a training program. How might a flow chart make the process easier to understand?

Following Directions

___ Reading a Science Selection _____

▶ **Background Information**

This selection discusses speed, velocity, acceleration, and Newton's Laws of Motion. It concludes with an experiment that demonstrates the relationships between force, mass, and acceleration, which are summarized by Newton's Second Law of Motion.

▶ **Skill Focus**

Following directions is an important skill. For example, to carry out an experiment in a science textbook, you must follow directions.

Directions for an experiment are often set up in a specific way. Most sets of directions have five parts: Problem, Aim, Materials, Procedure, and Observations or Conclusions. Science experiments are always set up the same way so that they can be repeated any number of times exactly as they were done the first time. This ensures that the results of the experiment are not affected by some slight variation in how it is carried out. The following describes each part of the directions for an experiment.

Problem
The question that you should be able to answer at the end of the experiment

Aim
What will be done in the experiment

Materials
Objects or equipment needed for the experiment

Procedure
The steps that must be carried out to complete the experiment

Observations or Conclusions
Questions to answer or conclusions to draw about the outcome of the experiment

Use the following steps to help you read a science selection with directions for an experiment.

1. Read the paragraphs that explain the experiment. Be sure that you understand the ideas.
2. Read through the five parts of the directions: Problem, Aim, Materials, Procedure, and Observations or Conclusions.
3. Study the pictures or diagrams. Be sure to read the captions and labels.

4. Reread the Problem, Aim, Materials, Procedure, and Observations or Conclusions. Be sure that you understand the steps in the procedure before you begin the experiment.

▶ **Word Clues**

Sometimes special words are explained in a paragraph and shown in a diagram. In this case, study both the text and the diagram to help you understand the words.

Use **diagram** clues as context clues to find the meanings of the three underlined words in the selection.

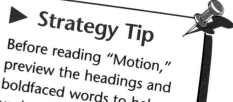

▶ **Strategy Tip**

Before reading "Motion," preview the headings and boldfaced words to help you understand how the facts are organized. After reading the selection, carefully study the directions for the experiment. Then perform the experiment.

Motion

Work is defined as **force**—a push or pull—acting over a distance. The phrase *acting over a distance* means that something is moving, or in **motion**; so whenever you move, you are doing work. Scientists have developed definitions and laws to describe this phenomenon.

Speed, Velocity, and Acceleration

<u>Speed</u> is defined as the distance covered in a specific amount of time, usually a second, minute, or hour, as shown in Figure 1. Speed limit signs tell drivers the maximum speed at which they may travel. These signs express speed in miles per hour (mph) or in kilometers per hour (kph). Speed can be calculated using the following formula.

$$\text{speed} = \frac{\text{distance}}{\text{time}} = \frac{\text{kilometers}}{\text{hour}}$$

By knowing any two of the three variables in the formula, you can find the third.

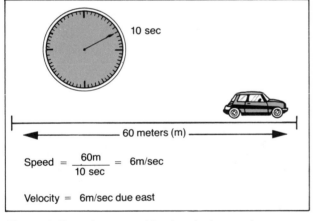

Figure 1. If you know an object's velocity, you have more information than if you only know its speed.

A second concept that is related to motion is <u>velocity</u>, which is closely related to speed, as indicated in Figure 1. Velocity is the speed of an object in a specific direction. For example, 35 kph is the speed of an automobile, while 35 kph due north is its velocity.

Any change in velocity is called <u>acceleration</u>. Acceleration occurs when velocity increases or decreases. Although people commonly call decreasing velocity

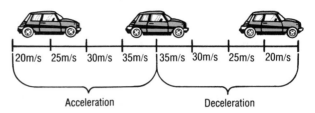

Figure 2. Acceleration indicates either an increase or a decrease in an object's velocity.

deceleration, scientists do not use this term. (See Figure 2.)

The formula below shows how acceleration is calculated.

$$a = \frac{v_2 - v_1}{t}$$

a = acceleration
v_1 = beginning velocity
v_2 = ending velocity
t = time

If a car is going north at 20 m/sec and 5 seconds later it is going 25 m/sec, the acceleration can be figured as follows.

$$a = \frac{25\text{m/sec} - 20\text{m/sec}}{5 \text{ sec}}$$

$$= \frac{5\text{m/sec}}{5 \text{ sec}} = 1\text{m/s/s}$$

Acceleration always indicates a change in velocity per unit of time. Since velocity is always expressed as distance covered per unit of time, acceleration can be expressed in terms of distance per unit of time per unit of time.

In this example, the answer is in meters per second per second. An answer might also be in kilometers per hour per hour.

Newton's Laws of Motion

Force and motion are related in specific ways. In the late 1600s, after studying the relationships between force and motion, English mathematician Isaac Newton developed three laws describing these relationships.

The first law is illustrated by the following example: If you are riding a bicycle and suddenly put on your brakes, the bicycle stops, but your body continues moving forward over the handlebars if you do not brace yourself. Newton's First Law of Motion explains the reason: A mass (anything made of matter) at rest tends to remain at rest, and a mass moving at a constant velocity tends to keep moving at that velocity, unless acted upon by an outside force. This law explains why a mass such as a rock or a wagon does not move until it is pushed, pulled, or thrown—that is, until a force is applied. This law also explains the bicycle example. When you put the brakes on a bicycle, you apply a force that changes the velocity of the bicycle, but your body continues to move forward unless you brace yourself.

Newton's first law is also called the law of **inertia** (in ER shə). Inertia is the tendency of a mass to resist having its motion changed. The greater an object's mass is, the greater is its inertia. Unless acted upon by an outside force, a mass at rest tends to remain at rest, and a mass moving at a constant velocity tends to keep moving at that velocity.

Newton's Second Law of Motion describes the relationship between force, mass, and acceleration. The law states that the acceleration of an object depends on the object's mass and on the amount of force applied to the object. The law is expressed in the following formula.

$$F = m \times a$$

F = force applied to an object
m = mass of the object
a = acceleration of the object

Newton's Third Law of Motion states that for every action, there is an equal and opposite reaction. A rocket taking off is a dramatic example of this law. However, a rocket is not the only example. Every time you lean against a wall, the wall pushes back against you. When you throw a ball against the sidewalk, the ball bounces back.

The concepts of speed, velocity, and acceleration, plus Newton's Laws of Motion, help scientists to predict the performance of moving objects.

The following experiment will help you to explore the relationship between mass and acceleration described in Newton's Second Law.

Experiment

Problem

When the same force is applied to objects with different masses, how does it affect the acceleration of each object?

Aim

In this experiment, the same force will be applied to balls of different masses. The acceleration of each ball will be approximated by measuring the distance it moves.

Materials

You will need a smooth, flat tabletop, a spring trigger, three balls of the same size but of different masses (one solid wood, one solid steel, one solid styrofoam), masking tape or chalk, and a meter stick.

Procedure

1. Place a piece of masking tape or chalk dot near the edge of the table. Each ball will be placed on this marker before force is applied.

2. Place the meter stick on the table and attach the spring trigger to the edge of the table, as shown in Figure 3.

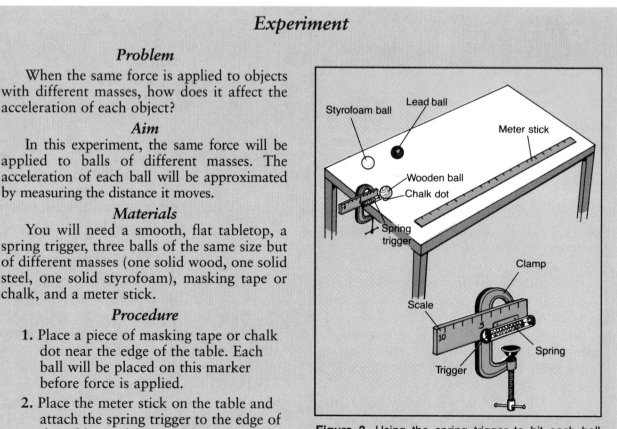

Figure 3. Using the spring trigger to hit each ball with a constant force.

3. Place the wooden ball on the marker.
4. Line up the trigger on the spring trigger with the wooden ball. Pull the spring back to number 5 on the scale: This is your constant force.
5. Release the trigger, and let it hit the wooden ball. Record the distance that the ball moves in the following chart.
6. Repeat steps 3–5 with the steel ball and again with the styrofoam ball.

Observations or Conclusions
With the constant force, the steel ball moves the shortest distance and the styrofoam ball moves the longest distance; the distance moved by the wooden ball is between the other two. The conclusion is that when a constant force is applied, an object with less mass moves farther (is accelerated more) than an object with great mass.

Ball	Force	Distance
Wooden	5	
Steel	5	
Styrofoam	5	

RECALLING FACTS

Recalling details
1. What is force?
a push or pull acting over a distance

Recalling details
2. What does the phrase *acting over a distance* mean?
that something is moving, or in motion

Recalling details
3. What is speed?
the distance covered in a specific amount of time, usually a second, minute, or hour

Recalling details
4. What is the formula for calculating speed?
$$speed = \frac{distance}{time}$$

Comparing and contrasting
5. How is velocity different from speed?
In addition to the information that calculating speed gives, velocity gives the direction of motion.

Recalling details
6. What is acceleration?
any change in velocity

Recalling details
7. What is the formula for calculating acceleration?
$$a = \frac{v_2 - v_1}{t}$$

Recalling details
8. What is deceleration?
decreasing velocity.

Recalling details
9. What is Newton's First Law of Motion?
Objects at rest tend to remain at rest; objects in motion tend to remain in motion unless acted upon by an outside force.

Recalling details
10. What is inertia?
the tendency of a mass to resist having its motion changed

Recalling details
11. What is Newton's Second Law of Motion?
The acceleration of an object depends on its mass and on the amount of force applied to the object.

12. What mathematical formula states Newton's Second Law of Motion?

F = m x a

13. What is Newton's Third Law of Motion?

For every action, there is an equal and opposite

reaction.

14. If you know the distance something travels and you want to find its speed, what else do you need to know?

the time it takes the object to travel over that distance

15. If you know the speed of something and you want to find the velocity, what else do you need to know?

the direction of the object's motion

16. If you want to find the acceleration of an object and you know the time period during which the object accelerated, what other two things do you need to know?

You need to know the beginning velocity (the velocity

at the beginning of the time period) and the ending

velocity (the velocity at the end of the time period).

17. Match each definition with the correct word from the list below:

velocity   a. increase or decrease in velocity

speed   b. rate and direction of velocity

acceleration   c. distance covered per unit of time

INTERPRETING FACTS

Circle the letter next to each correct answer.

1. If a car's speed is 60 km/hr and it travels for 6 hours, the distance it travels is —————.

   a. 10 km   b. 66 km   (c.) 360 km

2. If a rocket is going 30 km/sec and accelerates 2 km/s/s, its velocity after 10 seconds is ——.

   a. 20 km/sec   (b.) 50 km/sec   c. 60 km/sec

3. One object has a mass of 10 grams, and another object has a mass of 20 grams. If the same force is applied to both objects, the acceleration of the lighter object is —————.

   (a.) twice that of the heavy object

   b. half that of the heavy object

   c. the same as that of the heavy object

4. When amusement park rides start, the riders are often pushed backward in their seats. When the rides stop, the riders are often thrown forward in their seats. These two reactions illustrate Newton's —————.

   (a.) First Law   b. Second Law   c. Third Law

5. When you jump off a diving board, your downward push produces an upward push or springing-back in the diving board, which lifts you into the air. When you throw a ball against a wall, it bounces back toward you. These two reactions illustrate Newton's

   a. First Law   b. Second Law   (c.) Third Law

A. In your own words, summarize the experiment on pages 130–131. When you finish, check your summary by rereading the experiment, and make any corrections that are necessary.

Possible answer: Three balls of the same size but of different masses were hit with the same amount of force, and the distances they traveled were measured.

B. The following experiment shows how force must increase or decrease, relatively speaking, to accelerate three balls of different masses by the same amount. The distance that a ball moves is used to indicate the amount of its acceleration. Use the same materials as in the experiment on pages 130–131. Also using that experiment as a model, write the directions for this experiment on the lines provided. Be sure to number the steps in the procedure. Draw a chart to record the information you collect.

Experiment

Problem

What different relative forces must be applied to cause balls of different masses to accelerate the same amount?

Aim

In this experiment, you will determine the relative force necessary to move balls of different masses the same distance.

Materials

You need a smooth, flat tabletop, a spring trigger, three balls of the same size but different masses (one solid wood, one solid steel, one solid styrofoam), masking tape, and a meter stick.

Procedure

1. Place a piece of masking tape near the edge of the table. Place each ball on this tape before applying force.

2. Place the wooden ball on the tape, and lay the meter stick on the table.

3. Practice hitting the three balls with the spring trigger until you can move each one the same distance. You have to pull the spring back a different amount for each ball in order to move them all the same distance. Record the relative amount of force needed to move each ball.

Observations or Conclusions

The greater the mass of the ball, the more force is needed to move it a given distance.

Ball	Force	Distance
Wooden		
Steel		
Styrofoam		

Statistics

___ Reading a Mathematics Selection ___

▶ Background Information

Learning to work with tables of statistics can help you deal with many kinds of charts and tables in everyday life. For example, baseball statistics are presented in the box scores in newspapers. From this chart, you can find out a player's or a team's hits, runs, errors, put outs, and batting averages.

When you work with statistics, the starting point is generally a table, or sometimes just a list, of numbers. When reading tables, use a movable marker, such as a ruler, to make sure that you do not wander into the wrong column or row.

▶ Skill Focus

There are several ways to simplify or to make sense of large amounts of data. One way is to find the **average** of the numbers. The average, also called the **mean**, is a single number that represents an entire set of numbers. For example, you might read that the average income in the United States for a given year was $25,727. This number does not necessarily represent

anyone's income, but it tells you something about the incomes in the United States during that period.

Polls and surveys are frequently used to find out an average concerning some subject: the average salary of women in contrast to the average salary of men in the same line of work; the average age of people in a community; the average weekly grocery bill for a family of four with a certain income; the average attendance at types of movies during a year.

As our world becomes more and more a "global village," we probably will use statistics even more. It is a way of getting a "big picture" of a world made up of millions of different kinds of people.

Other kinds of averages, such as the **median** or the **mode**, are also used in **statistics**.

▶ Word Clues

The words *statistics, mean, median,* and *mode* all have their origin in Latin or Greek, but their meanings have changed over time.

Statistics originally meant the study of the state or nation; even today, much of the data that is analyzed concerns the populations, costs, and taxes of nations. Both *mean* and *median* come from the Latin word for *middle*. Both a *mean* and a *median* are averages. The word *mode* is from the Latin for *measure*. In statistics, the mode is most often useful when something is being measured or counted.

▶ Strategy Tip

As you read "Interpreting Statistics," you will learn how to find three kinds of averages: the mean, the median, and the mode. Study the examples carefully to be sure that you understand how these different averages are used.

Interpreting Statistics

Statistics is the mathematical method for extracting information from sets of numbers so as to better understand their meaning. One of the most important skills in interpreting statistics is finding a single number that in some way represents an entire set of numbers. One such number is commonly called an **average**. Different kinds of averages are used in statistics. The different kinds of averages are called **measures of central tendency**.

Mean

The most familiar measure of central tendency is the **mean**. The mean is found by adding the members of a set and dividing the sum by the number of members. The mean is especially useful if the average is to be later used in a computation.

For example, suppose that a small business employs ten part-time workers. Here is a list of the hours they work each week.

Ada Blanco	11	Frank DeLucca	20
Bill Martin	20	Keesha Miller	17
Cathy Donahue	20	Harold Smith	12
Don Sheng	2	Inge Pederson	18
Emily Goldberg	37	José Vazquez	20

To find the mean number of hours worked, add the number of hours for all ten workers and divide by ten. The sum is 177, so the mean number of hours is 17.7. For some purposes, you can use the mean instead of using the original set of numbers, or **data**.

One use of the mean would be to compare two different weeks. If you wanted to know whether the part-time workers were working more or less than they did the previous week, the mean would be an appropriate measure to use, since it reflects the total. If the number of workers changes from week to week, the mean would still indicate the average amount that each worked, even though the total amount of work done would be different.

Median

A different measure of central tendency would better express how many hours that the average person worked. This measure is the **median**, or the middle of the set; it shows that half the workers worked more than that amount, while the other half worked less. Notice that the mean is usually different from the median. In the example given, six workers worked more than 17.7 hours, while only four workers worked fewer than 17.7 hours.

There are two different ways to find the median, depending on whether the set of data has an even or an odd number of members. If the number of members is odd, the median is simply the middle number of the set. For example, suppose the set is 2, 9, 4, 1, 8, which has five members (an odd number). To find the middle number, arrange the set from least to greatest (or vice versa), and count to find the third member. From least to greatest, the set is 1, 2, *4*, 8, 9, so the median is 4.

When the number of members is even, there is no middle number in the set. To identify the median as a single number, *the mean of the two middle numbers* is used. For example, suppose the set is 2, 9, 4, 1, 8, 5, which has six members (an even number). The two middle numbers can be found by rearranging the set in order and taking the fourth and fifth numbers. From greatest to least, the set is 9, 8, *5*, *4*, 2, 1, so the median is the mean of 5 and 4. The mean is $(5 + 4) \div 2$, or 4.5.

Mode

The third measure of central tendency is the **mode**. This measure is simply the data item that occurs most in the set. Since 20 hours occurs 4 times and no other data item occurs more than once, the mode for the part-time workers is 20.

The mode is often used to show typical behavior. For example, if you were applying to the company for a part-time job, the manager might tell you, "The typical part-time worker works 20 hours a week."

Sometimes two different data items occur the same number of times, and both occur more often than any of the other data items. In this case, there are two modes, and the set of data is said to be **bimodal**.

Recalling details
1. What is statistics?
Statistics is the mathematical method for extracting

information from numbers.

Recalling details
2. What are the different types of averages called in statistics?
They are called measures of central tendency.

Recalling details
3. How do you find the mean of a set of numbers?
Add the numbers and divide by the number of

members in the set.

Recalling details
4. How do you find the mode of a set of data?
Count the number of times that each data item occurs.

The one that occurs the most often is the mode.

Recalling details
5. How do you find the median when the number of members in a set of numbers is even?
Arrange the set from either least to greatest or greatest

to least. The median is the mean of the two middle

numbers.

Recalling details
6. What do you call a set that has two modes?
A set with two modes is called bimodal.

Making inferences
1. If the same number of workers are employed by a company each month, which measure of central tendency is most appropriate for comparing the average salary from month to month? Explain.
The mean is the most appropriate measure of central tendency because the number of employees remains the

same.

Making inferences
2. A personnel director wants to give a young executive an idea of how her salary ranks among the company's other executives. With which measure of central tendency should the young executive's salary be compared to be most meaningful?
Her salary should be compared to the median, since half the executives make more and half make less.

Making inferences
3. The median of a set of five numbers is much smaller than the mean. What does this tell you about the set?
The two largest numbers in the set are much greater than the other three numbers in the set.

Alternatively, the actual numbers in the set are not close to the mean. There is more variation among the numbers

than similarity.

A. Use the table below to find the information asked for in each problem.

Records for the Acme Corporation			
Worker	**Hours Worked**	**Salary per Hour**	**Weekly Salary**
Matthew Smith	35	6.20	217.00
Ana Martinez	28	8.40	235.20
Tyrone Brown	40	8.80	352.00
Marie Sokoloski	35	7.20	252.00
Jean Gastineau	21	6.00	126.00
Ahmed Salaam	35	7.20	252.00
Walter Klecko	42	6.00	252.00
Naomi Simms	60	6.40	384.00
Umeko Tanaka	35	6.00	210.00
Marc Rutledge	14	7.20	100.80
Eduardo Fuentes	0	7.20	0.00
Rita Danelo	35	7.20	252.00

1. What is the mean number of hours worked? <u>31.7 (to the nearest hundredth)</u>

2. What is the median number of hours worked? <u>35 hours</u>

3. What is the mode of the number of hours worked? <u>35 hours</u>

B. Tell which measure of central tendency you would use for each situation and why.

1. You are looking for a model, a typical person, to represent your product. You know the heights of people who use your product. You want a model of average height.

You would use the median; half the people would be taller than your model, and half would be shorter.

2. You are purchasing a large order of shoes for your shoe store. You know the sizes of shoes that people wear, and you want to order extra pairs of the most popular size.

You would use the mode, since most people wear that size.

3. You are designing a passenger airplane, and you know how many passengers it will carry. You need to know the weight of the average passenger to determine the weight when the plane is fully loaded.

You would use the mean, since the number of passengers times the mean weight is the total weight of the

passengers.

▶ **Real Life Connections** Keep track of how many hours you watch television each day for a week. Then find the mean, the median, and the mode for your TV-watching time.

Lesson 35

Accented Syllable and Schwa Sound

When words contain two syllables, one of the syllables is stressed, or accented, more than the other. In most dictionaries, the **accent mark** ' is placed at the end of the syllable that is said with more stress. For example, the first syllable in the word *pilot* is said with more stress than the second syllable.

pi' lot

In words with three syllables, the accent is usually on one of the first two syllables. When you are trying to pronounce a word with three syllables, such as *conclusion*, stress the first syllable. If the word does not sound right, say it again, stressing the second syllable.

con' clu sion   con clu' sion

Say each of the following words to yourself. Write an accent mark after the syllable that should be stressed.

1. doz' en
2. im' i tate
3. at tend'
4. ad di' tion
5. a mount'
6. hi' ber nate
7. suc cess'
8. nu' cle us

Words of four or more syllables usually have two accented syllables. In the word *territory*, the first syllable has the most stress. This syllable has the primary accent mark '. The third syllable has more stress than the remaining two syllables but less than the first syllable. The lighter accent mark ' is placed after that syllable. This is called the secondary accent.

ter' ri to' ry

Say each of the following words to yourself. Write a primary accent mark after the syllable that has the most stress. Say the word again. Write a secondary accent mark after the syllable that has the second most stress.

1. e lec' tri fy' ing
2. hel' i cop' ter
3. op' er a' tion
4. sat' is fac' tion
5. dic' tion ar' y
6. sal' a man' der
7. dis' tri bu' tion
8. trans' por ta' tion

The vowels *a, e, i, o,* and *u* can all have the same sound. This is a soft sound like a short *u* pronounced lightly. This short, soft *u* sound is called the **schwa** sound. In dictionary respellings, the symbol ə stands for the schwa sound. If you look up the word *vitamin* in the dictionary, you will find it respelled this way.

vīt'ə min

Say each of the words below to yourself. Write a primary and secondary accent mark after the syllables that are stressed. Then circle the letter that stands for the schwa sound.

1. ad' ver tis' ing
2. e vap' o rate'
3. con' se quent' ly
4. i den' ti fy'
5. at' mos pher' ic
6. nec' es sar' y
7. in' di vid' u al
8. jus' ti fy' ing

Look at the words in the list above. Notice that the schwa sound always falls in an unaccented syllable of a word.

Lesson 36

Fact and Opinion

As you read books, newspapers, or magazines, you should be able to distinguish facts from opinions. A statement of **fact** is information that can be proven to be true. A statement of **opinion** is a personal belief or feeling.

As you read the following paragraphs, think about which statements are facts and which are opinions.

What Is a Paralegal?

Did you know that you could have an exciting career in law without becoming a lawyer? A paralegal, or legal assistant, does many of the things a lawyer does. A paralegal, however, cannot give legal advice, appear in court, or set fees. The duties of a paralegal include drafting, or preparing, legal documents, interviewing clients, and doing research. Most paralegals specialize in one kind of law, such as real estate or litigation, the actual conduct of a lawsuit. However, criminal law may be the most fascinating area of all.

Although law firms hire most paralegals, job opportunities are available in other fields. Corporations, banks, and insurance companies employ paralegals. In the public sector, legal-aid offices, the government, and the courts make use of paralegals. Jobs for legal assistants are also opening up in hospital and school administration and in legal publishing.

There continues to be a sharp rise in the number of paralegals. From 1992 to 2005, according to the U.S. Bureau of Labor Statistics, the number of paralegals will increase more than 85 percent, from 95,000 to about 175,000 professionals. Although some paralegals who are now employed have had no special training,

the competition for jobs will increase. Those people with formal paralegal training will have better chances of being hired in the future.

Hundreds of institutions in the United States offer formal paralegal training. Three main kinds of training programs exist. Junior colleges, as well as four-year universities and colleges, offer two-year programs. In addition to law-related and legal specialty courses, studies include general education. A few four-year colleges and universities have programs with a major or minor in legal assistant studies. Some universities, colleges, business schools, and special paralegal training schools also offer training programs.

Some of these programs require applicants to have finished at least one and one-half years of college. Other programs accept only college graduates with high grades. Classes may be given full time during the day or part time in the evening. The length of these programs is therefore anywhere from three months to two years. Students study either general law with some training in one or two specialty areas, or they specialize in one kind of law. The best training programs include internships so that students get on-the-job training.

Read the following statements, which are based on the selection. On the line before each statement, write *F* if it is a fact or *O* if it is an opinion.

_O_ 1. A career in law is exciting.

_F_ 2. A legal assistant does many of the things that a lawyer does.

_F_ 3. A person with formal paralegal training will have a better chance of getting a legal assistant job.

_F_ 4. Hundreds of institutions offer paralegal training.

_F_ 5. Legal assistants prepare documents.

_O_ 6. The most fascinating area of law is criminal law.

_F_ 7. Most legal assistants are hired by law firms.

_O_ 8. The best paralegal training programs include internships.

Lesson 37

The Dictionary

Each word, abbreviation, prefix, suffix, or group of words that your dictionary explains is called an **entry word**. The entry word and all the information about it is called an **entry**. Most of the dictionaries that you use include from 50,000 to 80,000 separate entries. These entries are arranged in alphabetical order, with biographical entries alphabetized by surnames, or family names.

To use a dictionary effectively, you need to know the function of each part of an entry. Study the following.

Guide words: Printed in boldfaced type at the top of the page, the left guide word shows the first full entry on the page and the right guide word shows the last.

Syllables: Centered dots in the entry word show where to divide a word when you cannot write it all on one line.

Respelling: Appearing in parentheses following the entry word, the respelling helps you to pronounce the word.

Etymology: Shown within brackets [ ], the etymology explains the origin and history of the word, using symbols and abbreviations. (For example, < means *derived from*, and OE means Old English.)

Definitions: Meanings for the entry word are listed together according to their part of speech.

Idioms: Included at the end of the entry that is the key word, an idiom is a group of words with a different meaning from the meaning of the words by themselves.

On the next page is part of a dictionary entry. Use it to answer the questions that follow.

1. What are the guide words for this page?
   eel, effulgence

2. Write the respelling of *eerie*. ir´ē

3. What is the ninth entry word on this page? efface

4. What is the fifth adjective meaning of *effective*? making a striking impression

5. How long does an eel grow to be?
   5 feet long

6. What key word is given in the pronunciation key for the long *o* sound?
   gō

7. What is the adjective form of the word *effervesce*? effervescent

8. How would you divide the word *efficiency* into syllables?
   ef•fi•cien•cy

9. How do you spell the plural of the word *effendi*? effendis

10. How do you spell the past tense of *efface*? effaced

11. What phrase is given as an example of the second adjective meaning of *efficient*?
    an efficient production method

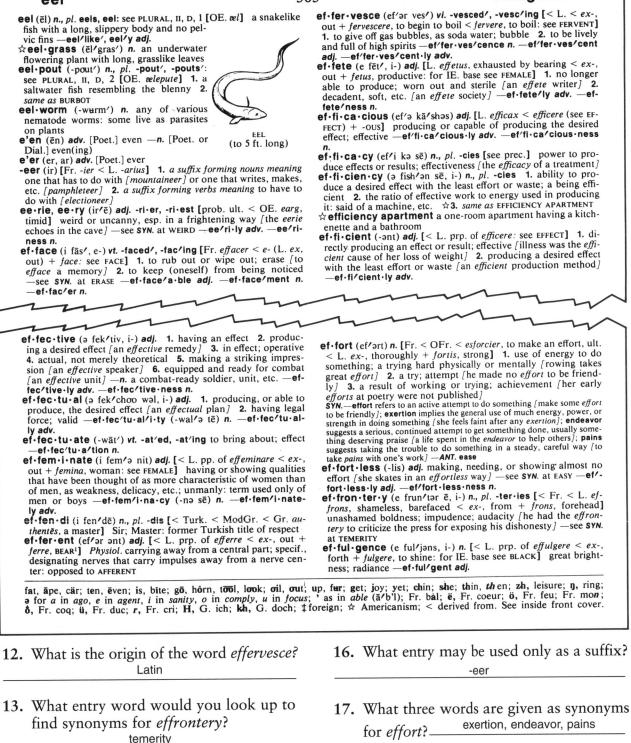

eel (ēl) *n., pl.* **eels, eel:** see PLURAL, II, D, 1 [OE. *æl*] a snakelike fish with a long, slippery body and no pelvic fins —**eel′like′, eel′y** *adj.*

☆**eel·grass** (ēl′gras′) *n.* an underwater flowering plant with long, grasslike leaves

eel·pout (-pout′) *n., pl.* **-pout′, -pouts′:** see PLURAL, II, D, 2 [OE. *ælepute*] **1.** a saltwater fish resembling the blenny **2.** *same as* BURBOT

eel·worm (-wurm′) *n.* any of various nematode worms: some live as parasites on plants

e'en (ēn) *adv.* [Poet.] even —*n.* [Poet. or Dial.] even(ing)

e'er (er, ar) *adv.* [Poet.] ever

-eer (ir) [Fr. *-ier* < L. *-arius*] **1.** *a suffix forming nouns meaning* one that has to do with [*mountaineer*] or one that writes, makes, etc. [*pamphleteer*] **2.** *a suffix forming verbs meaning* to have to do with [*electioneer*]

ee·rie, ee·ry (ir′ē) *adj.* **-ri·er, -ri·est** [prob. ult. < OE. *earg*, timid] weird or uncanny, esp. in a frightening way [the *eerie* echoes in the cave] —see SYN. at WEIRD —**ee′ri·ly** *adv.* —**ee′ri·ness** *n.*

ef·face (i fās′, e-) *vt.* **-faced′, -fac′ing** [Fr. *effacer* < *e-* (L. *ex*, out) + *face*: see FACE] **1.** to rub out or wipe out; erase [to *efface* a memory] **2.** to keep (oneself) from being noticed —see SYN. at ERASE —**ef·face′a·ble** *adj.* —**ef·face′ment** *n.* —**ef·fac′er** *n.*

ef·fec·tive (ə fek′tiv, i-) *adj.* **1.** having an effect **2.** producing a desired effect [an *effective* remedy] **3.** in effect; operative **4.** actual, not merely theoretical **5.** making a striking impression [an *effective* speaker] **6.** equipped and ready for combat [an *effective* unit] —*n.* a combat-ready soldier, unit, etc. —**ef·fec′tive·ly** *adv.* —**ef·fec′tive·ness** *n.*

ef·fec·tu·al (ə fek′choo wəl, i-) *adj.* **1.** producing, or able to produce, the desired effect [an *effectual* plan] **2.** having legal force; valid —**ef·fec′tu·al′i·ty** (-wal′ə tē) *n.* —**ef·fec′tu·al·ly** *adv.*

ef·fec·tu·ate (-wāt′) *vt.* **-at′ed, -at′ing** to bring about; effect —**ef·fec′tu·a′tion** *n.*

ef·fem·i·nate (i fem′ə nit) *adj.* [< L. pp. of *effeminare* < *ex-*, out + *femina*, woman: see FEMALE] having or showing qualities that have been thought of as more characteristic of women than of men, as weakness, delicacy, etc.; unmanly: term used only of men or boys —**ef·fem′i·na·cy** (-nə sē) *n.* —**ef·fem′i·nate·ly** *adv.*

ef·fen·di (i fen′dē) *n., pl.* **-dis** [< Turk. < ModGr. < Gr. *authentēs*, a master] Sir; Master: former Turkish title of respect

ef·fer·ent (ef′ər ənt) *adj.* [< L. prp. of *efferre* < *ex-*, out + *ferre*, BEAR¹] *Physiol.* carrying away from a central part; specif., designating nerves that carry impulses away from a nerve center: opposed to AFFERENT

ef·fer·vesce (ef′ər ves′) *vi.* **-vesced′, -vesc′ing** [< L. < *ex-*, out + *fervescere*, to begin to boil < *fervere*, to boil: see FERVENT] **1.** to give off gas bubbles, as soda water; bubble **2.** to be lively and full of high spirits —**ef′fer·ves′cence** *n.* —**ef′fer·ves′cent** *adj.* —**ef′fer·ves′cent·ly** *adv.*

ef·fete (e fēt′, i-) *adj.* [L. *effetus*, exhausted by bearing < *ex-*, out + *fetus*, productive: for IE. base see FEMALE] **1.** no longer able to produce; worn out and sterile [an *effete* writer] **2.** decadent, soft, etc. [an *effete* society] —**ef·fete′ly** *adv.* —**ef·fete′ness** *n.*

ef·fi·ca·cious (ef′ə kā′shəs) *adj.* [L. *efficax* < *efficere* (see EFFECT) + -OUS] producing or capable of producing the desired effect; effective —**ef′fi·ca′cious·ly** *adv.* —**ef′fi·ca′cious·ness** *n.*

ef·fi·ca·cy (ef′i kə sē) *n., pl.* **-cies** [see prec.] power to produce effects or results; effectiveness [the *efficacy* of a treatment]

ef·fi·cien·cy (ə fish′ən sē, i-) *n., pl.* **-cies** **1.** ability to produce a desired effect with the least effort or waste; a being efficient **2.** the ratio of effective work to energy used in producing it: said of a machine, etc. ☆**3.** *same as* EFFICIENCY APARTMENT

☆**efficiency apartment** a one-room apartment having a kitchenette and a bathroom

ef·fi·cient (-ənt) *adj.* [< L. prp. of *efficere*: see EFFECT] **1.** directly producing an effect or result; effective [illness was the *efficient* cause of her loss of weight] **2.** producing a desired effect with the least effort or waste [an *efficient* production method] —**ef·fi′cient·ly** *adv.*

ef·fort (ef′ərt) *n.* [Fr. < OFr. < *esforcier*, to make an effort, ult. < L. *ex-*, thoroughly + *fortis*, strong] **1.** use of energy to do something; a trying hard physically or mentally [rowing takes great *effort*] **2.** a try; attempt [he made no *effort* to be friendly] **3.** a result of working or trying; achievement [her early *efforts* at poetry were not published]
SYN.—**effort** refers to an active attempt to do something [make some *effort* to be friendly]; **exertion** implies the general use of much energy, power, or strength in doing something [she feels faint after any *exertion*]; **endeavor** suggests a serious, continued attempt to get something done, usually something deserving praise [a life spent in the *endeavor* to help others]; **pains** suggests taking the trouble to do something in a steady, careful way [to take *pains* with one's work] —**ANT.** ease

ef·fort·less (-lis) *adj.* making, needing, or showing almost no effort [she skates in an *effortless* way] —see SYN. at EASY —**ef′fort·less·ly** *adv.* —**ef′fort·less·ness** *n.*

ef·fron·ter·y (e frun′tər ē, i-) *n., pl.* **-ter·ies** [< Fr. < L. *effrons*, shameless, barefaced < *ex-*, from + *frons*, forehead] unashamed boldness; impudence; audacity [he had the *effrontery* to criticize the press for exposing his dishonesty] —see SYN. at TEMERITY

ef·ful·gence (e ful′jəns, i-) *n.* [< L. prp. of *effulgere* < *ex-*, forth + *fulgere*, to shine: for IE. base see BLACK] great brightness; radiance —**ef·ful′gent** *adj.*

fat, āpe, cär; ten, ēven; is, bīte; gō, hôrn, to͞ol, lo͝ok; oil, out; up, fur; get; joy; yet; chin; she; thin, then; zh, leisure; ŋ, ring; ə for *a* in *ago*, *e* in *agent*, *i* in *sanity*, *o* in *comply*, *u* in *focus*; ' as in *able* (ā′b'l); Fr. bál; ë, Fr. coeur; ö, Fr. feu; Fr. mon; ô, Fr. coq; ü, Fr. duc; r, Fr. cri; H, G. ich; kh, G. doch; ‡foreign; ☆ Americanism; < derived from. See inside front cover.

---

12. What is the origin of the word *effervesce?*
Latin

13. What entry word would you look up to find synonyms for *effrontery?*
temerity

14. What key word is given in the pronunciation key for the short *i* sound?
is

15. What is an antonym for *effort?*
ease

16. What entry may be used only as a suffix?
-eer

17. What three words are given as synonyms for *effort?*
exertion, endeavor, pains

18. What five key words are given in the pronunciation key for the schwa sound?
ago, agent, sanity, comply, focus

19. What entry word has two correct spellings?
eerie, eery

Reading a Floor Plan

A floor plan is a drawing that shows the layout of living or working space. The name and size of each room are marked on a floor plan. To save space, symbols are used on floor plans. For example, 14'1" × 20'0" means that the size of the room is 14 feet 1 inch wide by 20 feet 0 inches long. Note that the width of a room, measured from side to side, is written first. The length of a room is measured from top to bottom on a floor plan, and it is written second.

Study the following floor plan for a house.

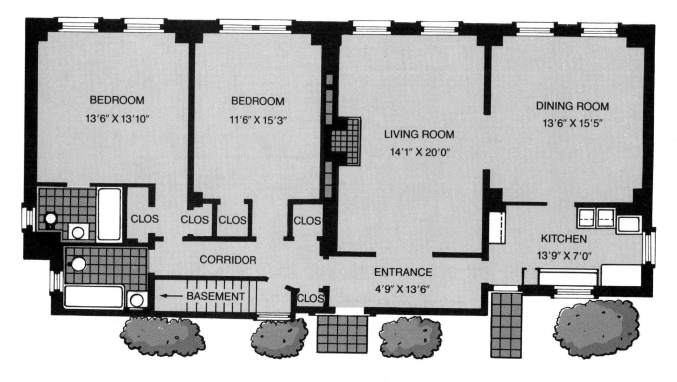

A. Use the floor plan to decide if each statement is true or false. Write *true* or *false* on the lines provided.

_____false_____ 1. There is one bathroom in the house.

_____false_____ 2. The two bedrooms are the same size.

_____true_____ 3. The bedroom that measures 11'6" × 15'3" has one closet.

_____false_____ 4. The kitchen can be entered from three different rooms.

_____true_____ **5.** The house has two doors to the outside.

_____false_____ **6.** The dining room is 15'5" × 13'6".

_____true_____ **7.** You enter the bedrooms from a corridor, or hallway.

_____true_____ **8.** You can enter the dining room only from the living room or the kitchen.

_____true_____ **9.** A doorway off the corridor leads downstairs to the basement.

_____false_____ **10.** The entrance is larger than the kitchen.

_____true_____ **11.** The bedroom that measures 13'6" × 13'10" is probably the master, or the parents', bedroom, because it has two closets and its own bathroom.

_____false_____ **12.** The 11'6" × 15'3" bedroom is the smallest room in the house.

B. Complete each of the following sentences using the information provided on the floor plan.

    1. The size of the dining room is __13'6" x 15'5"__.

    2. Of the dining room and the bedroom located next to the living room, the larger room is the __dining room__.

    3. The house has a total of ___5___ closets.

    4. You can enter the living room from the ___entrance___ or the ___dining room___.

    5. A fireplace is located in the __living room__.

    6. There are ___2___ windows in the kitchen.

    7. The narrowest room in the house is the __entrance__.

    8. The longest room in the house is the __living room__.

    9. The length of the kitchen is ___7'___.

    10. The two rooms with the same width are __the master bedroom and the dining room__.

    11. Give the width of the following rooms.

        a. master bedroom ___13'6"___   **c.** living room ___14'1"___

        b. other bedroom ___11'6"___   **d.** dining room ___13'6"___

    12. You can find the width of the entire house by adding the widths of the two bedrooms, the living room, and the dining room that you just recorded. Remember to always add inches to inches and feet to feet. Since 12 inches equal 1 foot, you need to change any measurements greater than 12 inches to feet. The width of the entire house is ___52'7"___.

Lesson 39 _____

Satire

Reading a Literature Selection _____

▶ Background Information

Our rapidly growing technology has had positive and negative effects on our environment. The future health of our fragile environment depends on the actions we take today.

▶ Skill Focus

Satire is a literary device used to ridicule, or poke fun at, an aspect of human nature or life in general. Almost any subject, from clothing fads to air pollution, can be the object of satire.

Through satire, writers and artists comment on the foolishness or weakness of people, institutions, or a current situation. In so doing, satirists also try to persuade people to make changes or improvements. Satire may be gentle, humorous, fierce, or scornful. While often amusing, its subject and intention are always serious.

To recognize satire, look for a serious topic treated in a humorous way. Satirists can exaggerate details and events to ridiculous proportions, or

they can jokingly imitate the language or style of an immediately recognizable literary or artistic form.

The following questions will help you to identify satire.

1. What is the subject matter?
2. How is the subject treated—gently? humorously? fiercely? scornfully?
3. What method or form does the satirist use to present his or her opinion?
4. At what is the satirist specifically poking fun?
5. What is the satirist saying about the subject being satirized?
6. What change or reform is the satirist trying to persuade the reader to accept as necessary?

▶ Word Clues

When you read, you may come across a word that names a person, place, or thing. If the paragraph or stanza has no context clues to explain the word, there may be a clue elsewhere. Read the lines that follow.

On the only patch of grass
In England, in England
(Except the grass by the hoardings[1]
Which doesn't count.)

The raised number after the word *hoardings* signals you to look at the bottom of the page for a footnote with the same number. A footnote gives a brief definition or explanation of the word. The footnote for *hoardings* tells you that it is a British word with a meaning quite different from the one Americans give it.

[1] hoardings: British billboards.

Use **footnote** context clues to find the meanings of the six other numbered words in the selections.

▶ Strategy Tip

As you read the following poems and study the cartoon, notice the light touch of their creators in dealing with serious topics. What environmental issues are they satirizing? Why is satire more effective than direct criticism?

We are going to see the rabbit . . .

Alan Brownjohn

We are going to see the rabbit.
We are going to see the rabbit.
Which rabbit, people say?
Which rabbit, ask the children?
Which rabbit?   5
The only rabbit,
The only rabbit in England,
Sitting behind a barbed-wire fence
Under the floodlights, neon lights
Sodium lights,   10
Nibbling grass
On the only patch of grass
In England, in England
(Except the grass by the hoardings[1]
Which doesn't count.)   15
We are going to see the rabbit
And we must be there on time.

First we shall go by escalator,
Then we shall go by underground.[2]
And then we shall go by motorway   20
And then by helicopterway,
And the last ten yards we shall have to go
On foot.

And now we are going
All the way to see the rabbit.   25
We are nearly there,
We are longing to see it,
And so is the crowd
Which is here in thousands
With mounted policemen   30
And big loudspeakers
And bands and banners,
And everyone has come a long way.
But soon we shall see it
Sitting and nibbling   35
The blades of grass
On the only patch of grass
In—but something has gone wrong!
Why is everyone so angry,

Why is everyone jostling   40
And slanging[3] and complaining?
The rabbit has gone,
Yes, the rabbit has gone.
He has actually burrowed down into the
    earth
And made himself a warren,[4] under the   45
    earth.
Despite all these people.
And what shall we do?
What can we do?

It is all a pity, you must be disappointed,
Go home and do something else for today, 50
Go home again, go home for today.
For you cannot hear the rabbit, under the
    earth,
Remarking rather sadly to himself, by
    himself,
As he rests in his warren, under the earth:
"It won't be long, they are bound to come, 55
They are bound to come and find me,
    even here."

---

[1] hoardings: British billboards.
[2] underground: British subway, or underground train.
[3] slanging: speaking to others in an abusive manner; a British expression.
[4] warren: a burrow under the earth with branching tunnels where rabbits live.

"THIS IS NEWS. NOTHING IS HARMFUL TO OUR HEALTH TODAY."

The Ingredients of Expedience[5]

Henry Gibson

There's a new recipe for water
That's caught on to such a degree
I now pass it on to others
The way it was passed on to me:
    Into an ocean of fluids   5
    Add a roentgen[6] of fallout or two,
    Aluminum cans, detergents
    (With the phosphates[7] most pleasing to you).
    Stir in ground glass, melted plastics,
    Any leftovers, sewage, rough waste.   10
    Thicken with chemical acids
    And mix to a pliable paste:
    Mercury, mustard or nerve gas
    Well blended with plenty of oil,

Insecticides, powdered or liquid,   15
Then slowly bring all to a boil.
That's it. Oh, yes, one reminder—
And forgive me for throwing a curve—
Fish die, but children prefer it
If you cool before you serve.   20

---

[5]expedience: the easy way of doing something, usually for personal advantage or self-interest and without regard for the consequences.
[6]roentgen (RENT gən): international unit for measuring radiation dosage.
[7]phosphates (FAHS fayts): salts derived from a kind of acid (phosphoric acid), used in various industrial products.

RECALLING FACTS

Identifying setting
1. Describe the setting of "We are going to see the rabbit . . ."

On the way to a crowded, highly lit, fenced-in

area with one small patch of grass.

Recalling details
2. Why is the rabbit a tourist attraction?
The rabbit is the only rabbit left in England.

Recalling details
3. The old recipe for making water (H_2O) includes hydrogen and oxygen. In the poem "The Ingredients of Expedience," what does the new recipe include?
The recipe includes radiation, cans, detergents,

glass, plastics, sewage, waste products, chemical

acids, gas, oil, and insecticides.

Recalling details
4. In the cartoon, what has the woman learned from reading the morning newspaper?
"Nothing is harmful to our health today."

Using context clues
5. Complete each sentence with the correct word below.

warren   expedience   roentgen   phosphates

a. The customer settled for a lower-quality product for the sake of ___expedience___.

b. The speedy animal negotiated the many turns and twists of the underground ___warren___.

c. Use the ___roentgen___ to measure the output of X-ray machines.

d. The company used ___phosphates___ to make fertilizer.

Inferring cause and effect

1. Why is the rabbit the last one left in England?

People have dug up and paved over most of its natural

habitat, eliminating all but one patch of grass.

Making inferences

2. a. What do you think happened to all the other rabbits?

The other rabbits probably died because they did not

have any food or any place to live.

b. What do you think happened to the grass?

The grass probably had no room to grow because the

land was used for buildings and roads.

Drawing conclusions

3. In the last line of "We are going to see the rabbit . . ." the rabbit remarks sadly to himself that "they" will find him. Who are "they"?

"They" are the people who will eventually catch up with

the rabbit and destroy the only place left in which

rabbits can live

Making inferences

4. a. In "The Ingredients of Expedience," what is the result of mixing together all the ingredients in the new recipe for water?

The result is polluted, dirty, contaminated water that is

harmful to human beings and fish alike.

b. Who do you think made up this new recipe?

Answers will vary. Possible answers include chemical,

food, and beverage companies, and careless individuals.

c. What does the poet mean when he says that the new recipe for water has "caught on"?

Answers may vary. Because so many water supplies

are polluted and harmful as a result of these

ingredients, the recipe is obviously very popular.

d. Reread lines 17–20. What is the meaning of these four lines?

Answers may vary. While polluted water is killing fish,

people nonchalantly continue drinking and using it—

doing nothing to improve its condition.

Drawing conclusions

5. Consider the meaning of the poem's title: "The Ingredients of Expedience." Who do you think might benefit by having water like that described in the poem?

Answers may vary. Those who benefit are companies and

individuals who find it easy, cheap, and expedient to

dispose of waste materials in waterways.

Making inferences

6. In the cartoon, why is it news that nothing new has been found harmful to one's health?

Answers may vary. It sometimes seems as though an

announcement is made daily that a commonly used

product has been judged dangerous to the public's health.

SKILL FOCUS

The purpose of most satire is to eliminate serious social problems by encouraging people to change their thinking or behavior. To answer the following questions, you may reread the poems and look back at the cartoon.

1. a. What is the subject of the first poem? the scarcity of wildlife

b. Of the second poem? the pollution of our water supply

2. a. What is the attitude of the poets in both poems? <u>serious</u>

   b. In both poems, is the satire gently humorous or bitterly humorous? <u>gently humorous</u>

3. a. What method does the first poet use to develop satire? <u>exaggeration</u>

   b. In the second poem, what special form does the poet imitate? <u>a cookbook recipe</u>

4. a. In the first poem, what issue does the poet satirize to increase the public's awareness?
The poet satirizes the careless and insensitive way in which people are destroying the natural habitats of animals.

   b. In the second poem? <u>He satirizes the knowing and harmful way in which people and institutions</u>
are polluting our waterways.

5. a. What action does the poet suggest the audience take to eliminate the problem in the first
   poem? <u>If people wish Earth to have abundant wildlife, they must stop destroying habitats, even at the cost</u>
of having fewer buildings and cities.

   b. In the second poem? <u>If people wish to have safe, clean water, they must stop dumping harmful waste</u>
products into lakes, rivers, and streams.

6. Do you think these poems are meant to be entertaining or persuasive? Explain.
The poems are meant to be both entertaining and humorous. They are humorous treatments of serious
environmental issues—the destruction of wildlife habitats and the pollution of our water supply. Both poets
feel that immediate attention must be given to these issues.

7. At what is the cartoonist poking fun? <u>He is poking fun at the frequent announcements</u>
that products we use—coffee, saccharin, chocolate—are dangerous to our health.

8. Find the year in which the cartoon was first published. How old is it now? Is the
   cartoonist's point still valid today? Explain.
The copyright date shows that the cartoon was first published in 1978. Students can calculate how old
the cartoon is. Answers will vary about its relevance. However, health issues undoubtedly will continue to
concern the U.S. population in the future.

▶ **Real Life Connections** Create a poem or cartoon about an environmental issue in your
area.

Making Generalizations

___ Reading a Social Studies Selection _____

▶ Background Information

Concerned scientists and citizens around the world are fighting to save plants and animals threatened with extinction. Four people who have made a difference in the survival of endangered wildlife are Pan Wenshi and Lü Zhi in China, Merlin Tuttle in the United States, and Chico Mendes in Brazil.

▶ Skill Focus

Facts are important in understanding a person or event that you read about. Facts, however, cannot provide a complete understanding or interpretation of a topic. You must be able to make **generalizations**, or draw principles from a sampling of facts. A generalization is a broad statement that goes beyond the specific information provided by facts.

Examine the following facts.

Pan Wenshi wrote to government officials requesting that they make the Qin Ling mountains panda reserves.

Pan persuaded officials to curtail habitat loss in Qin Ling by convincing them that pandas could die out.

The Chinese government declared that it would no longer allow people to take wild pandas into captivity.

Based on these three facts, the following generalization can be made.

Pan Wenshi's efforts have resulted in increased protection for wild pandas in China.

To be sound and reasonable, a generalization must be based on two or more facts, or information that is true and can be proven.

Often, more than one generalization can be made from a given set of facts.

▶ Word Clues

Read the sentences below. Look for the context clues that explain the underlined word.

Bats are, in fact, extremely <u>beneficial</u> to humans. They eat tremendous quantities of night-flying insects, including mosquitoes and agricultural pests. . . . Bats also help hundreds of plant species reproduce. . . . Fruit-eating bats are major dispersers of tree seeds.

If you do not know the meaning of the word *beneficial* in the first sentence, you can figure out the meaning by reading the details in the sentences that follow it: Bats eat harmful insects, they help plants reproduce, and they disperse seeds. From these details, you can infer that *beneficial* means "helpful."

Use **detail** context clues to find the meanings of the four underlined words in the selection.

▶ Strategy Tip

Before reading "Making a Difference," preview it. Read the section headings and look at the photographs. As you read, pay attention to the facts and the generalizations based on them.

Making a Difference

Pan Wenshi, Lü Zhi, and the Giant Pandas

At one time, large populations of giant pandas could be found throughout southern and eastern China. Today only about 1,200 wild pandas survive in a few small, scattered areas. Pan Wenshi, a zoology professor at Beijing University, and his colleague Lü Zhi have been studying wild pandas in China's Qin Ling mountains since 1984. Their discoveries about panda behavior, diet, and cub-rearing and their efforts to protect wild pandas offer new hope for saving these rare and elusive animals.

The major threat to wild pandas is not natural predators but humans. Poachers illegally kill pandas for their pelts, which sell

for more than $10,000 in Hong Kong, Taiwan, and Japan. A more serious threat, however, is destruction of the pandas' <u>habitat</u>. Loggers cutting timber and farmers clearing land for

fields have destroyed bamboo forests on which pandas depend for food and other resources. In addition, when logging and farming divide forested areas where pandas live, the separated panda <u>populations</u> may be too small to reproduce successfully. In small populations, <u>inbreeding</u> often produces weak offspring that cannot survive.

To protect what remains of the pandas' habitat, the Chinese government developed a 10-year plan to enlarge the 13 existing panda <u>reserves</u> and create 14 new ones. As part of the plan, loggers and farmers would be paid to relocate to areas that did not threaten pandas. To Pan Wenshi's dismay, the Qin Ling research area was not included in the plan.

Pan decided to take action. He wrote to government officials requesting that they include Qin Ling among the reserves. His request was honored, but Pan did not stop there. He next persuaded officials to curtail habitat loss in Qin Ling. In 1994, the roar of chain saws ceased when the government paid timber companies working there to move out of the area. "I think that Pan's story is a good example of how the researcher can make a difference," said Lü Zhi. In another major victory for pandas, the Chinese government recently declared that it would no longer allow people to take wild pandas into captivity.

About 130 pandas are now living in zoos throughout the world. Attempts to help save the giant panda through zoo breeding programs have been extremely discouraging. During the past 30 years, fewer than 100 panda cubs have been born in captivity, and most of them died in infancy. Pan Wenshi's and Lü Zhi's studies of infant pandas and their mothers in the wild may help improve the survival rate of panda cubs born in zoos.

Merlin Tuttle and Endangered Bats

Bats are the most endangered land mammals in the United States. Of the 44 species of bats native to North America, 6 species are already on the U.S. government's endangered list and 18 more are candidates for addition.

Since founding Bat Conservation International (BCI) in 1982, Merlin Tuttle has worked tirelessly to protect existing bat colonies and to change people's ideas about bats. For example, bats are not blind. They do not tangle themselves in people's hair. They do not attack people or pets, although they will bite in self-defense as any wild animal will do. Very few bats carry rabies. People are at far greater risk of contracting rabies from raccoons, foxes, skunks, dogs, and cats than from bats.

✗ Bats are, in fact, extremely beneficial to humans. They eat tremendous quantities of night-flying insects, including mosquitoes and agricultural pests such as moths and beetles. Just one little brown bat—the species most commonly found in attics and barns—can consume 600 mosquitoes in one hour. A large bat colony, such as the 20 million Mexican free-tailed bats inhabiting Bracken Cave in Texas, may devour 500 tons of insects in one night. Bats also help hundreds of plant species reproduce, including cactus and valuable fruit trees. Fruit-eating bats are major dispersers of tree seeds. They carry these seeds and spread them in many directions, to places they never would reach otherwise.

As people intentionally kill bats or carelessly destroy their caves, increasing numbers of bat colonies are seeking refuge in abandoned mines. But even there, bats are not safe. Although abandoned mines provide excellent shelter for bats, they pose safety hazards for people. Mines regarded as dangerous have been boarded up or filled with dirt, often without thought for bat colonies trapped inside. "BCI sounded the alarm on mine closures," said Tuttle. "A million bats can easily be buried alive and no one would even know it."

To protect both people and bats, Tuttle advocates closing off mine entrances with grid-like gates that allow bats to pass through but keep people out. Often built jointly by BCI, mining companies, and government agencies, such gates have saved millions of bats. In addition, some closed mines have been reopened and gated to provide new homes for bats. In some areas, local mine inspectors now cooperate with BCI in locating and protecting mines where bats live. In 1994, BCI and the U.S. Bureau of Land Management funded the North American Bats and Mines Project. The project's goal is to educate landowners and managers to survey for bats before closing mines and, if colonies are found, to construct bat-friendly gates.

✔ The largest urban bat colony in North America, numbering between 750,000 and 1.5 million bats, lives in the Congress Avenue Bridge in downtown Austin, Texas. When the bridge was renovated in 1980, thousands of bats that had lost their caves in the Austin area found that the bridge's new crevices provided an ideal roosting site. The people of Austin were horrified at first and demanded that the bats be exterminated.

Then Merlin Tuttle went to work. Through lectures, radio and television talk shows, and educational programs in schools, Tuttle changed people's attitude toward the bats. Now, when thick clouds of bats stream out of the bridge every evening, people gather to watch.

After Tuttle spoke at a bridge designer's conference, the Texas Department of Transportation funded major research to design more bat-friendly bridges. "We have about 6 million bats already living in 59 Texas bridges," said structural engineer Mark J. Bloschock, "and we'll be building 15 to 20 new bridges a year that together will accommodate a million new bats."

Chico Mendes and the Amazon Rain Forest

Many environmental activists encounter resistance, physical discomfort, and personal hardship in their fight to protect the world's endangered wildlife. In his fight, Chico Mendes lost his life.

Mendes was born into a poor, illiterate family of rubber tappers living and working in Brazil's Amazon rain forest. Rubber tappers cut small slits in the bark of rubber trees and collect the latex sap that oozes out. Tapping trees does not kill or injure trees.

By the age of 8, Mendes was already working in his family's grove. After an ex-army officer taught him to read and write at the age of 18, Mendes became convinced that the only way forest workers could improve their lives would be by organizing into a union.

In the 1970s, the Brazilian government started opening the rain forest to development by cattle ranchers, timber and mining companies, and farmers. Unlike rubber tappers, these developers destroy forests as they clear the land. The vast fires used in their "slash-and-burn" clearing method release huge quantities of carbon dioxide into the atmosphere and eliminate the plant life that normally consumes this heat-trapping gas. Amazon deforestation thus contributes to the greenhouse effect that threatens to alter Earth's climate.

Realizing that the rain forest and the rubber tappers' way of life were in danger, Mendes created a rural workers union. Besides raising money to build schools and medical clinics, Mendes pioneered the use of nonviolent tactics to block deforestation. Whenever work crews with bulldozers and chain saws threatened a parcel of land, Mendes called together rubber tappers and their families to form a human barrier against the machines. These peaceful blockades are estimated to have saved 3 million acres of rain forest.

Mendes fought to have large sections of the rain forest set aside as "extractive preserves," areas that could be used only for harvesting renewable resources such as rubber. He also helped persuade the Inter-American Development Bank to stop funding for a highway extension being cut through the rain forest. As a result of Mendes's efforts—and the international fame and support he was beginning to receive—the Brazilian government finally designated 5 million acres of rain forest for permanent preservation.

Mendes's successful efforts earned him the hatred of ranchers and developers determined to exploit the rain forest. Five times Mendes survived enemy attempts on his life. When new death threats were made in 1988, Mendes was assigned police guards to protect him. But on December 22 of that year, as he stepped out of his back door while his two guards played dominoes inside, Mendes was struck down by a shotgun blast. He died before reaching the hospital. Today his union colleagues carry on his work.

Shortly before he was murdered, Mendes wrote in a letter to a friend, "I wish no flowers after I die, for I know they would be taken from the forest."

Recalling details
1. How many giant pandas survive in the wild today? about 1,200

Recalling details
2. What organization did Merlin Tuttle found? Bat Conservation International (BCI)

Recalling details
3. What is an "extractive preserve"?

It is an area of the rain forest that can be used only

for harvesting such renewable resources as rubber.

Identifying cause and effect
4. Underline the cause in each of the following statements. Circle the effect.

   a. When logging and farming divide the forested areas where pandas live, the separated populations may be too small to reproduce successfully.

   b. Bat colonies seek refuge in abandoned mines because people have carelessly destroyed their caves.

Identifying the main idea and supporting details
5. Reread the paragraph with an X next to it. Underline the sentence that states its main idea. How many major details support the main idea? 2 Circle those details.

Recalling details
6. Write the letter of the correct meaning on the line next to each word.

   b habitat
   d populations
   a inbreeding
   c reserves

   a. reproduction among animals of the same kind
   b. the type of area in which a particular kind of animal lives
   c. protected areas set aside for certain animals
   d. groups of animals of the same kind

Making inferences
1. Why did developers hate Chico Mendes?

They hated him because he interfered with their efforts to exploit the rain forest.

Drawing conclusions
2. a. Why are abandoned mines boarded up or filled with dirt?

They are considered dangerous for humans.

   b. How does blocking or filling mines affect bat colonies?

The blocking, or filling, of mine traps the bats inside the mines, thereby killing them.

   c. What is the advantage of using grid-like gates to close off mines?

The grids protect people by keeping them out, while, at the same time, allowing the bats to pass through

and gather food.

Inferring the unstated main idea
3. Read the paragraph with a check mark next to it. Then write a sentence that describes its main idea.

Answers may vary. The widespread fear of bats can cause extreme reactions in people, especially when

the bats are numerous.

4. Describe Chico Mendes's attitude toward the Amazon rain forest.

Mendes wanted to make use of nature's resources, whether the labor of tappers or the rain forest itself,

without exploiting them.

SKILL FOCUS

---

1. Underline the statement below that is a generalization. Then circle the letter of each statement that supports the generalization.

(a.) Loggers and farmers have destroyed the pandas' habitat.

b. Most panda cubs born in captivity do not survive.

c. Humans are the major threat to giant pandas in the wild.

d. The Qin Ling research area was not originally included in China's panda protection plan.

(e.) Poachers kill pandas for their valuable pelts.

2. Circle the letter next to the more reasonable generalization for the following group of facts.

Facts Bats are not blind.

Very few bats are infected with rabies.

Bats do not tangle themselves in people's hair.

Generalization **a.** Bats are harmless creatures.

(b.) People have many inaccurate ideas about bats.

3. Locate three facts in the text to support the following generalization.

Generalization Harvesting renewable resources in the rain forest is better for the environment than developing the land.

Facts **a.** Tapping rubber trees does not injure or kill them.

b. Clearing the land to develop it destroys the forest.

c. Burning the forest helps kill plant life and change the climate.

4. Write a generalization for the following group of facts.

a. Chico Mendes formed a union for rural workers.

b. He raised money to build schools and clinics.

c. He fought to have large sections of rain forest set aside as "extraction preserves."

Generalization Mendes fought for workers' rights and to protect the rain forest.

5. Write a generalization about Merlin Tuttle and the closings of abandoned mines. Give at least two facts to support the generalization.

a. Generalization Merlin Tuttle worked to make abandoned mines safe for bats, as well as for people.

b. Fact Abandoned mines boarded up to protect people often killed bats.

c. Fact Tuttle proposed grid-like gates to protect both people and bats.

▶ **Real Life Connections** What animals or environments are threatened in your area? What could be done to save them?

Chemical Formulas

___ Reading a Science Selection _____

▶ Background Information

Chemical symbols, formulas, and equations are shorthand ways of conveying information in science. Symbols can be combined to make up formulas, and formulas can be grouped into equations to represent chemical reactions. To understand chemical equations, you need to know what the symbols stand for and how they are put together as formulas.

Understanding symbols will enable you to read information on the labels of grocery products and non-prescription drugs that tell you the amount of each ingredient they contain. For example, *g* stands for gram and *mg* stands for milligram. Many diets and recipes use these measurements for small amounts. Your ability to read these symbols can help you take care of your dietary and nutritional needs.

▶ Skill Focus

Science books often use symbols in place of words. In the expression 32°, for example, the raised ° is a symbol for the word *degrees*. Other common symbols include +, −, and %.

Sometimes a symbol or a group of symbols can be more precise than words, and they can give you as much information as a whole sentence or even a whole paragraph.

If you know the meanings of the symbols, you can understand a lot of information very quickly. In such subject areas as physics and chemistry, symbols are often grouped together to show a compound.

For example, the formula H_2O stands for water. When reading the symbols in a **chemical formula**, you can figure out the chemical composition of the substance as long as you know the meaning of each symbol. Symbols are the shorthand language scientists use in their work.

When you read material that includes chemical formulas, be sure that you understand the following:

1. the meaning of each letter and number symbol,
2. the relationships among the symbols in a formula, and
3. the meaning of the formula as a whole.

▶ Word Clues

Read the sentence below. Use context clues to explain the underlined word.

> Scientists have identified 90 different elements that are found in nature. They have synthesized, or made, another 19 in the laboratory.

If you don't know the meaning of the word *synthesized*, the word *made* can help you. The words *synthesized* and *made* are synonyms.

Use **synonym** word clues to find the meanings of the four underlined words in the selection.

▶ Strategy Tip

As you read "Symbols, Formulas, and Equations," study the chemical symbols, formulas, and equations carefully. Be sure that you understand how they are being used. If you do not understand them, use the three steps in the Skill Focus to help you.

Symbols, Formulas, and Equations

Scientists have identified 90 different elements that are found in nature. They have synthesized, or made, another 19 in the laboratory. Elements are composed of matter that cannot be subdivided into any other type of matter; they are pure substances. Carbon, oxygen, copper, iron, and gold are examples of elements.

Chemical Symbols

Early in the study of chemistry, scientists assigned symbols to the elements as a shorthand way of referring to them. The table on this page shows the symbols for some common elements. Notice that the symbols are one or two letters long, with the first letter always capitalized and the second letter in lower case.

The symbols for elements are not all selected in the same way. Many symbols are letters taken from the name of the element. For example, *O* is the symbol for oxygen, and *He* is the symbol for helium, a gas used in balloons. Other symbols have no relationship to their English names. For example, the symbol for sodium, an element found in table salt, is *Na*, and the symbol for iron is *Fe*. These symbols are taken from the Latin names for the elements. The Latin name for sodium is *natrium*, and the Latin name for iron is *ferrum*.

Chemical Formulas

When the atoms of two or more elements combine chemically, they form a **compound.** Elements in a compound, or a chemical bond, cannot be separated by physical means, such as sifting through a fine screen. In addition, compounds have characteristics that are <u>diverse</u>, or different, from the elements that they contain.

Hydrogen chloride is a liquid compound of two gases, hydrogen and chlorine. The formula for hydrogen chloride is written using the symbols for hydrogen and chlorine.

$$HCl$$

Notice that the formula takes much less space than the name of the compound. Also, a formula provides additional information, as you can see when you compare the preceding formula with the one below.

$$H_2O$$

In this formula for hydrogen oxide, or water, the numeral 2 is called a **subscript.** It tells you that, for every oxygen atom in the compound, there are two hydrogen atoms. The fact that the formula HCl has no subscripts means that this compound contains one hydrogen atom for every chlorine atom.

Element	Symbol	Latin Name If Different	Element	Symbol	Latin Name If Different
Calcium	Ca		Nitrogen	N	
Carbon	C		Oxygen	O	
Chlorine	Cl		Platinum	Pt	
Copper	Cu	cuprum	Phosphorus	P	
Fluorine	F		Potassium	K	kalium
Gold	Au	aurum	Silicon	Si	
Helium	He		Silver	Ag	argentum
Hydrogen	H		Sodium	Na	natrium
Iron	Fe	ferrum	Sulfur	S	
Nickel	Ni		Zinc	Zn	

The following is the formula for glucose, the sugar that your body uses to produce energy.

$$C_6H_{12}O_6$$

This compound contains three elements: carbon, hydrogen, and oxygen. In every molecule of glucose, there are 6 carbon atoms, 12 hydrogen atoms, and 6 oxygen atoms. A **molecule** is the smallest particle into which an element or compound can be divided without changing its properties.

Look at the following formula.

$$CuSO_4 \cdot 5H_2O$$

From the table, you can find that Cu is the symbol for copper, S for sulfur, and O for oxygen. You already know that H_2O is water. The group of atoms SO_4 is called a sulfate group, and the compound is named copper sulfate. This compound is a blue solid sometimes used to <u>exterminate</u>, or to kill, algae in ponds. Solid copper sulfate, however, also contains water molecules. For this reason, the formula also shows water, separated from the symbols for copper sulfate by a dot. The number 5 in front of the formula for water, which is called a **coefficient** (koh ə FISH ənt), indicates that 5 water molecules are attached to each unit of copper sulfate. Compounds that have water molecules attached to them are called **hydrated** compounds.

Chemical Equations

Besides being used to <u>denote</u>, or indicate, compounds in a shorthand form, chemical formulas are used in **chemical equations**. These equations are shorthand statements that show how elements and compounds react chemically with one another.

Look at the following chemical equation.

$$2Zn + O_2 \rightarrow 2ZnO$$

This equation for the formation of zinc oxide, a compound found in certain creams that protect the skin, contains much information. It says that two molecules of zinc, each of which has one atom, unite or react with one molecule of oxygen. The subscript 2 tells you that each molecule of oxygen is composed of two atoms of oxygen. The combination of these three molecules (two zinc plus one oxygen) forms two molecules of zinc oxide. The arrow is the symbol for *yields* or *forms*.

The formula for zinc oxide (2ZnO) shows its chemical composition. Each molecule of zinc oxide (ZnO) is composed of one atom of zinc that has joined with one atom of oxygen. The coefficient 2 tells you that two molecules of the compound are formed as a result of the chemical reaction.

The substances on the left side of the arrow are called **reactants** (ree AK tənts) because they chemically react, or combine, with one another. The substance to the right of the arrow is called the **product** because it is produced by the reaction. Coefficients are used so that the number of each type of atom is the same on both sides of the equation. Using coefficients balances the equation.

Here is a more complicated equation.

$$6CO_2 + 6H_2O \rightarrow C_6H_{12}O_6 + 6O_2$$

This equation is for the formation of glucose, a simple sugar. The equation is read as follows: six molecules of carbon dioxide (CO_2) unite with six molecules of water (H_2O) to produce one molecule of glucose ($C_6H_{12}O_6$) and six molecules of oxygen (O_2). This equation involves two products as well as two reactants. In addition, the reactants are both molecules of compounds rather than atoms, or molecules of elements.

In the previous examples, small molecules interact and unite into larger molecules; such equations represent **synthesis reactions**. A chemical equation can also show how a large molecule is <u>decomposed</u>, or broken down, into smaller ones. This is called a **decomposition reaction**. As an example, the following equation shows what happens when an electric current is passed through water. Two molecules of water are broken down to form two molecules of hydrogen gas and one molecule of oxygen gas.

$$2H_2O \rightarrow 2H_2 + O_2$$

Scientists use symbols for elements and for the interactions between elements. By grouping symbols, scientists can write chemical formulas and equations that communicate information more precisely and quickly than words alone. Because chemical symbols are the same in all languages, formulas and equations can be understood by scientists everywhere, and ideas and discoveries can be easily communicated.

Recalling details
1. What is the function of a subscript in a chemical formula?

It tells the number of atoms of an element present

in a molecule or compound.

Recalling details
2. What is a chemical equation?

It is a group of formulas and symbols representing how

elements and compounds interact to form new substances.

Recalling details
3. What is a balanced equation?

It is one with the same number of atoms of each

element on either side of the arrow.

Recalling details
4. What is a decomposition reaction?

It is a reaction in which a large molecule is broken

down into smaller molecules.

Recalling details
5. What is a hydrated compound?

It is a compound that has one or more water molecules

attached to it.

Recalling details
6. What are the reactants in a chemical equation?

They are the elements and/or compounds that

chemically combine to form a new compound.

Using context clues
7. Complete each sentence by filling in the correct word from the list below.

diverse denote exterminate decomposed

a. A sign showing a cigarette with a diagonal line over it is used to _____denote_____ an area where smoking is not allowed.

b. Poisons are used to _____exterminate_____ pests.

c. There were many _____diverse_____ types of books on the shelves.

d. The wet paper _____decomposed_____ while the dry paper did not break down into pieces.

Circle the letter of the correct answer.

Making inferences
1. The number of atoms in H_2SO_4 (sulfuric acid) is _____.
   a. 6
   b. 4
   c. 7 (circled)

Making inferences
2. The balanced equation for the formation of NaCl (sodium chloride, or table salt) is _____.
   a. $Na + Cl_2 \rightarrow NaCl$
   b. $2Na + Cl_2 \rightarrow NaCl$
   c. $2Na + Cl_2 \rightarrow 2NaCl$ (circled)

Making inferences
3. The hydrated compound in this list is _____.
   a. H_2O
   b. NaOH
   c. $Na_2CO_3 \cdot 10H_2O$ (circled)

Making inferences
4. In the equation $2H_2O \rightarrow 2H_2 + O_2$, the coefficients are _____.
   a. the 2's in front of the H's (circled)
   b. the 2's under the H's
   c. the 2's under the H's and the 2 under the O

1. For each compound listed below, identify the elements and give the number of atoms for each element. The first one is done for you.

H_3PO_4
hydrogen phosphate

3 hydrogen

1 phosphorus

4 oxygen

Na_2O
sodium oxide

2 sodium

1 oxygen

$CaCl_2$
calcium chloride

1 calcium

2 chlorine

Fe_2O_3
iron oxide

2 iron

3 oxygen

SiO_2
silicon dioxide

1 silicon

2 oxygen

$CaSO_4$
calcium sulfate

1 calcium

1 sulfur

4 oxygen

2. Write the formulas for and name the chemical compounds described below. Use the table on page 156 to help you.

1 sodium

1 fluorine
NaF

sodium fluoride

1 potassium

1 nitrogen

2 oxygen
KNO_2

potassium nitrate

2 hydrogen

1 carbon

3 oxygen
H_2CO_3

hydrogen carbonate

1 sodium

1 nitrogen

3 oxygen
$NaNO_3$

sodium nitrate

3 potassium

1 phosphorus

4 oxygen
K_3PO_4

potassium phosphate

1 potassium

1 chlorine

3 oxygen
$KClO_3$

potassium chlorate

3. Add coefficients on the lines in the equations below to make balanced equations.

__2__ K + H_2SO_4 → K_2SO_4 + H_2

H_2CO_3 + __2__ NaOH → Na_2CO_3 + $2H_2O$

N_2 + __3__ H_2 → __2__ NH_3

CCl_4 + O_2 → CO_2 + __2__ Cl_2

▶ **Real Life Connections** Look up the symbols or equations for some of the foods that you eat daily, such as salt, sugar, soda water (used in soft drinks).

Equations

__ Reading a Mathematics Selection __

► Background Information

Algebra is becoming more and more important in school and in the workplace. This is because it is such a useful tool for finding out unknown facts from facts that are known. If you are able to set up the facts in an equation, that means you have understood a basic relationship among the facts that you know and the information you need to know. Your ability to analyze information in this way will help develop your reasoning skills in general.

In fact, algebra has come to be regarded as a primary means of gaining better jobs. Many jobs, whether factory or office work, now require the understanding of relationships among numbers and facts that is a major focus of algebra. The famous Algebra Project, founded some years ago by the civil rights activist, Robert Moses, has helped many inner-city youths find better careers.

This selection deals with one of the basic skills in algebra, reading and solving equations.

► Skill Focus

When you solve a word problem in mathematics, you use a plan for a solution that is stated in the form of a mathematical sentence, or **equation**. Equations used in problem solving involve unknown numbers, which are represented by letters called **variables,** such as *x, n, A,* or *t.* A variable is a symbol for a number whose value can vary. To solve the equations, you must find numbers to assign to the variables.

You can solve most simple equations by using the operations opposite to the ones shown in the equation. You subtract the number that is being added in the equation and divide by the number that multiplies the variable. A simple equation that is formed by subtraction can be solved by addition. An equation that uses division can be solved by multiplication.

Problems in algebra often involve equations that either include negative numbers or that have negative numbers as the solution. You can solve these equations in the same way as other simple equations. Just keep in mind the methods of adding, subtracting, multiplying, and dividing negative numbers.

► Word Clues

The word *equation* comes from the word *equal;* an equation is a statement in which two numbers or quantities are equal. Two equations that are **equivalent** have the same solution. *Equivalent* means "equal valued." The equations $n + 2 = 5$ and $n = 3$ are not the same, but they are equivalent because n has the same value in each of them. Therefore, the equivalent equation $n = 3$ is called the **solution** to the original equation, $n + 2 = 5$.

► Strategy Tip

As you read each equation in the following selection, notice the signs of operation: addition, subtraction, multiplication, and division. Also be alert for negative numbers in equations. Learning how to use them is essential in doing algebra. The more you understand the different parts of algebra, the more you will be able to use it.

Reading Equations

The plan for solving many word problems includes one or more **equations**, depending on the number of steps in the problem. An equation is a statement that two numbers or quantities are equal. The branch of mathematics that includes solving equations is called **algebra**.

In algebra, equations use various letters, such as N, x, y, or p, as **variables**. The object of solving equations is to find the numerical values of the variables. A solution to an equation, then, is found when an **equivalent** equation is produced. An equivalent equation shows the variable isolated, or set apart, on one side of an equation and a number on the other, such as $N = 3$. In other words, the equation is true when N has the value 3. Equations are equivalent when the same variable in both has the same value. Read the following problem.

Calvin is 4 years older than twice his sister's age. If Calvin is 16, how old is his sister?

You need to write two different expressions that describe Calvin's age and then combine the expressions into an equation. (An equation states that two expressions are equal.) The solution to the equation will be an equivalent equation that tells his sister's age.

Let x equal the sister's age. The two expressions for Calvin's age are $2x + 4$ (4 years older than twice his sister's age) and 16. Therefore, the equation is as follows.

$$2x + 4 = 16$$

To solve the equation, first subtract the number that was added, 4, from both sides of the equation.

$$2x + 4 - 4 = 16 - 4$$
$$2x + 0 = 12$$

Then divide both sides by the number, 2, that is used as a **factor**. Factors are numbers that form a product when multiplied together. Here, 2 is a number that is multiplied by x, the variable, to produce the product 12. So you divide both sides by 2.

$$\frac{2x + 0}{2} = \frac{12}{2}$$
$$x = 6$$

These two steps produce an equivalent equation of the following form: $x =$ "some number."

The equation $x = 6$ is equivalent to the original equation, but it is in a form that directly tells you the value of x. Therefore, Calvin's sister is 6 years old.

Read the following problem.

Lucia told Carlos that if it were three times as cold as the thermometer showed and then got one degree colder, or $-1°$, it would be ten degrees below zero, or $-10°$. What was the temperature?

An equation with negative numbers is solved in the same way as any other simple equation. When a negative number is added to the product, the effect is the same as subtraction. So $3x + (-1) = -10$ is the same as $3x - 1 = -10$. In this case, the equation is as follows.

$$3x - 1 = -10$$
$$3x - 1 + 1 = -10 + 1$$
$$3x = -9$$
$$x = -3$$

The thermometer showed 3 degrees below zero, or $-3°$.

Read the following problem.

If Mei-yu used to have five times as many trading cards as she now has plus three more, she would have the same number of cards as if she had three times as many cards plus five more. How many cards does she have now?

Let x equal the number of cards now. The equation is as follows.

$$5x + 3 = 3x + 5$$

First you can subtract $3x$ from each side of the equation to get the variable expressions all on one side.

$$5x - 3x + 3 = 3x - 3x + 5$$
$$2x + 3 = 5$$
$$2x + 3 - 3 = 5 - 3$$
$$2x = 2$$
$$x = 1$$

Mei-yu has only one trading card now.

RECALLING FACTS

Recalling details
1. What is an equation?
An equation is a statement in which two numbers or quantities are equal.

Recalling details
2. When is a solution to an equation found?
A solution is found when an equivalent equation is produced.

Recalling details
3. What is another way of writing $1x$**?** x

Recognizing sequences of events
4. If two expressions with variables occur on different sides of an equation, what should your first step be in solving the equation?
Apply an expression to both sides of the equation that will eliminate the variable on one side.

Recalling details
5. What is the difference between $5 + (-3)$ **and** $5 - 3$**? Explain.**
The two expressions are the same because adding a negative number is the same as subtracting that number.

INTERPRETING FACTS

Making inferences
1. To solve the equation $3x = 12$**, would you multiply or divide both sides of the equation?**
          divide   **By what number?**   3

Making inferences
2. To solve the equation $-4x = -32$**, would you multiply or divide both sides of the equation?**
          divide   **By what number?**   -4

Making inferences
3. Suppose you multiply both sides of an equation by two different numbers. Why does this result in an equation that is not equivalent to the original equation?
Because the expressions are supposed to be equal in the original equation, multiplying the two sides by

different numbers results in unequal expressions.

SKILL FOCUS

Solve each equation. Use the space to the right of each equation to work it out.

1. $x + 7 = 10$

$x = 3$

2. $x - 3 = 15$

$x = 18$

3. $7x = 56$

$x = 8$

4. $4x - 12 = 24$

$x = 9$

5. $x - 9 = -2$

$x = 7$

6. $3x + 3 = 12$

$x = 3$

7. $3x + 15 = 12$

$x = -1$

8. $25 = 39 - 2x$

$x = 7$

9. $x + 8 = 15$

$x = 7$

10. $4x + 6 = 22$

$x = 4$

11. $3x - 7 = 23$

$x = 10$

12. $42 - x = 28$

$x = 14$

13. $16 = 24 - x$

$x = 8$

14. $65 = 75 - 2x$

$x = 5$

15. $5x + 4 = -21$

$x = -5$

16. $9 = -6 + 5x$

$x = 3$

17. $3x + 4x = 49$

$x = 7$

18. $5x - x = 24$

$x = 6$

19. $-24 = 7x - x$

$x = -4$

20. $8x - 3x = 20$

$x = 4$

21. $5x + 7 = 3x - 5$

$x = -6$

22. $x - 5 = 3x - 1$

$x = -2$

23. $5x + 3 = 2x - 9$

$x = -4$

24. $24 = 16 + 4x$

$x = 2$

25. $-12 = 2x - 2$

$x = -5$

26. $3x + 3 = x + 9$

$x = 3$

27. $10x + 1 = 8x - 3$

$x = -2$

28. $x - 7 = 2x - 17$

$x = 10$

29. $-25 = 5x + 10$

$x = -7$

30. $6x - 1 = x + 4$

$x = 1$

▶ **Real Life Connections** In your own words, explain to a partner the meaning of *equation* and *equivalent equation*. Then see if together you can set up and solve an equation based on a real-life situation, where you know certain facts and want to find out other facts.

Lesson 43

Inferences

Sometimes you can **infer**, or figure out, information that is not stated directly in a selection.

Read the following selection about two female pioneers.

Pioneers in the Sky

In 1948, Blanche Stuart Scott made history. She was the first woman to fly as a passenger in a jet airplane. But this was only the latest in a lifetime of firsts. She was born in 1892 to a prominent family in Rochester, New York. Always adventurous, she became an expert ice skater and took up bicycling as a trick rider. As a teenager, she terrorized Rochester with one of her first automobiles. When she was about 18, she became the first car saleswoman in New York. Soon after, she persuaded an auto manufacturer to sponsor her to be the first woman to drive cross-country. The year was 1910, and there were only 218 miles of paved roads in the United States!

On her trip across the country, she saw a demonstration flight by Orville Wright and one of his students. She was captivated by the idea of flying, and by October of that year she was the first woman to become a professional pilot. In those days, most planes were flown around a field in exhibitions. One day, angry at her boss, she made a 60-mile round trip to another town and back. Newspapers called it the first long-distance flight by a woman. In 1919, as part of Glenn Martin's Flying Circus, she agreed to test new airplanes that Martin built. Blanche Stuart Scott was the first woman test pilot.

Christa McAuliffe never dreamed of glory, but of what she could do for others. Described by a friend as "your basic, ordinary person," McAuliffe was a mother, a wife, and a dedicated social studies teacher from Concord, New Hampshire. Then, on July 19, 1985, Vice President George Bush named 36-year-old McAuliffe to be the "first private citizen passenger in the history of space flight." Overcome by such an honor, she deftly commented, "It's not often that a teacher is at a loss for words." Overnight, the name Christa McAuliffe became known, and America's schoolchildren were filled with pride and anticipation.

In preparation for her journey into space on the spaceship *Challenger*, McAuliffe trained for many months. While in space, she was to broadcast two live lessons on television to the nation's schoolchildren.

Finally, on January 28, 1986, after several days of poor weather conditions, the *Challenger* took off. But 73 seconds after takeoff, the spacecraft exploded, killing all seven members, including the popular social studies teacher who, nevertheless, was a pioneer in the frontier of space.

Put a check mark next to each of the statements below that can be inferred.

Blanche Stuart Scott

✔ Blanche Stuart Scott loved adventure.

✔ Cross-country travel was difficult for anyone in 1910.

___ It was easy to learn how to fly in the old days.

Christa McAuliffe

✔ Christa McAuliffe accomplished much in her life.

___ Only trained astronauts should travel in space.

✔ Christa McAuliffe served as a model for America's schoolchildren.

164 Lesson 43 *Making inferences*

Cause and Effect

Many ideas that you read about in textbooks are connected by **cause and effect**. A cause is an underlying reason, condition, or situation that makes something happen. An effect is the result or outcome of a cause. Several causes can bring about a single effect, and several effects can result from a single cause.

Causes and effects are usually directly stated in a selection. Sometimes, however, you have to infer, or figure out, a cause or an effect.

As you read the selection, try to understand how the ideas are connected. Think about both the causes and the effects of particular actions.

The Great Blackout

At 5:15 P.M. on November 9, 1965, the lights suddenly went out—first in Toronto, next in Boston, and then in New York City. Before anyone knew what was going on, 30 million people in eight states and some of Canada were in the dark. It was the greatest blackout in history.

Somewhere north of New York City, the complex power network that supplies electricity to the Northeast broke down. Nobody is sure exactly how the power failure happened. A big city's rush hour demands extra power. During such periods of high demand, a power system may not be able to supply enough power, and it borrows power from a neighboring system. That is what the power systems of the Northeastern net did on the day of the blackout. Even with borrowing, however, the failing systems could not generate enough power.

Linked to the net and guided by computers, each electric system began to fight for more electricity. A chain effect followed. After trying to borrow power from neighboring systems and finding none, each system was forced to shut off its power, resulting in a blackout. Toronto failed at 5:15 P.M., Rochester at 5:18 P.M., and Boston at 5:21 P.M.

Within minutes, all the communities still connected to the net were drawing on one system, Consolidated Edison, a giant utility serving New York City and Westchester County. During the rush hour, Consolidated Edison usually transmitted 300,000 kilowatts

New York shown during a power failure; the building lit is a hospital with emergency generators.

into New York City to run elevators, commuter trains and subway cars, electric stoves, and television sets. On the day of the blackout, Con Ed pumped that power out to other systems. Within minutes, automatic safety devices stopped the straining Con Ed generators.

At 5:28 P.M., New York elevators stopped hustling thousands of people to the streets. Those inside were stuck—joking, singing, and fortunately not panicking. Many people who hadn't yet embarked on elevators walked down many flights of stairs in the dark or by the light of matches.

Commuters on the streets, in subways, and in airplanes immediately felt the impact of the blackout. Because drivers had to drive without traffic signals and street lights, police set out flares on busy highways. Commuter trains couldn't leave the stations without power, and stranded, tired riders ended up sleeping in their seats. One by one, police and firefighters led

600,000 to 800,000 people who were stuck on subways from the cars' emergency exits. By midnight, 90% of the subway riders were out.

Because stranded people grew exhausted as the dark night wore on, they flopped down on hotel lobby chairs and floors. Some weary commuters even slept in reclining barbershop chairs. Luckily, there were no aviation disasters; the moon was bright and airport personnel guided every plane to a safe landing.

People remained calm and an air of cheerfulness prevailed as everyone listened to battery-powered radios. Radio stations switched to emergency generators, so they stayed on the air with continuous coverage. Television stations required too much power to transmit.

The 1965 Northeast blackout became a perfect story for people to tell their yet unborn grandchildren one day.

Answer the following questions based on the many cause and effect relationships described in the selection.

1. Give two effects for each cause listed below.
   a. Cause Elevators hustling thousands of people to the street suddenly stalled.
   Effect The people inside the elevator were stuck.

   Effect Those who hadn't yet gotten on the elevators had to walk down the stairs.

   b. Cause Stranded people grew exhausted as the dark night wore on.
   Effect They flopped down on hotel lobby chairs and floors.

   Effect Some slept in reclining barbershop chairs.

2. Give two causes for each effect listed below.
   a. Cause The moon was bright.

   Cause Airport personnel guided every plane to a safe landing.

   Effect There were no aviation disasters.
   b. Cause They were not connected to the net.

   Cause They cut themselves off from the net before other systems borrowed from them.

   Effect Some communities were able to maintain power.

3. When effects are not directly stated, they have to be inferred, or figured out. Answer each of the following questions by inferring an effect.
   a. What would happen if people continued to use more and more electrical appliances and neglected to turn them off when they were not in use?
   Sources of power would be stretched to the limit, and more blackouts or brownouts would occur.

   b. What would happen if the whole country were eventually hooked together in one power network and a failure occurred in one system?
   A blackout could spread across the entire United States.

   c. How could a power company conserve energy for a short period without totally inconveniencing users of electricity?
   It could reduce the supply of electricity to a certain area during a time when people's needs are less.

Synonyms and Antonyms

The word *synonym* comes from two Greek word parts, *syn* meaning together and *onyma* meaning a name. A **synonym** is a word having the same or nearly the same meaning as another word. For example, *hurry* is a synonym for *rush*.

The word *antonym* comes from two Greek word parts, *anti* meaning opposite and *onyma* meaning a name. An **antonym** is a word that is opposite in meaning to another word. As an example, *clear* is an antonym of *muddy*.

A. Underline the word that is the best synonym of the italicized word. If you do not know the meaning of the word, look it up in a dictionary.

1. *pledge*
   a. vote   c. joke
   b. promise   d. wealth

2. *brood*
   a. flock   c. stream
   b. alloy   d. jewelry

3. *skeptic*
   a. bones   c. instrument
   b. doubter   d. measurement

4. *client*
   a. noise   c. smartness
   b. slogan   d. customer

5. *uncouth*
   a. divide   c. open
   b. careless   d. crude

6. *relic*
   a. relief   c. remains
   b. satisfaction d. happiness

7. *spontaneous*
   a. expressed c. dependent
   b. clean   d. automatic

8. *accessible*
   a. entrance   c. available
   b. occupied   d. agreeable

B. Underline the word that is the best antonym of the italicized word. If you do not know the meaning of the word, look it up in a dictionary.

1. *dominant*
   a. humble   c. tired
   b. aggressive d. unclear

2. *retired*
   a. quiet   c. respond
   b. arrive   d. working

3. *migratory*
   a. mild   c. permanent
   b. seasonal   d. plain

4. *amateur*
   a. vagueness   c. beginner
   b. professional d. affectionate

5. *typical*
   a. usual   c. exceptional
   b. powerless d. copied

6. *likely*
   a. probable   c. admire
   b. overdo   d. impossible

7. *valiant*
   a. fearlessly c. miserly
   b. cowardly   d. blooming

8. *chronic*
   a. temporary c. classified
   b. persistent d. kindness

Analogies

An **analogy** is a comparison. It shows that a relationship between one pair of words is similar to the relationship between another pair of words. For example, the relationship between *apple* and *fruit* is similar to the relationship between *spinach* and *vegetable*. In other words, an apple is a kind of fruit, as spinach is a kind of vegetable.

One way to express an analogy is to use words.

Apple is to *fruit* as *spinach* is to *vegetable*.

Another way to express an analogy is to use dots for the words *is to* (:) and *as* (::).

apple : fruit :: spinach : vegetable

Each word pair in this analogy contains a specific item and the category to which it belongs. Other relationships can show cause and effect (such as earthquake : destruction :: germ : disease) or part to whole (knob : door :: handlebar : bike).

Read the incomplete analogies below. On the first line provided, write the word that completes the analogy. Then, on the line at the right, identify the analogy as either *cause and effect, part to whole,* or *category.*

1. chill : cold :: exhaustion : _____sleep_____   cause and effect
   a. tired   **b.** trip   **c.** doctor   **d.** sleep

2. sleeves : shirt :: wings : _____airplane_____   part to whole
   a. engine   **b.** airplane   **c.** flying   **d.** clothes

3. purple : color :: dogwood : _____tree_____   category
   a. animal   **b.** lilac   **c.** tree   **d.** green

4. attic : house :: finger : _____hand_____   part to whole
   a. hand   **b.** toe   **c.** nail   **d.** basement

5. drawers : bureau :: spokes : _____wheel_____   part to whole
   a. bristles   **b.** bedroom   **c.** clothes   **d.** wheel

6. sweater : clothing :: dictionary : _____book_____   category
   a. book   **b.** library   **c.** store   **d.** encyclopedia

7. bath : relaxing :: shower : _____invigorating_____   cause and effect
   a. clean   **b.** invigorating   **c.** towel   **d.** water

8. iris : eye :: stem : _____flower_____   part to whole
   a. leaf   **b.** flower   **c.** pupil   **d.** summer

9. canary : bird :: poodle : _____dog_____   category
   a. mammal   **b.** dog   **c.** breed   **d.** collie

Lesson 47

Improving Reading Rate

A good reader is able to read at several speeds, depending on the material being read. When reading difficult or unfamiliar material, a good reader reads slowly. For example, social studies, science, mathematics, and poetry may be more difficult to read than most stories. So these materials are read more slowly. Even some literary selections can be difficult. Sometimes it is necessary to reread a paragraph to understand a complex idea. A good reader slows down when words or sentences are difficult or unfamiliar. A good reader also stops to read diagrams and maps, which require increased attention and make a slower reading rate necessary.

The following selection can be used to check your reading rate. Use a watch or a clock with a second hand to time yourself. Start right on a minute, such as five minutes past ten o'clock. Write your starting time at the beginning of the selection, and then read the selection. Write your ending time at the end of the selection.

Starting time ———————————

A Spear for Omar

Twelve-year-old Omar knelt at the bottom of a small dugout canoe and let his hand drift in the balmy water of the Red Sea. He loved this hour of the day. It usually made him feel peaceful and happy. Today, however, there was no peace in Omar's heart, for he had failed again.

Omar's father was the best at spear fishing from Suez all the way down to Port Sudan. Omar's brother, Abdel, promised to be as excellent as his father. At 15, Abdel was already exceptionally skillful with the spear and fearless in skin diving.

Abdel went to the sea daily with his father, and his catch contributed much to the support of the family. Omar accompanied his father and brother each day. He did whatever he could to help, but he had not yet learned how to spear fish. He was even afraid to dive. Abdel poked fun at his fear of drowning.

Omar's father was more understanding. "You'll learn in time," he said to Omar, "and when you do, I'll give you a beautiful spear of your own."

Yet this night, as the three rowed home, the spear seemed very far off. As usual, Omar had failed miserably in his diving. He was discouraged and deeply troubled.

The next morning, Abdel and Omar traveled to the sea alone. Abdel gripped his heavy spear immediately, shot far down into the water, and came back with an unusually large fish.

Lesson 47 *Improving reading rate* **169**

"How about you coming down?" he asked Omar.

"I will, I will in a minute," replied Omar a bit unwillingly as Abdel plunged down for another fish.

Suddenly Omar became aware of something happening. As he looked to the right, a huge shark emerged from the deep water and began circling the boat. Omar scanned the clear deep water for his brother. About 15 feet below, half hidden by a ridge in a coral reef, was Abdel.

Omar uttered a cry of horror. His brother's hand had been caught in the jaws of a mammoth clam, and he was trying desperately to free himself.

Omar felt his mouth go dry as he fearfully lowered himself into the water. He did not turn his head when the shark moved in closer. Without any outward sign of his deadly fear, he plunged straight downward.

Never before had Omar dived so deep as that, and he felt as if his lungs would burst. For a second, everything looked black. Then he saw his brother in front of him with his hand in the clam's jaws. Abdel, almost out of breath, looked at Omar with horror-stricken eyes.

Omar acted quickly. With deft fingers, he pried the stubborn clam loose from the coral. He left it attached to Abdel's hand because he didn't want to waste precious time.

The monstrous shark swam toward them. Trying to ignore the great fish, Omar grabbed Abdel by the armpits and started upward. Suddenly the shark's murderous yellow eyes seemed to focus directly at Omar. The shark came in closer, its powerful, fanlike fins almost brushing against Omar.

In desperation, Omar did what his father had taught him to do in such an emergency. He let go of Abdel with his right hand and slapped the shark across its pointed nose. Relentlessly he struck again and again.

For a long moment, the shark seemed stunned. Then it churned about in confusion, finally turning toward the deep water.

Omar grabbed Abdel with both hands again, swam swiftly to the top, and pushed him into the canoe. He whipped out a knife with a strong handle and chipped away sections of the shell. Abdel winced with pain, but Omar worked feverishly until he pried the clam open.

"It's only a flesh wound and will heal rapidly," Omar said. He wrapped his dry shirt around Abdel's arm to stop the bleeding. Abdel opened his eyes weakly and smiled at Omar with gratitude and admiration.

"Thank you, my brother," he said. "Thank you."

The next morning, when Omar awoke, he discovered a spear next to his sleeping mat. His father stood looking down at him, with warm approval and affection in his eyes. Omar jumped to his feet, gripping the spear tightly in his hand.

"You will be fine at spear fishing, my son," his father said. Omar lowered his head, a great surge of happiness rising through him.

To find the total time it took you to read the selection, do the following: (1) Subtract your starting time from your ending time. (2) Divide the number of words in the selection by the remainder expressed in seconds.

If it took you 4 minutes and 3 seconds (4 × 60 + 3 = 243 seconds) to read the selection, you would have read 3 words per second (729 ÷ 243 = 3). (3) To find the number of words per minute (WPM), multiply your rate per second by 60. Your answer would be 180 WPM.

Words in selection: 729

	Hr.	Min.	Sec.
Ending time:	_____	_____	_____
Starting time:	_____	_____	00
Total time:	_____	_____	_____

$$\frac{\text{No. words: } 729}{\text{No. seconds: \_\_\_\_\_}} = \frac{\quad}{\quad} \times 60 = \_\_\_\_\_ \text{ WPM}$$

To check your understanding of the selection, underline the answer to each question.

1. What is the setting of this selection?
   a. the Red Sea
   b. the Suez Canal
   c. Port Sudan

2. Why was Omar discouraged at the beginning of this selection?
   a. His father had poked fun at him.
   b. He had caught only a few small fish.
   c. He had failed in skin diving.

3. What promise did Omar's father make?
   a. He promised to teach Omar to swim.
   b. He promised to take Omar to the city for a week of sightseeing.
   c. He promised to give Omar a spear of his own one day.

4. How did Omar know there was a shark in the area?
   a. Omar could see the shark 15 feet down in the water.
   b. The shark began circling the boat.
   c. His brother warned Omar of the shark.

5. Why didn't Abdel return to the boat?
   a. His hand was caught in the jaws of a clam.
   b. He was busy spearing a large fish.
   c. He thought he should stay hidden in the coral reef until the shark went away.

6. What did Omar do when he reached Abdel?
   a. He gave Abdel a supply of oxygen.
   b. He pried the clam loose from the coral.
   c. He took a knife and cut the coral loose.

7. How did Omar deal with the shark?
   a. He attacked the shark with his knife.
   b. He ignored the shark, and it swam away.
   c. He kept slapping the shark across the nose.

8. Why did Omar wait until he and Abdel were in the boat before he cut away the clam?
   a. Abdel might have drowned before Omar could have freed his hand.
   b. Abdel told Omar to wait until they were away from the shark.
   c. Omar knew that the clam would open easily when it was out of the water.

9. How did Omar know that he had become a skillful diver?
   a. He discovered a spear next to his sleeping mat.
   b. His brother invited Omar to go deep-sea fishing with him.
   c. His father let him take the dugout canoe by himself.

Using an Index

The quickest way to find specific information in a text or reference book is to use the **index**. An index alphabetically lists the important topics of the book. The index is usually located at the end of a text or reference book.

On the next page is part of an index from a world history textbook. Look at the index, and find the main topic or entry **Agriculture**. The subtopics that follow the entry are arranged chronologically, that is, in the order in which they happened. This kind of arrangement is common to history books since the contents of such books are usually arranged chronologically. In this entry, for example, the most recent event in agriculture, the Green Revolution, is listed last.

The numbers after each topic or subtopic are the page numbers on which related information is found. Numbers separated by dashes indicate that the information begins on the page before the dash and ends on the page after the dash. Numbers separated by commas show that information appears only on the pages for which numbers are given. Study the index on the next page. Then answer the questions on the lines provided.

1. On which page(s) would you find information about the Alliance for Progress? __646, 718__

2. How many subtopics are listed under the topic Architecture? __9__

3. On which page(s) would you find information about Konrad Adenauer? __631, 635–36__

4. How many pages does the book have on Arabic numerals? __5__

5. On which page(s) would you find information about the Algonquin Indians? __318__

6. On which page(s) would you find a map of Albania? __548, 610, 760__

7. What four subtopics are listed after the topic *Alexander the Great*? __Aristotle and, conquests,__ successors, Hellenistic culture and

8. On which page(s) would you find information on the American Revolution? __369, 371–72, 527__

9. On which page(s) would you find a picture of Greek architecture? __80__

10. On which page(s) would you find a picture of Ajanta? __153__

11. If you wanted information about agriculture in medieval Europe, which page(s) would you not read between 175 and 180? __176, 179__

12. Which topic comes between *Appeasement* and *Apprentice*? __Appian Way__

13. On which page(s) would you find a chart about agriculture in developing countries? __742__

14. On which page(s) would you find a footnote about annulment? __297__

15. If the book had information about Samuel Adams, after which topic would it be listed? __Act of Union__

16. If the book had information about Susan B. Anthony, before which topic would it be listed? __Anthropology__

17. On which page(s) would you find a map of the climate in Africa? __240, 756__

INDEX

Italicized page numbers refer to illustrations. The *m*, *c*, or *p* preceding the number refers to a map (*m*), chart (*c*), or picture (*p*) on that page. An *n* following a page number refers to a footnote.

Abbassid dynasty, *m232,* 233
Abraham, 230
Absolute monarch, 326, 331, 334, 337, 341, 352, 377
Abstract expressionism, 749
Abu Bakr, 232
Achaean civilization, *m82,* 82–85, 111
Acre, *m196,* 198
Acropolis, *p80,* 85, 92, 93, 97, 100
Actium, battle of, 122
Act of Settlement, 367, *c368*
Act of Supremacy, 297
Act of Toleration, 366
Act of Union, *m367,* 367
Addams, Jane, 462
Adelaide, 208
Adenauer, Konrad, 631, 635–36
Adowa, battle of, 494, *p494*
Adrianople, battle of, 138–39
Aegean Sea, 81, *m82*
Aeneid (Virgil), 110–11, 131
Aeschylus, 98
Afghanistan, 669, *m690;* Soviet invasion of, 690, 728, 730, 733; today, *m759*
Africa, *m758;* climate, 239, *m240,* 241, 655–56, *m756;* diseases, 239, 491, *p660;* geography, 241; early peoples, 241; empires, 242–43, *m243,* 244–46; Asians in, 245, 581, 662; Portuguese explorations, 305, *m306,* 320, 489; Age of Imperialism, 488, 489, *m490,* 502, 651; explorations of interior, 491, *p504;* colonial rule, 502–5, 651; World War I, 556, 561, 583; mandates, 583; nationalists, 583, 650–52; new nations, 650–54, *m653;* UN and, 651, 652, 654, 664; cold war and, 651–52, 664–65; colonial heritage, 655; economic development, 655–56, 664; social change, 656–57, *p656,* 657, 658, 660, 662; education, *p505,* 656–57; political stability, 657–58; today, 664–66, 730. See *also* East Africa; North Africa; South Africa; West Africa.
Afrikaner, 662, 663
Agamemnon, 83, *p84,* 98
Age grade, 246
Age of Exploration, 303, *m306,* 321–22
Age of Imperialism, 486–87, 489, *m490,* 491, 503, 504,

508, *m510, m515, m538,* 651, 671
Agra, 261, *m261, c750*
Agricultural cooperatives, 661, 692
Agricultural revolution: in Neolithic Age, 22–23, 31; in Africa, 241; in Europe in 1700s, 411, 414–15, 421, 424
Agriculture: in New Stone Age, 22–24; Nile Valley, 30, *p41,* Mesopotamia, 48, 50, 52; Indus Valley, 65; Greek, 81, 87; Roman, 111, 112, 119, 125, 175; in medieval Europe, 175, 177–78, 180, 213; Islamic, 233; in New World, 251, 255; Chinese, 265, 266; Japanese, 269; Renaissance, 291; Russian, 477–78; after World War I, 574, *p575;* in USSR, 589–90, 591–92; African, 655–56, 661; Middle Eastern, 669, 672, 681; Indian, 688; in Communist China, 692; in Latin America, 707, 708, 715, 716–17; in developing countries, *c742,* 742–43; Green Revolution, 743–44, *c744,* 750
Ahriman, 56
Ahura Mazda, 56
Aiken, Howard, 738
Aircraft, airplanes, 553, 625; medieval drawings, 194, 195; Wright brothers flight, 420; Lindbergh flight, 566–67; passenger service, 566, 570–71; in World War II, 612–13, 614, 616, 621–22, 623
Aix-la-Chapelle, treaty of, 338
Ajanta, *m151,* 153, *p153*
Akbar, Mogul emperor, 261, *p262*
Akenaton, Egyptian pharaoh, 39, 42
Akkadian Empire, 52
Alaric, Visigoth general, 139
Alaska, 457, 646, *m761*
Albania, *m548,* 549, *m610,* 633, *m760*
Albigensians, 181–82, 206–7
Albuquerque, Affonso de, 309
Alchemy, 194, *p348*
Alcuin, Anglo-Saxon monk, 168–69
Aldrin, Buzz, 737
Alexander I, czar of Russia, 393, 397, 398, 399, 478

Alexander II, czar of Russia, 478–79
Alexander III, czar of Russia, 479
Alexander the Great, 40, 52, 56, 103–7, *p105,* 111, 118; Aristotle and, 103, 104; conquests, 104–5, *m106,* 150; successors, 105, 106; Hellenistic culture and, 105–7
Alexandra, czarina of Russia, 587
Alexandria, 104–6, *m106,* 122, 129, 136
Algeria, 483, *m490,* 491, 493, 619, 620, *m653,* 726; French control, 493, 583; war in 1954, 637, 652; independence, 652
Algonquin Indians, 318
Alhambra Palace, *p211*
Ali, Muhammed, 492
Allah, 230
Allende, Salvador, 711–12, 718
Alliance for Progress, 646, 718
Allied Powers: World War I, 552, 554, *m555,* 555–56, 559, 589; World War II, 611, 618, 619, *m620,* 624, 628, 629
All Quiet on the Western Front (Remarque), 544–45, 571
Almoravids, 243
Alphabet: Phoenician, 57, 81, 85; Greek, 57, 81, 85; Roman, 57, 112; Slavic, 226. See *also* Writing.
Alps, 111, *m112,* 117, *m118, m760*
Alsace, 336, *m336,* 454
Alsace-Lorraine: German control of, 454, 473, *m473;* French control of, 545, 561, *m563*
Amaterasu, 270
Amazon River, *m250, p648–49, m761*
America, naming of, 308. See *also* North America; South America; Central America; Latin America.
American Revolution, 369, 371–72, 527
Amin, Idi, 658
Amon-Re, 32–33, 36, 39
Amorites, 52
Amritsar Massacre, 581
Amsterdam, 326, *m760*
Anabaptists, 297
Ancestor worship, 71, 72, 248, 271
Andean Common Market, 717
Andes Mountains, 255, *m761*
Andorra, *m760*
Angkor Wat, 521
Angles, *m139,* 167

Anglican Church. *See Church of England.*
Anglo-Saxons, 171, 203
Angola, *m653,* 654, 662, 730, *m758*
Anne, queen of England, 367
Annulment, 297, 297*n*
Anschluss, 608–9
Anthropology, 19, 24
Antigone (Sophocles), 96, 98
Antigonus, Macedonian general, 105
Antigua and Barbuda, *m761*
Antioch, *m106,* 136, *m196,* 197
Anti-Semitism: during Crusades, 199–200; in France, 455; nationalism and, 599. See *also* Jews.
Antony, Mark, 121–22
Antwerp, *m186,* 326
Anyang, 70, *m71,* 72, 73
Apartheid, 662, 663
Apennine Mountains, 111, *m112, m760*
Aphrodite, 97, 116
Apollo, 97
Apollo 10 and 11, 736, 737, 739
Appeasement, 609
Appian Way, 116
Apprentice, 188
Aqueduct, 130, *p130*
Aquitaine, 202, *m207*
Aquinas, Thomas, 194, 236
Arabian Desert, 47, *m48,* 669, *m675,* 744
Arabian Peninsula, *m759*
Arabian Sea, *m759*
Arabic language, 230, 234, 260
Arabic numerals, 153–54, 194, 234, 349
Arab-Israeli wars, 631, 677, 678, 681–83, *m682;* peace treaty, 683, *p683*
Arab oil embargo, 682, 699, 725, *c725,* 732
Arabs, Arabia, 229, *m232,* 483, 670; in World War II, 556; nationalism, 580, 581. See *also* Islam; Muslims.
Arafat, Yasir, 684
Aragon, 211, *m212*
Archaeology, 19–20
Archbishop, 135, 179
Archimedes, 107
Architecture: Egyptian, 37, 43; Sumerian, 51; Indian, *p65, p220–21,* 260, 261, *p262;* Greek, *p80,* 99–100, 108; Roman, 129; in Middle Ages, 189–90, *p190,* 191; Islamic, *p211,* 235; Renaissance, 285; in Europe in 1800s, 442–43
Archon, 87
Arctic Ocean, *m759*
Argentina: independence, 529, *m531,* 532; economy, 533–34, 537; since 1945,

Reading a Budget

A budget is a plan that shows how much money you will receive, or your income, and how much you will spend, or your expenses, in a given period. To plan a monthly budget, you must first know how much money you receive each month. Although you may receive more income by working overtime or getting a raise, your income usually doesn't change each month. Next you must figure out your expenses on a monthly basis.

Many expenses, such as rent, loan payments, and insurance payments, are the same each month; they are **fixed expenses**. Other fixed expenses, like electricity, may not be the same amount each month. However, you know when these costs must be paid and about how much they will be.

Other expenses may change each month; they are **variable expenses**. The cost of clothing, for example, is a variable expense because you may spend more on clothing in some months than in other months. To plan a budget, you must estimate, or guess the amount of, your variable expenses. The best way to estimate these expenses is to record how much they are for a few months and then find the average for one month. Last of all, you should determine how much money you can save each month. The amount you can save will vary from month to month also.

The following monthly budget shows how Wayne's income will be used during the month of May. Wayne shares an apartment with two friends, and he needs to budget his share of expenses along with his individual expenses. Study his budget carefully.

Wayne's Budget for May			
Fixed Expenses		**Variable Expenses**	
Rent ($\frac{1}{3}$ share)	$210.00	Gasoline & car repair	$85.00
Electricity ($\frac{1}{3}$ share)	22.00	Food ($\frac{1}{3}$ share)	120.00
Car loan payment	150.00	Telephone ($\frac{1}{3}$ share)	11.50
Car insurance	75.00	Clothing	60.00
Money owed to Dad	25.00	Summer swimming	
	$482.00	pool membership	50.00
		Entertainment	120.00
			$446.50
Total fixed expenses	$482.00	Monthly income after taxes	$1,007.25
Total variable expenses	+ 446.50	Monthly expenses	-928.50
Total monthly expenses	$928.50	Savings	$78.75

A. Fill in the circle next to the phrase or sentence that correctly answers each question.

1. How much money does Wayne receive each month?
- ○ $928.50
- ● $1,007.25
- ○ $482.00

2. What are some fixed expenses on Wayne's budget?
- ○ rent, telephone, and food
- ○ telephone, car loan payment, and gasoline
- ● rent, car loan payment, and electricity

3. Why is entertainment listed on the budget as a variable expense?
   - ● The amount spent on entertainment changes from one month to another.
   - ○ The same amount is spent on entertainment every month.
   - ○ Wayne spends a lot of money on entertainment.

4. How much money is Wayne planning to spend in May?
   - ○ $482.00   ○ $446.50   ● $928.50

5. What one expense does Wayne have in the month of May that he will probably not have in any other month of the year?
   - ○ clothing   ● swimming pool membership   ○ entertainment

6. What is the greatest single expense on the budget?
   - ● rent   ○ food   ○ fixed expenses

7. Why is Wayne able to save some money in May?
   - ● His total monthly expenses are less than his income.
   - ○ His fixed expenses are less than his income.
   - ○ His variable expenses are less than his income.

8. How much money can Wayne save in May?
   - ○ $928.50   ○ $446.50   ● $78.75

9. If Wayne's variable expenses for June are less than those for May, how will his June budget be affected?
   - ○ His fixed expenses will be greater.
   - ● He will be able to save more money than he did in May.
   - ○ He will save less money than he did in May.

B. Complete Wayne's budget for June by using the information from Wayne's May budget. Then answer the questions below the budget.

Wayne's Budget for June

Fixed Expenses		Variable Expenses	
Rent (1/3 share)	$210.00	Gasoline & car repair	$60.00
Electricity (1/3 share)	22.00	Food (1/3 share)	100.00
Car loan payment	150.00	Telephone (1/3 share)	13.00
Car insurance	75.00	Entertainment	80.00
Money owed to Dad	25.00	Dental check-up	45.00
	$482.00	CD player repair	85.00
			$383.00

Total fixed expenses	$482.00	Monthly income after taxes	1,007.25
Total variable expenses	+383.00	Monthly expenses	-865.00
Total monthly expenses	$865.00	Savings	$142.25

1. Which expenses stayed the same for both months? Why? Rent, electricity, car loan payment, car insurance, money owed stayed the same. They are fixed expenses.

2. In which month was Wayne able to save more money? Why? He saved more in June, because his monthly expenses were less than they were in May.

Context Clue Words

The following words are treated as context clue words in the lessons indicated. Lessons that provide instruction in a particular context clue type include an activity requiring students to use context clues to derive word meanings. Context clue words appear in the literature, social studies, and science selections and are underlined for ease of location.

Word	Lesson	Word	Lesson	Word	Lesson	Word	Lesson
acceleration	33	dwellings	11	labor force	24	sarcasm	1
alcoves	11	egotistical	16	mattock	1	seething	16
allotted	17	elixirs	23	modulated	12	segregated	18
alternating	12	elude	16	nomads	11	slanging	39
anteroom	10	emitted	12	nonchalantly	31	slate	17
applicants	24	environment	18	nonentity	16	speed	33
ascertain	25	esoteric	25	nostrums	23	stagnate	24
autres temps, autres moeurs	23	expedience	39	obligatory	17	subcommittee	32
beneficial	40	expended	3	overtly	31	surge	2
calculates	3	exterminate	41	pantomimed	1	susceptible	3
candor	31	farthingale	23	phosphates	39	synchronize	10
cessation	2	foraged	11	pigeonholed	32	synthesized	41
chaos	2	forecast	24	pomander	23	transmitted	25
ciphers	23	gauntlet	31	populations	40	underground	39
decomposed	41	genial	10	potentially	12	utmost	31
denote	41	habitat	40	preceding	3	valid	2
depleted	11	hoardings	39	procrastinating	10	velocity	33
designated	18	hopper	32	resemble	18	veto	32
diverse	41	imperative	25	reserves	40	warren	39
dulcimer	23	inbreeding	40	revoke	17		
		knoll	1	roentgen	39		

Concept Words

In lessons that feature social studies, science, or mathematics selections, words that are unique to the content and whose meanings are essential to the selection are treated as concept words. Many of these words appear in boldface type and are often followed by a phonetic respelling and a definition.

Word	Lesson	Word	Lesson	Word	Lesson	Word	Lesson
adobe	11	faulting	3	mano	11	right	19
aeronautical	25	first filial generation	18	mean	34	right angle	19
algebra	42	focus	3	measures of central		scalene	19
Anasazi	11	force	33	tendency	34	second filial generation	18
anatomists	25	frequency	12	median	34	seismograph	3
animal keepers	25	gamma rays	12	metate	11	seismologists	25
assayers	25	gem cutters	25	meteorologists	25	similar	19
astronomers	25	genes	18	microwaves	12	solution	42
astrophysicists	25	genetic counselors	25	mode	34	speech/language	
automotive engineers	25	genetics	18	molecule	41	pathologists	25
average	34	geologists	25	motion	33	speed	33
bimodal	34	-gon	19	nuclear physicists	25	statistics	34
botanists	25	heredity	18	opticians	25	stonemasons	25
bryologists	25	herpetologists	25	organic chemistry	25	structural engineers	25
cartographers	25	hertz	12	paleontologists	25	subscript	41
chance	26	hexa-	19	parental generation	18	sum	4
chemical equations	41	hexagon	19	penta-	19	surveyors	25
coefficient	41	hybrid	18	pentagon	19	synthesis reactions	41
compound	41	hydrated	41	per	4	technicians	25
congruent	19	hypotenuse	19	pharmacologists	25	tiltmeter	3
criminologists	25	ichthyologists	25	physical therapists	25	time zone	13
cytologists	25	incomplete dominance	18	physiologists	25	total	4
data	34	inertia	33	pithouses	11	transverse	12
decomposition reaction	41	infrared radiation	12	poly-	19	tree diagram	26
difference	4	inheritance	18	polygon	19	tri-	19
dominant	18	inverse	12	possibility	26	triangle	19
electromagnetic spectrum	12	isosceles	19	probability	26	tsunami	3
entire	4	kiva	11	product	41	ultraviolet waves	12
entomologists	25	laboratory technicians	25	pueblo	11	variables	42
epicenter	3	landscapers	25	Punnett square	18	vertex	19
equations	42	Law of Dominance	18	purebred	18	visible light	12
equilateral triangle	19	Law of Independent		reactants	41	wavelength	12
equivalent	42	Assortment	18	recessive	18	X rays	12
factor	42	Law of Segregation	18	regular	19		
fault	3	legs	19	repair technicians	25		
		lichenologists	25	research chemists	25		

Read the following selection. Then choose the best answer for each question. Mark your answer on the answer sheet.

The Long Haul

1. Oscar and Lydia Torres received an urgent call Wednesday night from the dispatcher at the Freight Lines truck terminal in east Los Angeles, California. They were scheduled to leave Thursday morning with a cargo of avocados and assorted citrus fruits for a produce market in New York City.

2. Oscar and Lydia Torres worked together as a husband-and-wife driver team. Oscar had been a professional truck driver for four years, while Lydia was still an apprentice driver. Nevertheless, she was as enthusiastic about her job as when she first started driving with Oscar almost a year ago.

3. Arriving at the truck terminal at 7:30 the next morning, Oscar and Lydia immediately checked in at the dispatcher's office.

4. "The cargo has to be in New York City by 5:00 A.M. Monday," the dispatcher said.

5. "Where do we load up?" Lydia asked.

6. "At Watsonville," the dispatcher replied.

7. Oscar and Lydia headed out of the office. Outside, Lydia turned to Oscar. "We have only 3 1/2 days to get to New York City. That's not much time, is it?"

8. Oscar smiled. "We've had tight schedules before. We'll make this one, too." Lydia certainly hoped so.

9. Oscar and Lydia climbed into the cab of their trailer truck. Oscar slid behind the steering wheel and was soon guiding the truck north on Route 5 through heavy city traffic. Approaching the outskirts of Los Angeles, Oscar eased the truck into the next forward gear and the truck sped faster because of lighter traffic. At 11:10 A.M., the truck reached Watsonville. Oscar backed up the 55-foot trailer truck to the loading platform.

10. As their truck was being loaded with packed crates, another truck backed up alongside them. Another husband-and-wife team—Sally and Jason Arkowitz—got out of the truck and headed for the loading platform.

Spotting their former neighbors Oscar and Lydia, Sally and Jason walked over to them.

11. "Where are you heading this time?" Sally asked her friends.

12. "New York City," responded Lydia.

13. "That's where Sally and I are going," said Jason.

14. "Do you have to be there at five on Monday morning?" queried Sally. Lydia nodded.

15. "You're on the same run we're on," said Sally. "How about that!"

16. "Bet Sally and I can get there before you," responded Jason.

17. Oscar and Lydia glanced at each other. Lydia wasn't as sure as Oscar seemed to be. Then Oscar commented, "You're on. The last team to arrive in New York treats the other team to a Dodgers game when we get back." Sally and Jason nodded enthusiastically.

18. Later, with Lydia seated next to him, Oscar eased the truck into first gear and headed northeast toward Sacramento. Oscar and Lydia sat motionlessly, staring at the long ribbon of road ahead of them. Lydia wished she could be as calm as Oscar was.

19. Although he didn't say anything to Lydia, Oscar kept thinking about the schedule. He was not as confident as Lydia thought he was. He was preoccupied with thoughts about the 3,000 miles they had to log in 3 1/2 days. It would be the usual race against the clock.

20. Within a few hours, the Torreses would be approaching Donner Pass near the California-Nevada border. As the sun started to go down behind the mountains, they crossed into Nevada and pulled over to a truck stop outside of Reno. After a hurriedly eaten supper at the truck stop's restaurant, they were in transit again, heading into the vast stretch of Nevada desert.

21. The truck's headlights pierced the eerie blackness of the desert night. The only sound was the drone of the truck's exhaust stacks. The

monotonous low humming was a reassuring sound in the emptiness that engulfed them.

22. Approaching the Utah border, Lydia took over driving from Oscar. Each driver usually drove for five hours and then rested for five hours.

23. As dawn lit up the sky, the Torreses were moving across Utah. Several hours later, they paused long enough for breakfast in Salt Lake City. As they entered the diner, they caught sight of Sally and Jason, who were just leaving. Both Lydia and Oscar suddenly felt discouraged.

24. "What took you so long?" Sally inquired. Before Oscar or Lydia could reply, the Arkowitzes were out of the diner.

25. To keep on schedule, Oscar and Lydia hurried through their breakfast. Neither spoke very much. Each was lost in thought, pondering the long haul still ahead. Within 20 minutes they were back on the interstate highway and by mid-afternoon were crossing the Utah-Colorado border. Ahead of them loomed the awesome peaks of the Rocky Mountains.

26. "Traveling cross-country and seeing all this natural beauty and landscape is better than programming and running a computer all day long," said Lydia, trying to sound casual. They continued steadfastly on Route 6 as it climbed 12,000 feet in a series of steep, zigzag grades through the mountains.

27. By midday Saturday they had crossed the Colorado-Kansas border and were deep into Kansas. Crossing the flat, unchanging countryside was the part of the trip that Oscar and Lydia dreaded most. It always seemed to take forever to cross this portion of the country.

28. The Torreses zoomed past a man working on a disabled trailer parked on the shoulder of the highway. Lydia looked back.

29. "Shouldn't we stop?" she asked Oscar, who was driving again. Oscar shook his head.

30. "No way, Lydia. It's too risky to stop. A favorite trick of hijackers is to fake a breakdown. When truck drivers stop to offer help, they often have their cargo hijacked. I just hope our rig never breaks down, and we have to pull over." Lydia couldn't have agreed more.

31. The sun was rising Sunday as the Torreses approached the Mississippi River.

Lydia was driving. Soon her attention was completely taken with the heavy traffic on the bridge over the river. As the traffic slowed, she grew more and more anxious. Glancing at the clock on the dashboard, she started drumming her fingers on the steering wheel.

32. "How are we doing?" asked Oscar apprehensively.

33. "You're supposed to be sleeping," said Lydia, smiling.

34. "Couldn't sleep," Oscar replied.

35. "Worried?"

36. "A little," Oscar said, trying to sound convincing. "We'll make it. I know we will."

37. Keeping to the speed limit of 55 miles an hour, Oscar and Lydia drove through Illinois, Ohio, and West Virginia in 10 hours. It was bleak and misty when they stopped briefly Sunday night at a roadside diner in Wheeling, West Virginia. Once back in their rig, they resumed their trip, driving through Pennsylvania over slick roads in a chilling rain.

38. By 2:00 A.M. Monday they were bucking the heavy truck traffic moving north on the New Jersey Turnpike. Despite the bottleneck caused by an earlier accident, they reached their destination, the Hunts Point Terminal Market in New York City, at 4:43 A.M. on Monday, 17 minutes ahead of their deadline. The terminal market was jammed with trucks from practically every state.

39. As their trailer was being unloaded, Oscar nudged Lydia. "Look! Sally and Jason are pulling in."

40. After they backed up their truck to the unloading platform, Sally and Jason walked past Lydia and Oscar, pretending not to see them.

41. "What took you so long?" called Lydia. Sally and Jason stopped.

42. "For a while there we thought we had lost you. We couldn't see you behind us. At any rate, we're glad you were able to follow us in. We're ready any time you are for the Dodgers game," said Oscar as he smiled at Lydia.

43. Both Lydia and Oscar seemed at ease. Despite the long journey and the inclement weather along the way, they had beaten the clock and were looking forward to the baseball game with their friends when they all arrived back in Los Angeles.

1. Who are the main characters in the story?
   a. Sally and Jason Arkowitz
   b. Lydia and Oscar Torres
   c. Sally, Jason, Lydia, and Oscar

2. Choose the words that best describe Oscar and Lydia during the cross-country truck trip.
   a. determined but uninterested
   b. relaxed but determined
   c. worried but confident

3. How does the author reveal the kind of person Oscar is?
   a. through his actions
   b. through his thoughts
   c. through his reaction to other characters

4. How would you describe Sally and Jason's attitude toward Lydia and Oscar?
   a. skeptical but pleasant
   b. playful but aggressive
   c. friendly but competitive

5. The main conflict that Oscar and Lydia face is with
   a. themselves.
   b. other characters.
   c. an outside force.

6. Which sentence best describes this conflict?
   a. As they entered the diner, they bumped into Sally and Jason, who were just leaving the diner.
   b. "We have only 3 1/2 days to get to New York City."
   c. As their truck was being loaded with packed crates, another truck backed up alongside them.

7. How is the conflict resolved?
   a. Jason and Sally arrive in New York City before Lydia and Oscar.
   b. Oscar and Lydia arrive in New York City ahead of schedule.
   c. Oscar and Lydia remind Jason and Sally about their bet.

8. Lydia and Oscar first encounter Sally and Jason at
   a. the dispatcher's office.
   b. a diner in Salt Lake City.
   c. the loading station.

9. The part of the cross-country trip that Oscar and Lydia dreaded most was crossing the
   a. desert.
   b. Rocky Mountains.
   c. Kansas plains.

10. The story's climax occurs when
    a. Oscar does not stop to help a trucker by the side of the highway.
    b. Oscar and Lydia reach the Hunts Point Terminal Market 17 minutes before the deadline.
    c. Sally and Jason walk past Lydia and Oscar, pretending not to see them.

11. What is the theme of the story?
    a. Truck driving is difficult work.
    b. Women truck drivers are better then men drivers.
    c. Long-haul truck drivers work under the pressure of time.

12. Which title would be appropriate for the story?
    a. "Driving Cross-Country"
    b. "Racing the Clock"
    c. "Transporting Cargo"

13. What is the unstated main idea of paragraph 25?
    a. Lydia and Oscar still had a long way to go before they met their New York deadline.
    b. Lydia and Oscar were beginning to fall behind schedule.
    c. Lydia and Oscar had time for a leisurely meal.

14. What is the unstated main idea of paragraph 31?
    a. Lydia was a careless driver.
    b. Lydia did not like driving in heavy traffic.
    c. Lydia was concerned about the schedule.

15. Why did the Torreses eat hurriedly when they stopped for supper outside of Reno?
    a. They knew there were no more truck stops in Nevada.
    b. They were approaching Donner pass.
    c. They wanted to get back on the road again as soon as possible.

16. What does Lydia's statement about computers in paragraph 26 tell you about her?
    a. She used to work as a computer programmer.
    b. Programming is more difficult than driving a truck.
    c. She has always wanted to be a truck driver.

17. Why does Oscar say, "I just hope our rig never breaks down, and we have to pull over"?
    a. Neither Oscar nor Lydia is a good mechanic.
    b. Other truckers would not stop to offer help.
    c. Hijackers often use a disabled truck as a decoy.

18. In this story, the narrator is
    a. an outsider who observes the events but does not know what the characters feel.
    b. a participant who is actively involved in the events of the story.
    c. an outsider who sees into the mind and thinking of some of the characters in the story.

19. Why is this point of view a good one from which to tell this story?
    a. The narrator explains all the actions of all the characters.
    b. The narrator gives details of all that happened.
    c. The narrator is able to describe the thoughts and feelings of the main characters.

20. In order to drive 3,000 miles in 3 1/2 days, how many miles must the Torreses average each day?
    a. about 1,000
    b. about 850
    c. about 650

21. Choose the correct definition of *ribbon* as it is used in paragraph 18.
    a. a narrow strip
    b. a military decoration
    c. a band of fabric

22. Choose the correct definition of *grades* as it is used in paragraph 26.
    a. rising or descending slopes
    b. ratings in a classification scale according to quality or value
    c. marks on examinations or in courses

23. What is the meaning of *drone* in paragraph 21?
    a. click
    b. hum
    c. roar

43. What document referred to in this selection is a primary source?
   a. article   **b.** letter   **c.** book

44. When was this primary source published?
   a. 1962   **b.** 1991   **c.** 1992

45. This document was used in the selection to
   a. describe the economy of South Africa.
   b. point out that South Africa's beauty and economic wealth are not shared by all who live there.
   c. provide a detailed description of South Africa's problems.

46. Based on the facts in this selection, which of the following generalizations can be made about Nelson Mandela as a political leader?
   a. Mandela used the political process in South Africa to improve the lives of black South Africans.
   b. Mandela had to resort to illegal activities to get his way.
   c. Mandela became a strong leader, even as a prisoner, by refusing to give up his ideals.

47. Based on the facts in this selection, which of the following generalizations can be made about Nelson Mandela as a person?
   a. Mandela was a man of conviction.
   b. Mandela was ambitious for power.
   c. Mandela was a victim of circumstances.

48. Based on the facts in this selection, which of the following generalizations can be made about ending apartheid in South Africa?
   a. Apartheid would have ended eventually of its own accord.
   b. A long struggle was necessary to end apartheid.
   c. Nonviolent protest was effective in ending apartheid.

49. Choose the correct definition of *strike* as it is used in paragraph 14.
   a. a stoppage of normal activity, as a form of protest
   b. an attack, such as a military air attack
   c. a sudden discovery, such as a gold strike

50. Choose the correct definition of *reserves* as it is used in paragraph 5.
   a. supplies that are put aside for future use
   b. minerals, like coal and oil, that are known to exist but are still in the ground
   c. lands set aside for a particular use

51. What is the meaning of *isolated* in paragraph 3?
   a. separated or remote from others
   b. containing only a few houses
   c. very small

52. What is the meaning of *heritage* in paragraph 4?
   a. written history
   b. traditions handed down from previous generations
   c. culture of a particular place or time

53. What is the meaning of *bigotry* in paragraph 8?
   a. prejudice
   b. oppression
   c. poverty

Use the map to answer the following questions.

54. South Africa has three capitals. Which of the following is *not* one of the capitals?
   a. Pretoria
   b. Johannesburg
   c. Bloemfontein

55. Which ocean borders the Transkei?
   a. Indian Ocean
   b. Atlantic Ocean
   c. neither of these

56. Which country lies completely inside the borders of South Africa?
   a. Swaziland
   b. Orange Free State
   c. Lesotho

57. How far is it from Cape Town to Pretoria?
   a. about 600 miles
   b. about 900 miles
   c. about 800 miles

Read the following selection. Then choose the best answer for each question. Mark your answer on the answer sheet.

The World of Inner Space

1. Scientists are discovering an invisible realm. Until relatively recently, this region has been hidden from view. Now, because of very powerful microscopes, scientists are discovering a whole new world of atoms, molecules, genes, bacteria, and viruses.

2. Learning about the realm of inner space is extremely important. "Within this invisible world lie the keys to every life process and many diseases," says scientist Humberto Fernández-Morán.

The Electron Microscope

3. Scientists are learning about this invisible realm through the use of electrons, which are tiny particles of matter. With the electron microscope, scientists are exploring the far reaches of inner space, and what they are seeing there is beautiful and awesome.

4. The electron microscope can reveal this invisible world because of its tremendous magnification power. Until recent times, scientists had to rely on the optical microscope, which cannot rival the electron microscope in magnification power. The optical microscope can magnify no more than 2,000 times. By contrast, the electron microscope can magnify 20 million times. Since the seventeenth century, optical microscopes have been used to observe bacteria. Optical microscopes, however, cannot distinguish the tiny viruses that cause many kinds of diseases. Electron microscopes, on the other hand, make it possible to see viruses that are measured in billionths of a centimeter.

Impact on Science

5. Because of its tremendous magnification capabilities, the electron microscope has revolutionized research. Biologists can now see viruses that are as small as 60 angstroms in diameter. One angstrom is about 100 millionths of a centimeter. It is even possible now for biologists to see normal cells changing into cancerous cells and to identify genes that cause hereditary diseases.

6. The electron microscope is also extending the research capabilities of other scientists. The metallurgist now can study the structure of crystals and learn how metals corrode and crack. The materials expert can look into the heart of a rubber molecule and determine how well a tire will perform. The ecologist is using the electron microscope to track down the causes of pollution.

How the Electron Microscope Works

7. The electron microscope was first used in 1931. The electron microscope is similar in principle to the optical microscope. To magnify objects, the optical microscope uses beams of light and glass lenses. The electron microscope uses beams of electrons instead of light beams, and its lenses are formed by magnetic coils. As glass lenses focus light beams, magnetic coils focus electron beams. Because the coils condense, or focus, they are called condensing lenses.

8. The scanning electron microscope (SEM) is a more recent form of the electron microscope. At the upper end of the SEM, a high-voltage electron gun shoots a beam of electrons that travel with almost the speed of light. The electrons are focused by the condensing lenses into a very fine beam, which rapidly scans, or moves across, the specimen. As the beam moves over the specimen's surface, it knocks loose showers of electrons from the specimen. These secondary electrons are picked up by a signal detector and formed into images on a cathoderay tube, which resembles a television screen.

9. The images produced by the SEM have a great deal of detail and clarity, so scientists can get an incredibly complete look at minuscule organisms. These organisms appear enormous on the SEM viewing screen. For example, when magnified by the SEM, the tardigrade, a tiny insect, looks like a giant

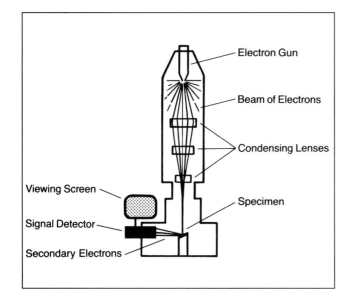

58. Choose the main idea of paragraph 10.

    a. For example, pollen grains can be closely examined.

    b. With the SEM, scientists can study many ordinary things close up.

    c. On a SEM viewing screen, pollen grains look like huge balloons.

59. Choose the main idea of paragraph 4.

    a. By contrast, the electron microscope can magnify 20 million times.

    b. The electron microscope can reveal this invisible world because of its tremendous magnification power.

    c. Since the seventeenth century, optical microscopes have been used to observe bacteria.

60. The main idea of paragraph 7 is that the electron microscope is similar in principle to the optical microscope. Which detail supports the main idea?

    a. The electron microscope was first used in 1931.

    b. As glass lenses focus light beams, magnetic coils focus electron beams.

    c. Because the coils condense, or focus, they are called condensing lenses.

61. Find the main idea of paragraph 9. Then choose the detail that best supports the main idea.

    a. The images produced by the SEM have

monster in a science fiction movie. This speck-size organism is found in water drops on plants.

10. With the SEM, scientists can study many ordinary things close up. For example, pollen grains can be closely examined. On an SEM viewing screen, pollen grains look like huge balloons. Human antibodies can be magnified a million times, and the images can be photographed and filmed. Scientists have been able to make a movie of uranium atoms in motion.

a great deal of detail and clarity, so scientists can get an incredibly complete look at minuscule organisms.

    b. This speck-size organism is found in water drops on plants.

    c. For example, when magnified by the SEM, the tardigrade, a tiny insect, looks like a giant monster in a science fiction movie.

62. The SEM's magnetic coils are called condensing lenses because

    a. they scan the specimen.

    b. they condense electron beams.

    c. they focus light beams.

63. Because of the tremendous magnification capabilities of the electron microscope, scientists can now

    a. see tiny viruses that cause many kinds of diseases.

    b. identify human cells.

    c. study the structure of roots.

64. Earlier forms of the electron microscope

    a. lacked the clarity and detail of the SEM.

    b. were more expensive than the SEM.

    c. had smaller viewing screens than the SEM.

65. How did the SEM get its name?

    a. It can observe atoms and molecules.

    b. It can greatly enlarge images.

    c. It can scan a specimen.

66. Until the electron microscope was developed, scientists
    a. had a limited view of the world of inner space.
    b. were totally unaware of the world of inner space.
    c. could observe the entire world of inner space.

67. What do optical microscopes and electron microscopes have in common?
    a. They both have a viewing screen.
    b. They both use glass lenses.
    c. They both operate on the same principle.

68. How does the electron microscope differ from the optical microscope?
    a. The electron microscope is less powerful than the optical microscope.
    b. The electron microscope uses light beams.
    c. The electron microscope does not have glass lenses.

69. How does the optical microscope differ from the electron microscope?
    a. The optical microscope is a newer form of the electron microscope.
    b. The optical microscope can magnify viruses as small as 60 angstroms in diameter.
    c. The optical microscope uses light beams.

70. What purpose is shared by magnetic coils and glass lenses?
    a. They both magnify objects.
    b. They both focus a beam.
    c. They both condense light beams.

71. Choose the correct definition of *rival* as it is used in paragraph 4.
    a. be less than
    b. be equal to or as good as
    c. have an unfair advantage

72. Choose the correct definition of *heart* as it is used in paragraph 6.
    a. organ of the body
    b. courage
    c. central or main part

73. Choose the correct definition of *fine* as it is used in paragraph 8.
    a. skilled
    b. slender
    c. sharp

74. What is the meaning of *realm* in paragraph 1?
    a. kingdom
    b. region
    c. activity

75. What is the meaning of *scans* in paragraph 8?
    a. studies
    b. closely views
    c. moves across

76. What is the meaning of *minuscule* in paragraph 9?
    a. monstrous
    b. tiny
    c. deadly

77. The electron beam moves in a direct line from the _____ to the _____.
    a. specimen, electron gun
    b. viewing screen, signal detector
    c. electron gun, specimen

78. Before reaching the condensing lenses, the beam is
    a. comparatively wide.
    b. extremely powerful.
    c. comparatively narrow.

79. From what does the beam knock loose a shower of electrons?
    a. condensing lenses
    b. specimen
    c. signal detector

80. The secondary electrons are transmitted to the
    a. condensing lenses.
    b. specimen.
    c. signal detector.

AT12

Questions 81 through 84 are word problems. Use the space below for your calculations. For problems 83 and 84 use the following formula: distance = rate × time.

81. Suppose a specimen appeared to be 3 millimeters wide when magnified 2,000 times. How many millimeters wide would it appear when magnified 20 million times?
    a. 3,000,000
    b. 300,000
    c. 30,000

82. There are ten million angstroms in a millimeter. A millimeter is one-tenth of a centimeter. How many angstroms are in one centimeter?
    a. 100,000,000
    b. 100,000
    c. 10,000

83. Two trucks leave a truck terminal at the same time. Truck A travels at 65 kilometers per hour. Truck B travels at 60 kilometers per hour. After 3 hours, Truck A has to stop because of engine trouble. How long will it be before Truck B passes the stalled Truck A?
    a. 1 hour
    b. 15 minutes
    c. 40 minutes

84. A driver team drives around the clock and averages 840 kilometers a day. They have to transport goods a distance of 3,005 kilometers. They will leave on Monday at 2:00 A.M. They know that in 3 days, on Thursday at 2:00 A.M., they will have traveled 2,520 kilometers. Approximately when will they arrive at their destination?
    a. Thursday at 9:00 A.M.
    b. Thursday at 4:00 P.M.
    c. Friday at 1:00 A.M.

Use the following dictionary entry to answer questions 85 through 88.

---

neu·tral (n$\overline{oo}$′trəl, ny$\overline{oo}$′-) *adj.* [Fr. < ML. < L. < *neuter*, NEUTER] **1.** not taking part in either side of a quarrel or war [a *neutral* nation] **2.** of or characteristic of a nation not taking part in a war or not taking sides in a power struggle [a *neutral* position] **3.** not one thing or the other; indefinite, middling, etc. [a *neutral* state between joy and sadness] **4.** having little or no decided color [gray is a *neutral* color] **5.** *Biol.* same as NEUTER **6.** *Chem.* neither acid nor alkaline **7.** *Elec.* neither negative nor positive; uncharged **8.** *Phonet.* pronounced as the vowel is in most unstressed syllables, which tends to become (ə) *—n.* **1.** a nation not taking part in a war **2.** a neutral color **3.** a neutral person **3.** a neutral color **4.** *Mech.* the position of gears when they are not meshed together and therefore cannot pass on power from the engine —**neu′tral·ly adv.**

---

85. What is the second respelling of the entry word?
    a. neu · tral   **b.** n$\overline{oo}$′ trəl   **c.** ny$\overline{oo}$′ trəl

86. What is the first noun meaning?
    a. not one thing or the other
    b. neither negative nor positive
    c. a nation not taking part in a war

87. Which phrase uses the second *adj.* meaning?
    a. a neutral nation
    b. a neutral position
    c. gray is a neutral color

88. Which meaning applies to chemistry?
    a. neither negative nor positive
    b. neither acid nor alkaline
    c. pronounced as the vowel is in most unstressed syllables

Use the following history book index to answer questions 89 through 92.

Churchill, Winston, *p613,* 614, 619, *p629;* Dunkirk and, 612; on battle of Britain, 613; World War II and, 618, 623; Iron Curtain speech, 628, 633
Church of England, 298, *m299,* 361–66, 449, 450
Cicero, 131, 283, 292
Cincinnatus, Lucius Quinctius, 114
Climate zones, in Africa, 239, *m240;* worldwide, *m756*
Clive, Robert, 509

Committee of Public Safety, 387
Common law, 205
Common Market, 639–40, 717, 724, 725–26
Communes, in China, 692
Compass. *See* Magnetic compass.
Compiègne, 606–7, 612
Computers, 738–39, *p739,* 750
Concentration camps, 500, 601, 623–24, *p624,* 631, 680
Concert of Europe, 399–400
Concordat of 1801, 391

---

89. How many pages does the book have on the Common Market?
    a. 6   **b.** 4   **c.** 7

90. On which page(s) is information on Churchill's Iron Curtain Speech?
    a. 618, 623   **b.** 613, 614   **c.** 628, 633

91. For information about the compass, under which topic would you look?
    a. *Magnetic compass*
    b. *Compass*
    c. *Navigation*

92. On which page would you find a map of worldwide climate zones?
    a. 239
    b. 240
    c. 756

You will have to think about word parts to answer questions 93 through 100.

93. To evaluate again is to
    a. disevaluate.
    b. misevaluate.
    c. reevaluate.

94. The middle part of the day is
    a. preday.   **b.** midday.   **c.** biday.

95. Which word completes the following sentence?
    The story did not have a _____ ending.
    a. believable   **b.** believeable   **c.** believiable

96. Which word completes the following sentence?
    Bill _____ helped rake leaves.
    a. happyily   **b.** happyly   **c.** happily

97. Choose the correct way to divide the word *misunderstanding* into syllables.
    a. mis under standing
    b. mis under stand ing
    c. mis un der stand ing

98. In which word below is the accent mark correctly placed?
    a. dis′ trib ute
    b. dis trib′ ute
    c. dis trib ute′

99. Choose the root in the word *prescription.*
    a. pre   **b.** ion   **c.** script

100. Choose the root in the word *detainment.*
    a. de
    b. tain
    c. ment

Name _____

Student Answer Sheet

	Test 1				Test 2				Test 3				Test 4		
	a	b	c		a	b	c		a	b	c		a	b	c
1	○	○	○	24	○	○	○	58	○	○	○	85	○	○	○
2	○	○	○	25	○	○	○	59	○	○	○	86	○	○	○
3	○	○	○	26	○	○	○	60	○	○	○	87	○	○	○
4	○	○	○	27	○	○	○	61	○	○	○	88	○	○	○
5	○	○	○	28	○	○	○	62	○	○	○	89	○	○	○
6	○	○	○	29	○	○	○	63	○	○	○	90	○	○	○
7	○	○	○	30	○	○	○	64	○	○	○	91	○	○	○
8	○	○	○	31	○	○	○	65	○	○	○	92	○	○	○
9	○	○	○	32	○	○	○	66	○	○	○	93	○	○	○
10	○	○	○	33	○	○	○	67	○	○	○	94	○	○	○
11	○	○	○	34	○	○	○	68	○	○	○	95	○	○	○
12	○	○	○	35	○	○	○	69	○	○	○	96	○	○	○
13	○	○	○	36	○	○	○	70	○	○	○	97	○	○	○
14	○	○	○	37	○	○	○	71	○	○	○	98	○	○	○
15	○	○	○	38	○	○	○	72	○	○	○	99	○	○	○
16	○	○	○	39	○	○	○	73	○	○	○	100	○	○	○
17	○	○	○	40	○	○	○	74	○	○	○				
18	○	○	○	41	○	○	○	75	○	○	○				
19	○	○	○	42	○	○	○	76	○	○	○				
20	○	○	○	43	○	○	○	77	○	○	○				
21	○	○	○	44	○	○	○	78	○	○	○				
22	○	○	○	45	○	○	○	79	○	○	○				
23	○	○	○	46	○	○	○	80	○	○	○				
				47	○	○	○	81	○	○	○				
				48	○	○	○	82	○	○	○				
				49	○	○	○	83	○	○	○				
				50	○	○	○	84	○	○	○				
				51	○	○	○								
				52	○	○	○								
				53	○	○	○								
				54	○	○	○								
				55	○	○	○								
				56	○	○	○								
				57	○	○	○								

	Test 1	Test 2	Test 3	Test 4			
Number Possible	23	34	27	16	Total	100
Number Incorrect	_____	_____	_____	_____	Total	_____
Score	_____	_____	_____	_____	Total	_____

Class Record–Keeping Chart

Test Item	Skill	Name								
1–4	Understanding character									
5–7	Identifying conflict and resolution									
8–10	Identifying plot									
11–12	Identifying theme									
13–14, 27–28	Identifying the stated or unstated main idea									
15–17, 40–42 64–66	Making inferences									
18–19	Identifying omniscient point of view									
20, 81–84	Solving word problems									
21–22, 49–50, 71–73	Recognizing multiple meanings of words									
23, 51–53, 74–76	Using context clues									
24–26, 58–59	Identifying the main idea									
29–30, 60–61	Identifying the main idea and supporting details									
31–33, 62–63	Identifying cause and effect									
34–36	Comparing and contrasting									
37–39	Distinguishing fact from opinion									
43–45	Using a primary source									
46–48	Making generalizations									
54–57	Reading a map									
67–70	Classifying									
77–80	Reading text with diagrams									
85–88	Using the dictionary									
89–92	Using an index									
93–100	Recognizing prefixes, suffixes, syllables, and roots									
	Total Incorrect									
	Score (subtract total incorrect from 100)									

AT16